JUMPER

JUMPSCARS

JUMPER

JUMPSCARS

written by **NUNZIO DEFILIPPIS** & **CHRISTINA WEIR**

illustrated by **BRIAN HURTT**
(with assistance from **CHRIS SCHWEIZER**)

colored by JARED M. JONES, DEAN TRIPPE & POP ART STUDIOS

lettered by DOUGLAS E. SHERWOOD

oni
PRESS

edited by JAMES LUCAS JONES
design by KEITH WOOD
cover by BRIAN HURTT and DAN JACKSON

Thanks to DEBBIE OLSHAN, CATHY BUNNIN,
DOUGLAS DABBS, CHRIS HUFF, and GUSTAVO
PETER. Special thanks to STACY MAES for her
invaluable assistance on this project.

ONI PRESS, INC.
JOE NOZEMACK, publisher
JAMES LUCAS JONES, editor in chief
RANDAL C. JARRELL, managing editor
DOUGLAS E. SHERWOOD, editorial assistant
CHRIS HUFF, editorial intern

onipress.com
jumperthemovie.com

Oni Press, Inc.
1305 SE Martin Luther King Jr. Blvd.
Suite A
Portland, OR 97214

First Edition: January 2008
ISBN-13 978-1-932664-93-5
ISBN-10 1-932664-93-9

1 3 5 7 9 10 8 6 4 2

Printed in Canada

CHAPTER 1

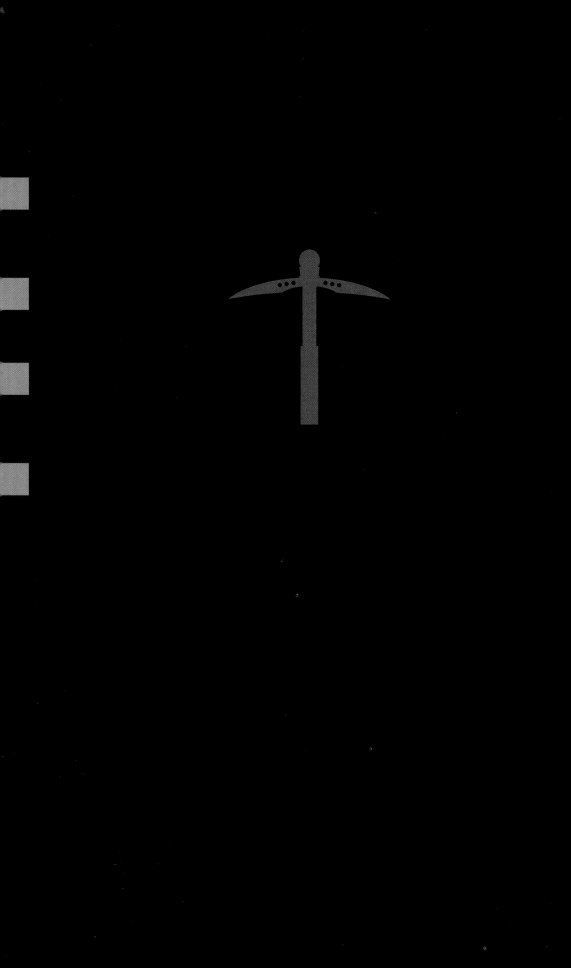

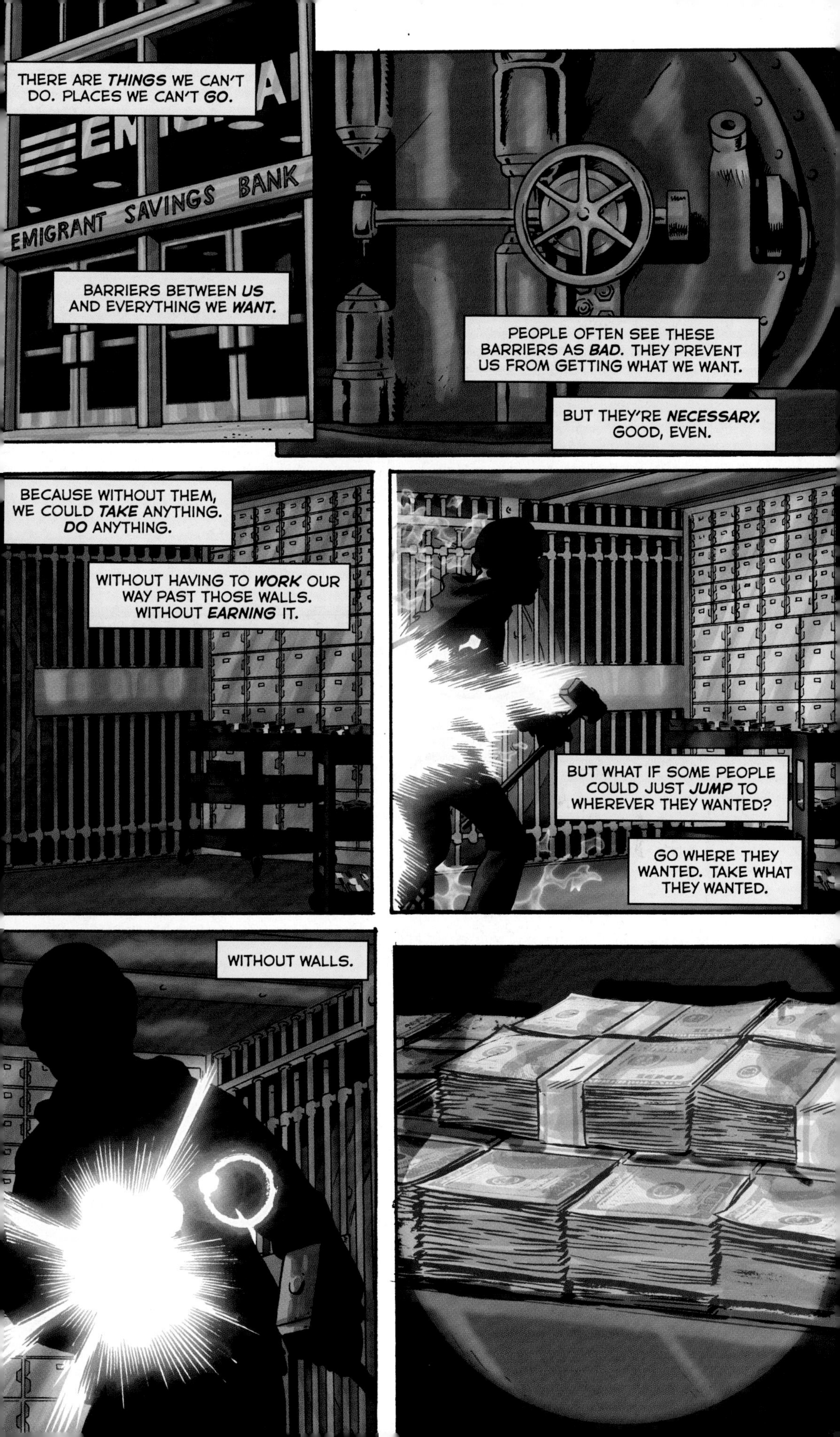
EMIGRANT SAVINGS BANK
THERE ARE *THINGS* WE CAN'T DO. PLACES WE CAN'T *GO*.
BARRIERS BETWEEN *US* AND EVERYTHING WE *WANT*.
PEOPLE OFTEN SEE THESE BARRIERS AS *BAD*. THEY PREVENT US FROM GETTING WHAT WE WANT.
BUT THEY'RE *NECESSARY*. GOOD, EVEN.
BECAUSE WITHOUT THEM, WE COULD *TAKE* ANYTHING. *DO* ANYTHING.
WITHOUT HAVING TO *WORK* OUR WAY PAST THOSE WALLS. WITHOUT *EARNING* IT.
BUT WHAT IF SOME PEOPLE COULD JUST *JUMP* TO WHEREVER THEY WANTED?
GO WHERE THEY WANTED. TAKE WHAT THEY WANTED.
WITHOUT WALLS.

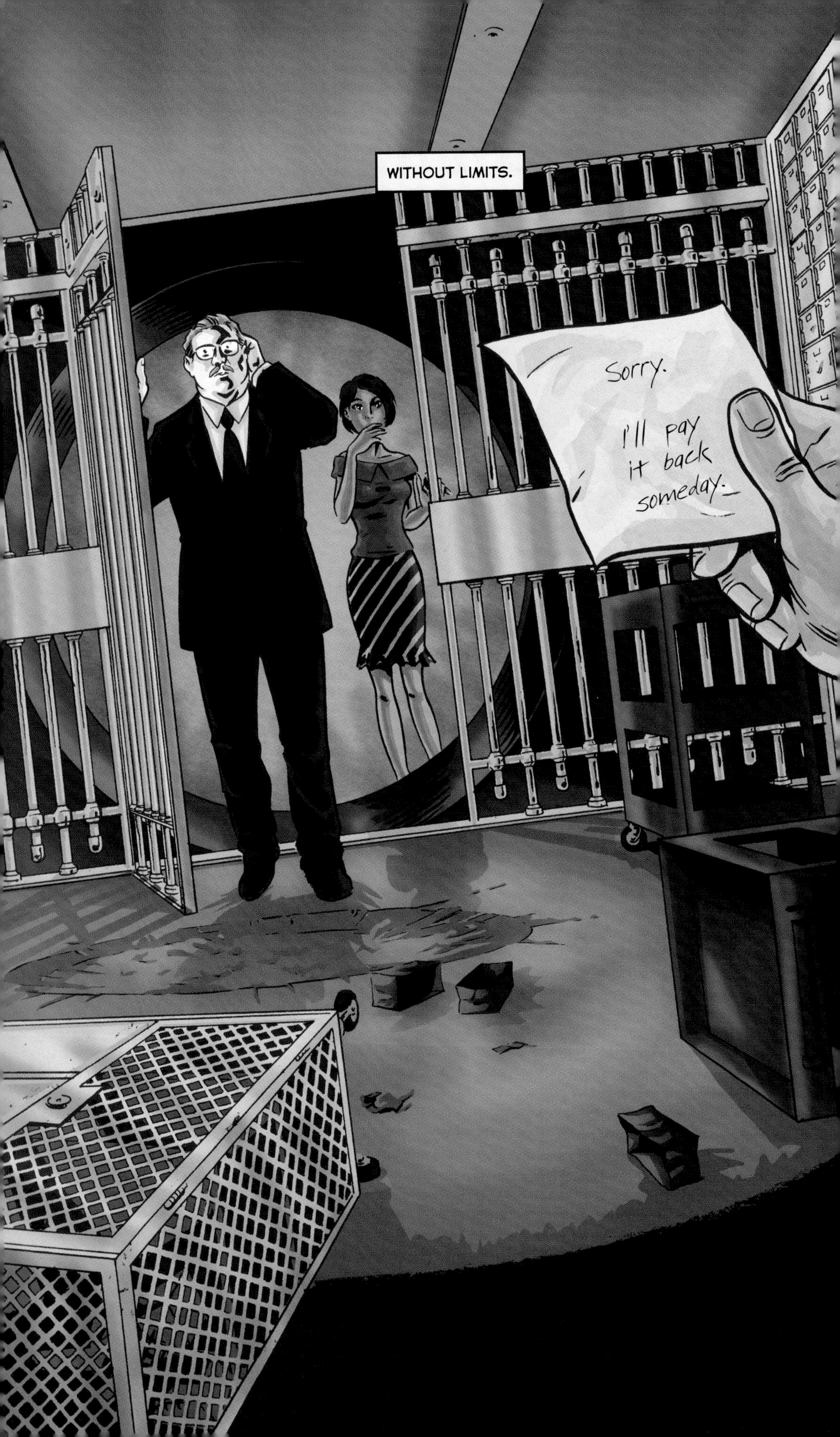
WITHOUT LIMITS.
Sorry.
I'll pay it back someday.

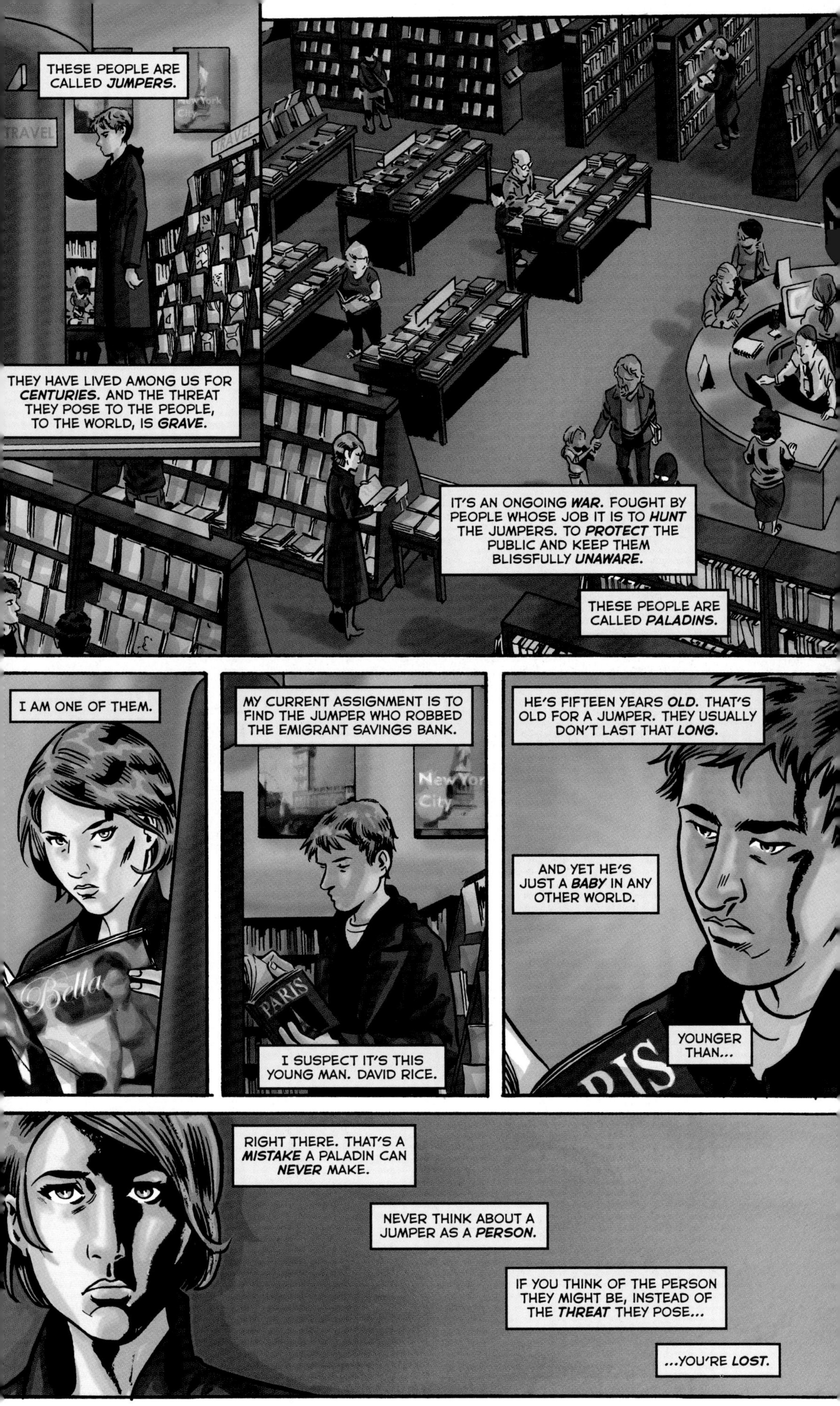
THESE PEOPLE ARE CALLED JUMPERS.
TRAVEL
TRAVEL
New York City
THEY HAVE LIVED AMONG US FOR CENTURIES. AND THE THREAT THEY POSE TO THE PEOPLE, TO THE WORLD, IS GRAVE.
IT'S AN ONGOING WAR. FOUGHT BY PEOPLE WHOSE JOB IT IS TO HUNT THE JUMPERS. TO PROTECT THE PUBLIC AND KEEP THEM BLISSFULLY UNAWARE.
THESE PEOPLE ARE CALLED PALADINS.
I AM ONE OF THEM.
Bella
MY CURRENT ASSIGNMENT IS TO FIND THE JUMPER WHO ROBBED THE EMIGRANT SAVINGS BANK.
PARIS
I SUSPECT IT'S THIS YOUNG MAN. DAVID RICE.
HE'S FIFTEEN YEARS OLD. THAT'S OLD FOR A JUMPER. THEY USUALLY DON'T LAST THAT LONG.
AND YET HE'S JUST A BABY IN ANY OTHER WORLD.
YOUNGER THAN...
RIGHT THERE. THAT'S A MISTAKE A PALADIN CAN NEVER MAKE.
NEVER THINK ABOUT A JUMPER AS A PERSON.
IF YOU THINK OF THE PERSON THEY MIGHT BE, INSTEAD OF THE THREAT THEY POSE...
...YOU'RE LOST.

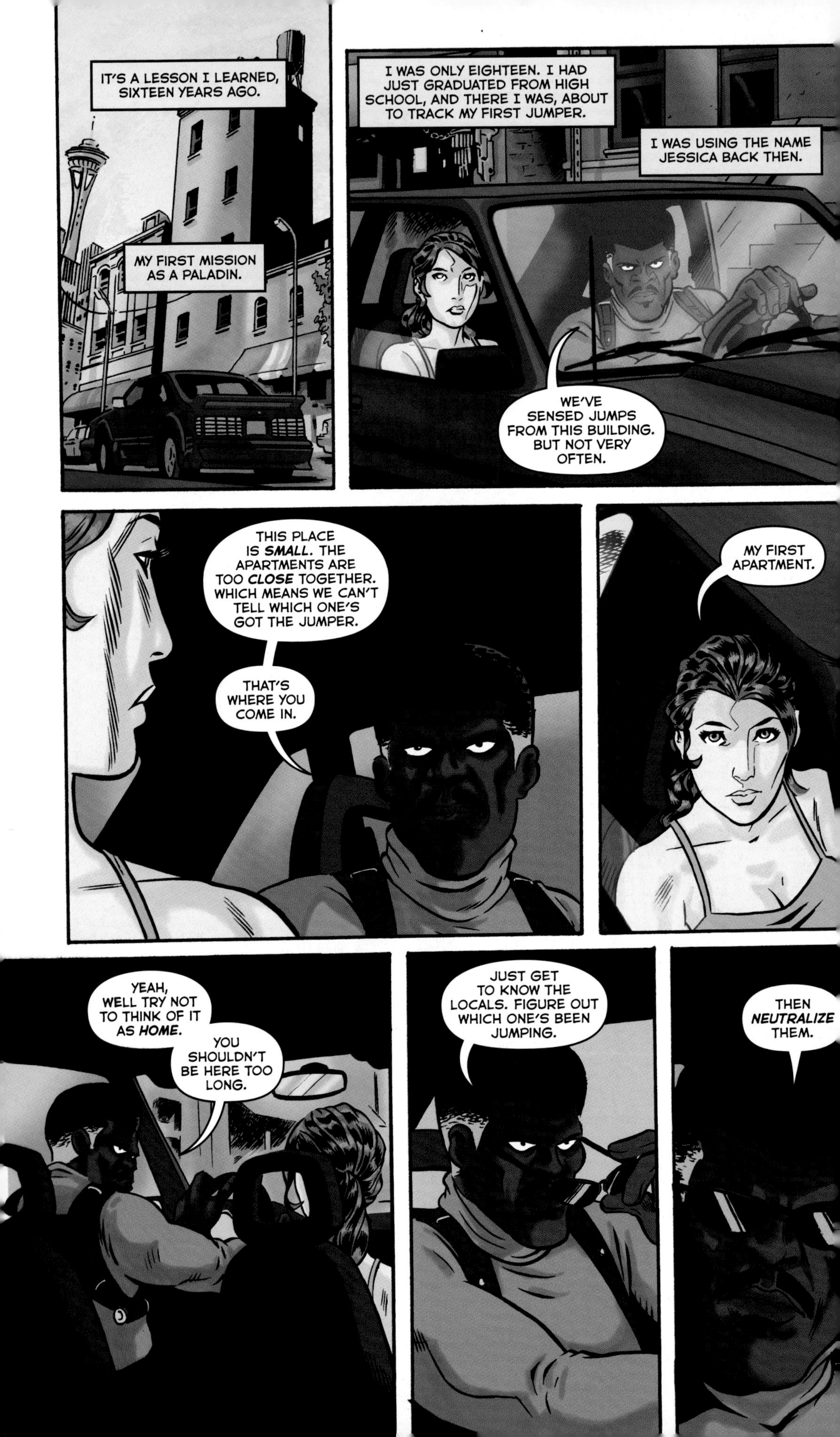
IT'S A LESSON I LEARNED, SIXTEEN YEARS AGO.
MY FIRST MISSION AS A PALADIN.
I WAS ONLY EIGHTEEN. I HAD JUST GRADUATED FROM HIGH SCHOOL, AND THERE I WAS, ABOUT TO TRACK MY FIRST JUMPER.
I WAS USING THE NAME JESSICA BACK THEN.
WE'VE SENSED JUMPS FROM THIS BUILDING. BUT NOT VERY OFTEN.
THIS PLACE IS ***SMALL***. THE APARTMENTS ARE TOO ***CLOSE*** TOGETHER. WHICH MEANS WE CAN'T TELL WHICH ONE'S GOT THE JUMPER.
THAT'S WHERE YOU COME IN.
MY FIRST APARTMENT.
YEAH, WELL TRY NOT TO THINK OF IT AS ***HOME***.
YOU SHOULDN'T BE HERE TOO LONG.
JUST GET TO KNOW THE LOCALS. FIGURE OUT WHICH ONE'S BEEN JUMPING.
THEN ***NEUTRALIZE*** THEM.

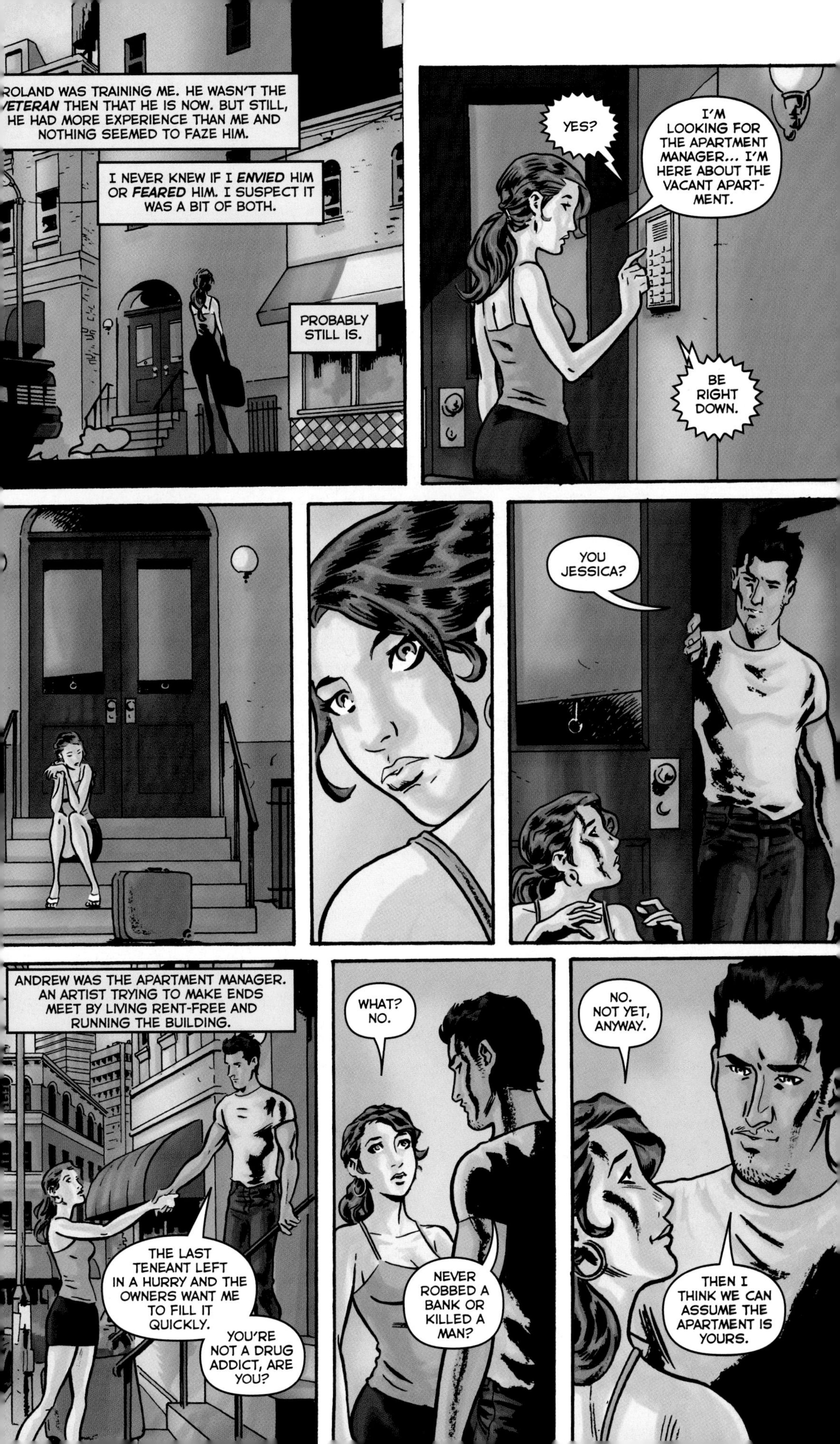

ROLAND WAS TRAINING ME. HE WASN'T THE VETERAN THEN THAT HE IS NOW. BUT STILL, HE HAD MORE EXPERIENCE THAN ME AND NOTHING SEEMED TO FAZE HIM.
I NEVER KNEW IF I *ENVIED* HIM OR *FEARED* HIM. I SUSPECT IT WAS A BIT OF BOTH.
PROBABLY STILL IS.
YES?
I'M LOOKING FOR THE APARTMENT MANAGER... I'M HERE ABOUT THE VACANT APARTMENT.
I'M BE RIGHT DOWN.
YOU JESSICA?
ANDREW WAS THE APARTMENT MANAGER. AN ARTIST TRYING TO MAKE ENDS MEET BY LIVING RENT-FREE AND RUNNING THE BUILDING.
THE LAST TENEANT LEFT IN A HURRY AND THE OWNERS WANT ME TO FILL IT QUICKLY.
YOU'RE NOT A DRUG ADDICT, ARE YOU?
WHAT? NO.
NEVER ROBBED A BANK OR KILLED A MAN?
NO. NOT YET, ANYWAY.
THEN I THINK WE CAN ASSUME THE APARTMENT IS YOURS.

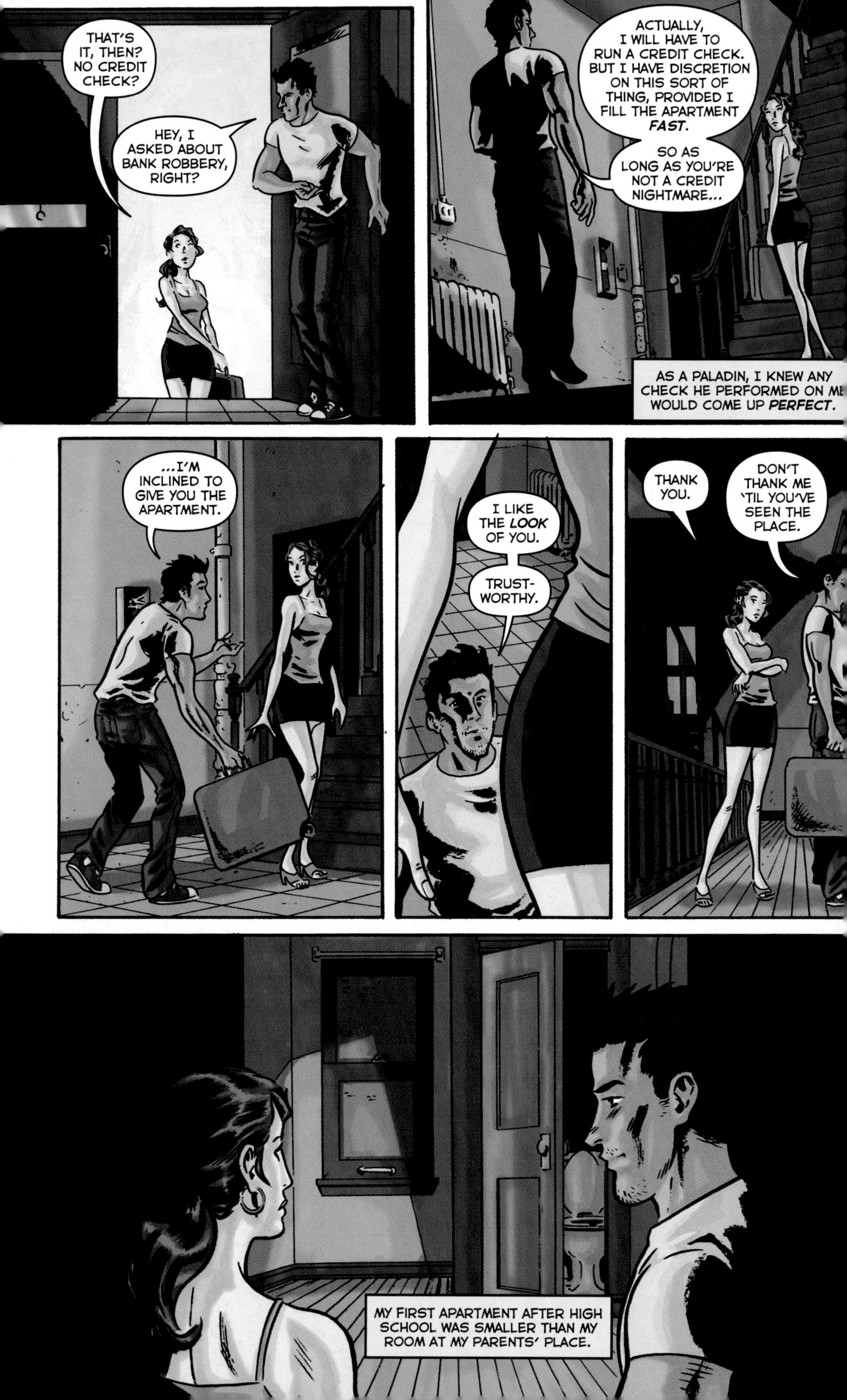

THAT'S IT, THEN? NO CREDIT CHECK?
HEY, I ASKED ABOUT BANK ROBBERY, RIGHT?
ACTUALLY, I WILL HAVE TO RUN A CREDIT CHECK. BUT I HAVE DISCRETION ON THIS SORT OF THING, PROVIDED I FILL THE APARTMENT *FAST*.
SO AS LONG AS YOU'RE NOT A CREDIT NIGHTMARE...
AS A PALADIN, I KNEW ANY CHECK HE PERFORMED ON ME WOULD COME UP *PERFECT*.
...I'M INCLINED TO GIVE YOU THE APARTMENT.
I LIKE THE *LOOK* OF YOU.
TRUST-WORTHY.
THANK YOU.
DON'T THANK ME 'TIL YOU'VE SEEN THE PLACE.
MY FIRST APARTMENT AFTER HIGH SCHOOL WAS SMALLER THAN MY ROOM AT MY PARENTS' PLACE.

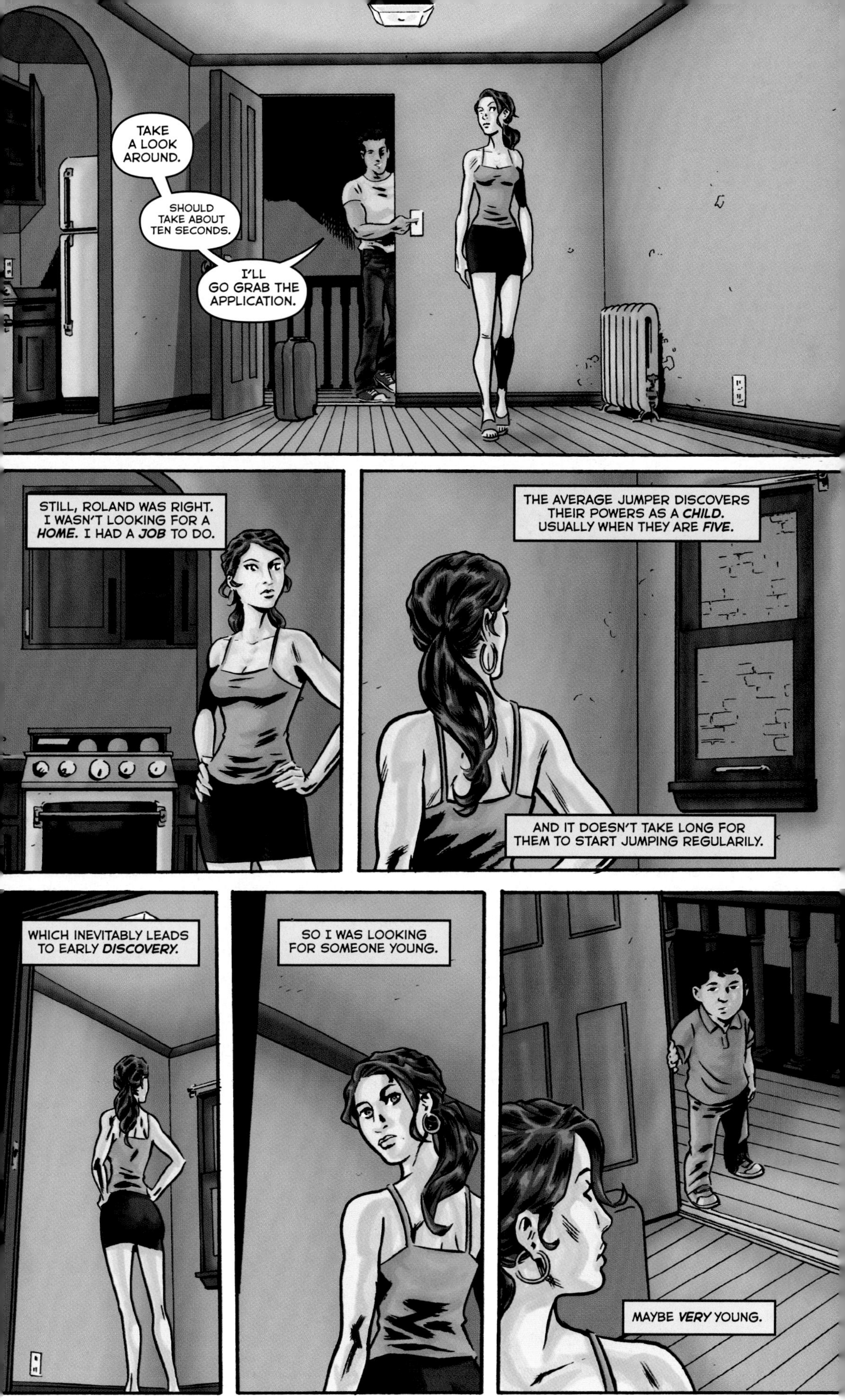
TAKE A LOOK AROUND.
SHOULD TAKE ABOUT TEN SECONDS.
I'LL GO GRAB THE APPLICATION.
STILL, ROLAND WAS RIGHT. I WASN'T LOOKING FOR A *HOME*. I HAD A *JOB* TO DO.
THE AVERAGE JUMPER DISCOVERS THEIR POWERS AS A *CHILD*. USUALLY WHEN THEY ARE *FIVE*.
AND IT DOESN'T TAKE LONG FOR THEM TO START JUMPING REGULARILY.
WHICH INEVITABLY LEADS TO EARLY *DISCOVERY*.
SO I WAS LOOKING FOR SOMEONE YOUNG.
MAYBE *VERY* YOUNG.

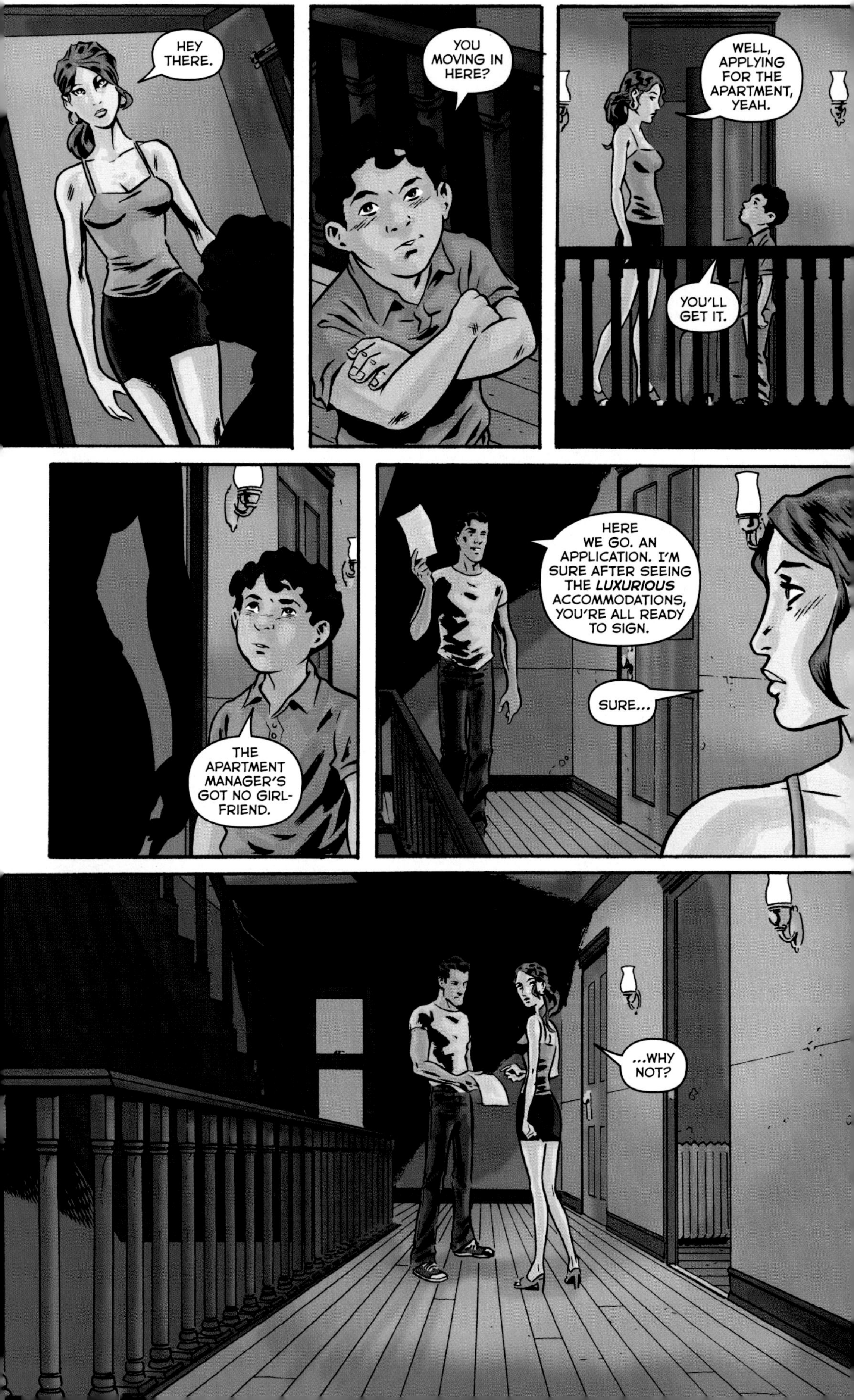
HEY THERE.
YOU MOVING IN HERE?
WELL, APPLYING FOR THE APARTMENT, YEAH.
YOU'LL GET IT.
THE APARTMENT MANAGER'S GOT NO GIRL-FRIEND.
HERE WE GO. AN APPLICATION. I'M SURE AFTER SEEING THE *LUXURIOUS* ACCOMMODATIONS, YOU'RE ALL READY TO SIGN.
SURE...
...WHY NOT?

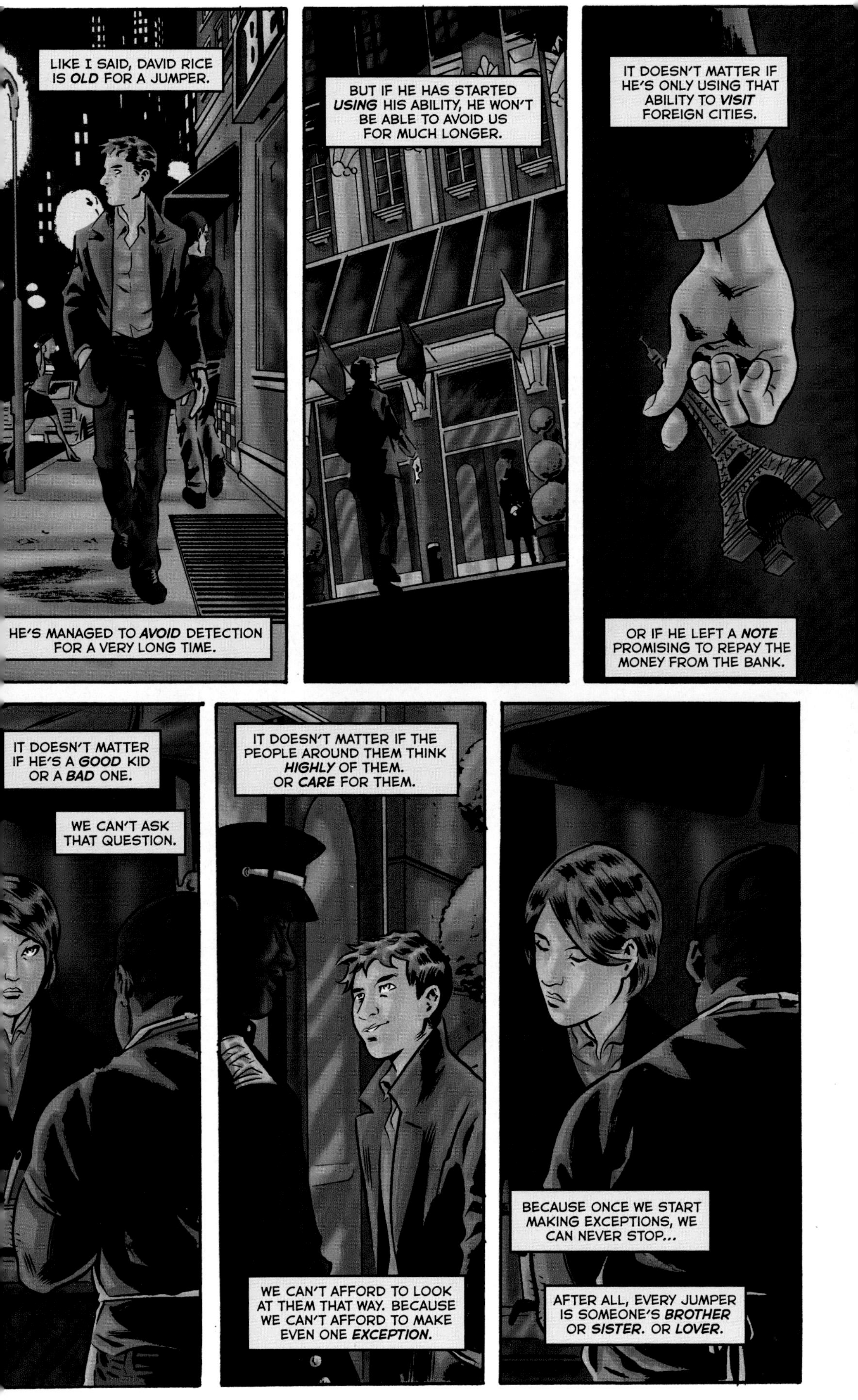
LIKE I SAID, DAVID RICE IS OLD FOR A JUMPER.
HE'S MANAGED TO AVOID DETECTION FOR A VERY LONG TIME.
BUT IF HE HAS STARTED USING HIS ABILITY, HE WON'T BE ABLE TO AVOID US FOR MUCH LONGER.
IT DOESN'T MATTER IF HE'S ONLY USING THAT ABILITY TO VISIT FOREIGN CITIES.
OR IF HE LEFT A NOTE PROMISING TO REPAY THE MONEY FROM THE BANK.
IT DOESN'T MATTER IF HE'S A GOOD KID OR A BAD ONE.
WE CAN'T ASK THAT QUESTION.
IT DOESN'T MATTER IF THE PEOPLE AROUND THEM THINK HIGHLY OF THEM. OR CARE FOR THEM.
WE CAN'T AFFORD TO LOOK AT THEM THAT WAY. BECAUSE WE CAN'T AFFORD TO MAKE EVEN ONE EXCEPTION.
BECAUSE ONCE WE START MAKING EXCEPTIONS, WE CAN NEVER STOP...
AFTER ALL, EVERY JUMPER IS SOMEONE'S BROTHER OR SISTER. OR LOVER.

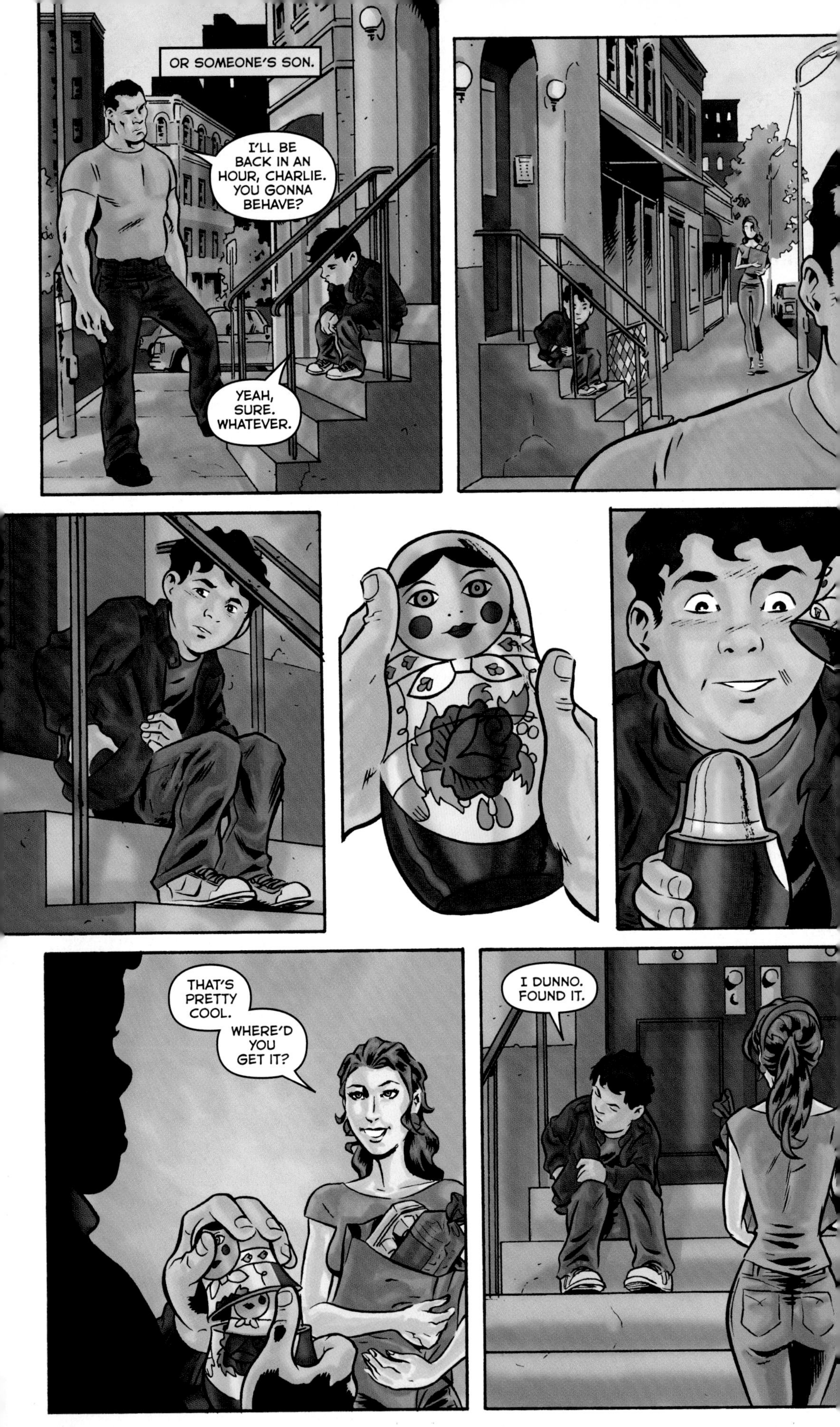
OR SOMEONE'S SON.
I'LL BE BACK IN AN HOUR, CHARLIE. YOU GONNA BEHAVE?
YEAH, SURE. WHATEVER.
THAT'S PRETTY COOL.
WHERE'D YOU GET IT?
I DUNNO. FOUND IT.

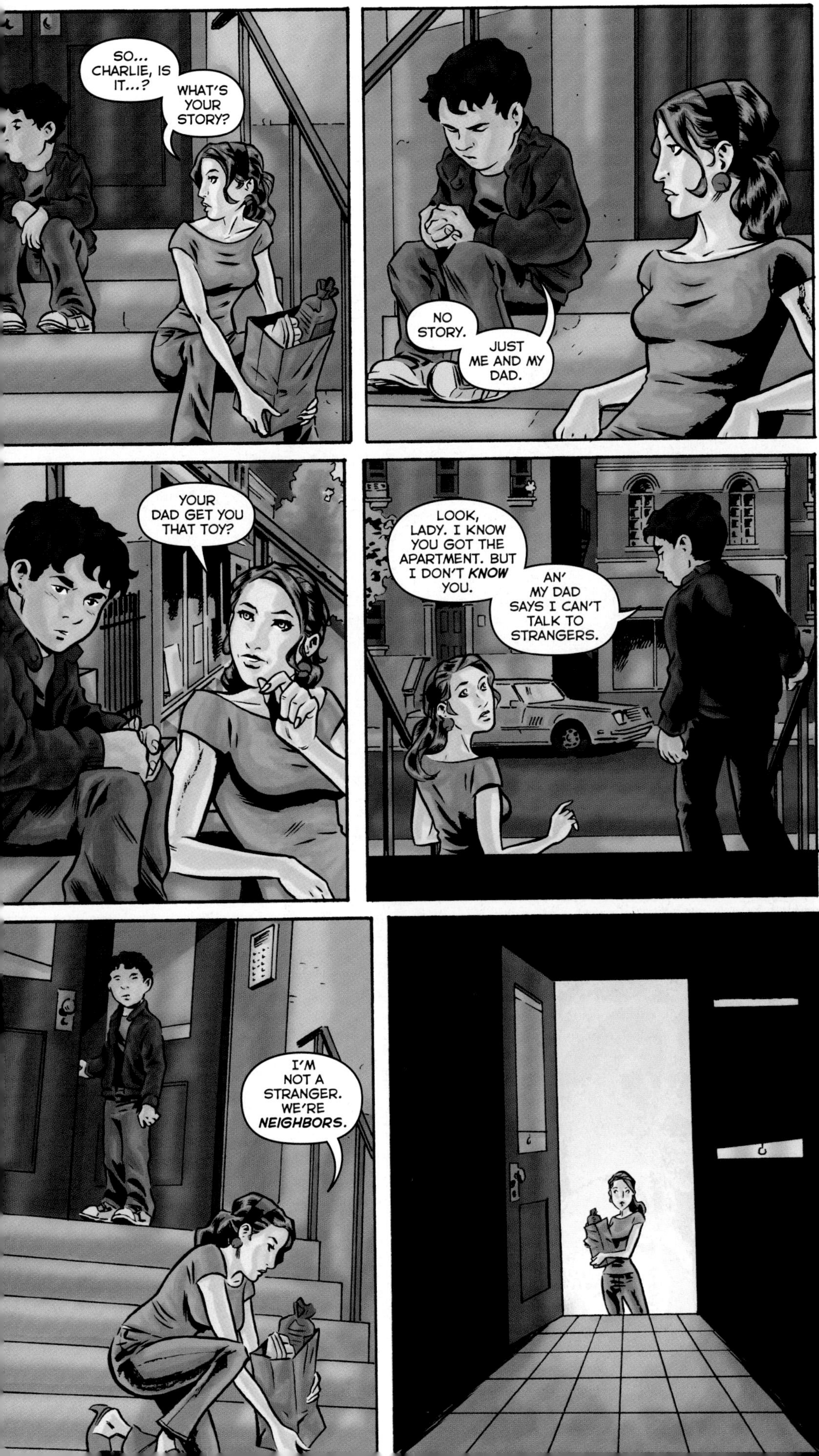
SO... CHARLIE, IS IT...?
WHAT'S YOUR STORY?
NO STORY.
JUST ME AND MY DAD.
YOUR DAD GET YOU THAT TOY?
LOOK, LADY. I KNOW YOU GOT THE APARTMENT. BUT I DON'T KNOW YOU.
AN' MY DAD SAYS I CAN'T TALK TO STRANGERS.
I'M NOT A STRANGER. WE'RE NEIGHBORS.

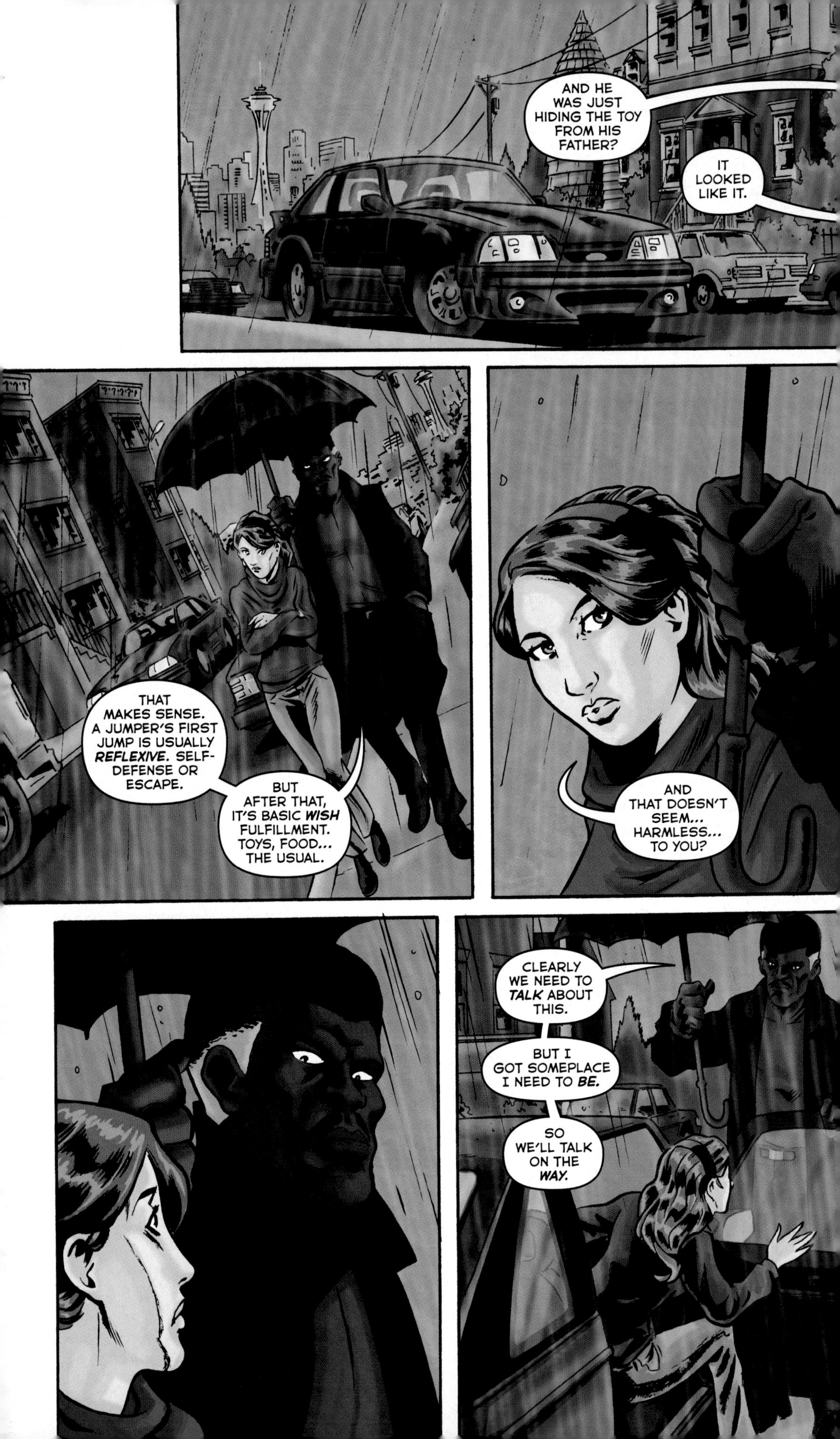
AND HE WAS JUST HIDING THE TOY FROM HIS FATHER?
IT LOOKED LIKE IT.
THAT MAKES SENSE. A JUMPER'S FIRST JUMP IS USUALLY REFLEXIVE. SELF-DEFENSE OR ESCAPE.
BUT AFTER THAT, IT'S BASIC WISH FULFILLMENT. TOYS, FOOD... THE USUAL.
AND THAT DOESN'T SEEM... HARMLESS... TO YOU?
CLEARLY WE NEED TO TALK ABOUT THIS.
BUT I GOT SOMEPLACE I NEED TO BE.
SO WE'LL TALK ON THE WAY.

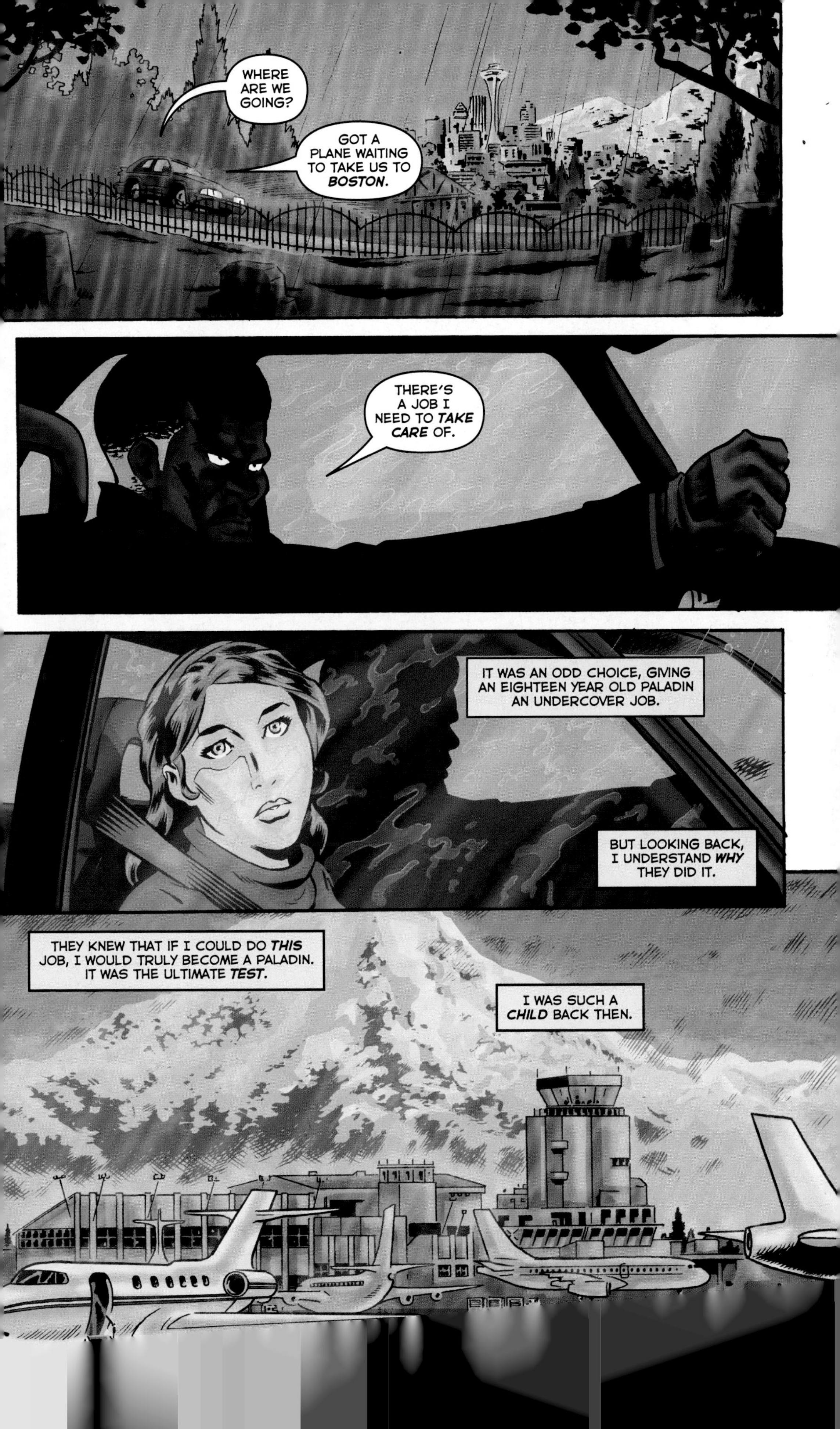

WHERE ARE WE GOING?
GOT A PLANE WAITING TO TAKE US TO BOSTON.
THERE'S A JOB I NEED TO TAKE CARE OF.
IT WAS AN ODD CHOICE, GIVING AN EIGHTEEN YEAR OLD PALADIN AN UNDERCOVER JOB.
BUT LOOKING BACK, I UNDERSTAND WHY THEY DID IT.
THEY KNEW THAT IF I COULD DO THIS JOB, I WOULD TRULY BECOME A PALADIN. IT WAS THE ULTIMATE TEST.
I WAS SUCH A CHILD BACK THEN.

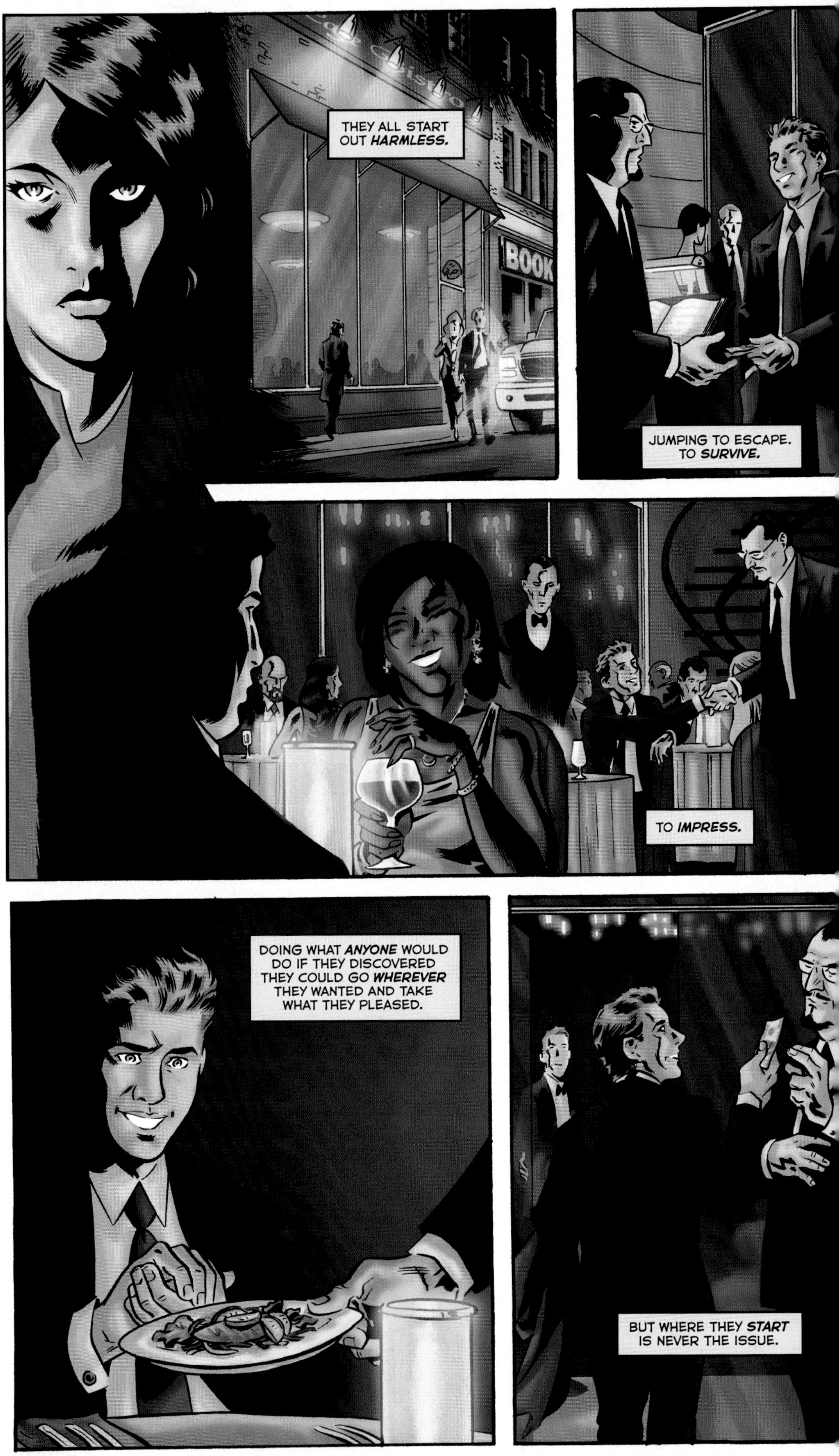
THEY ALL START OUT HARMLESS.
BOOK
JUMPING TO ESCAPE. TO SURVIVE.
TO IMPRESS.
DOING WHAT ANYONE WOULD DO IF THEY DISCOVERED THEY COULD GO WHEREVER THEY WANTED AND TAKE WHAT THEY PLEASED.
BUT WHERE THEY START IS NEVER THE ISSUE.

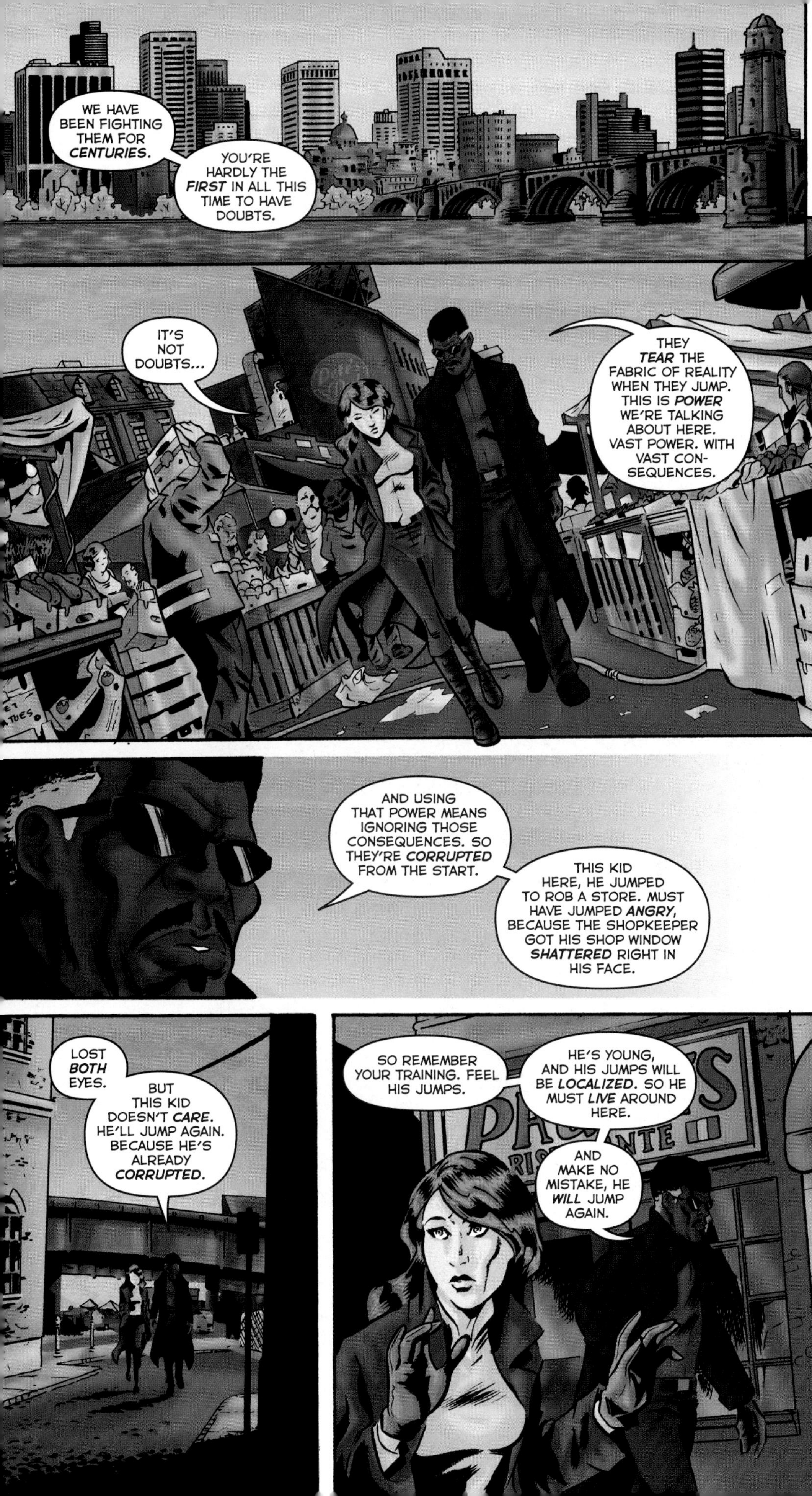
WE HAVE BEEN FIGHTING THEM FOR *CENTURIES*.
YOU'RE HARDLY THE *FIRST* IN ALL THIS TIME TO HAVE DOUBTS.
IT'S NOT DOUBTS...
THEY *TEAR* THE FABRIC OF REALITY WHEN THEY JUMP. THIS IS *POWER* WE'RE TALKING ABOUT HERE. VAST POWER. WITH VAST CON-SEQUENCES.
AND USING THAT POWER MEANS IGNORING THOSE CONSEQUENCES. SO THEY'RE *CORRUPTED* FROM THE START.
THIS KID HERE, HE JUMPED TO ROB A STORE. MUST HAVE JUMPED *ANGRY*, BECAUSE THE SHOPKEEPER GOT HIS SHOP WINDOW *SHATTERED* RIGHT IN HIS FACE.
LOST *BOTH* EYES.
BUT THIS KID DOESN'T *CARE*. HE'LL JUMP AGAIN. BECAUSE HE'S ALREADY *CORRUPTED*.
SO REMEMBER YOUR TRAINING. FEEL HIS JUMPS.
HE'S YOUNG, AND HIS JUMPS WILL BE *LOCALIZED*. SO HE MUST *LIVE* AROUND HERE.
AND MAKE NO MISTAKE, HE *WILL* JUMP AGAIN.

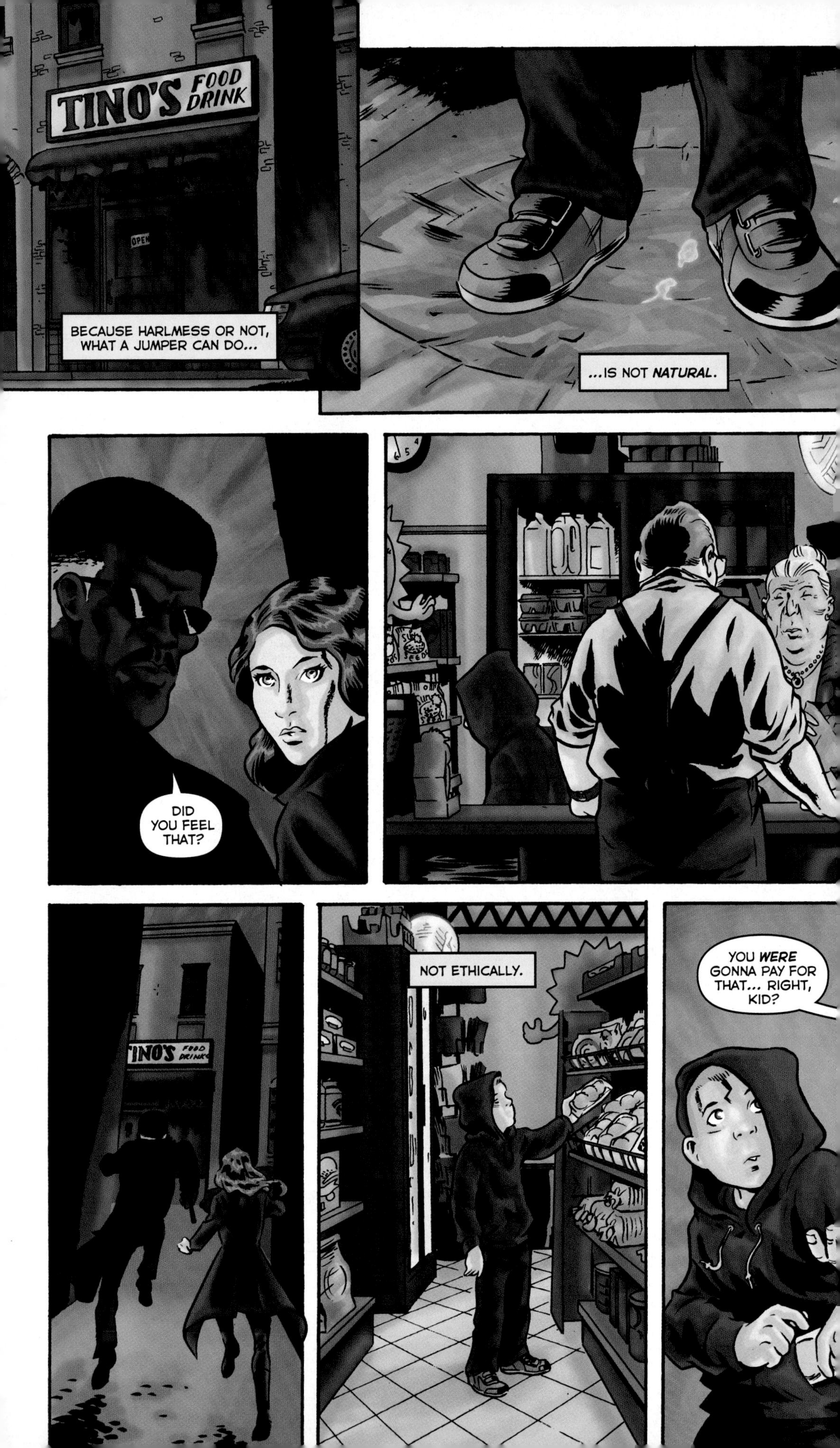
TINO'S FOOD DRINK
OPEN
BECAUSE HARLMESS OR NOT, WHAT A JUMPER CAN DO...
...IS NOT NATURAL.
DID YOU FEEL THAT?
TINO'S FOOD DRINK
NOT ETHICALLY.
YOU WERE GONNA PAY FOR THAT... RIGHT, KID?

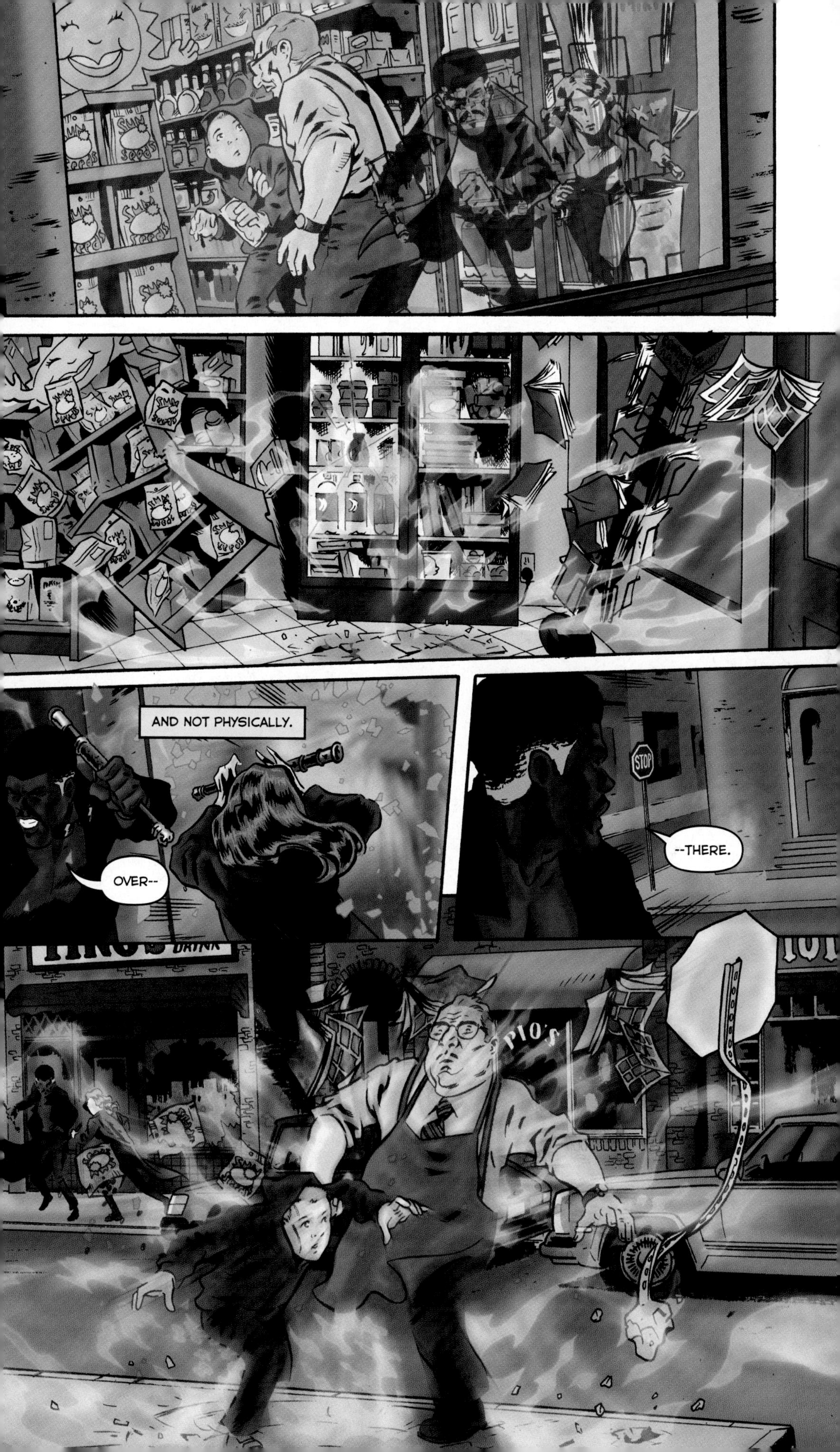
AND NOT PHYSICALLY.
OVER--
--THERE.

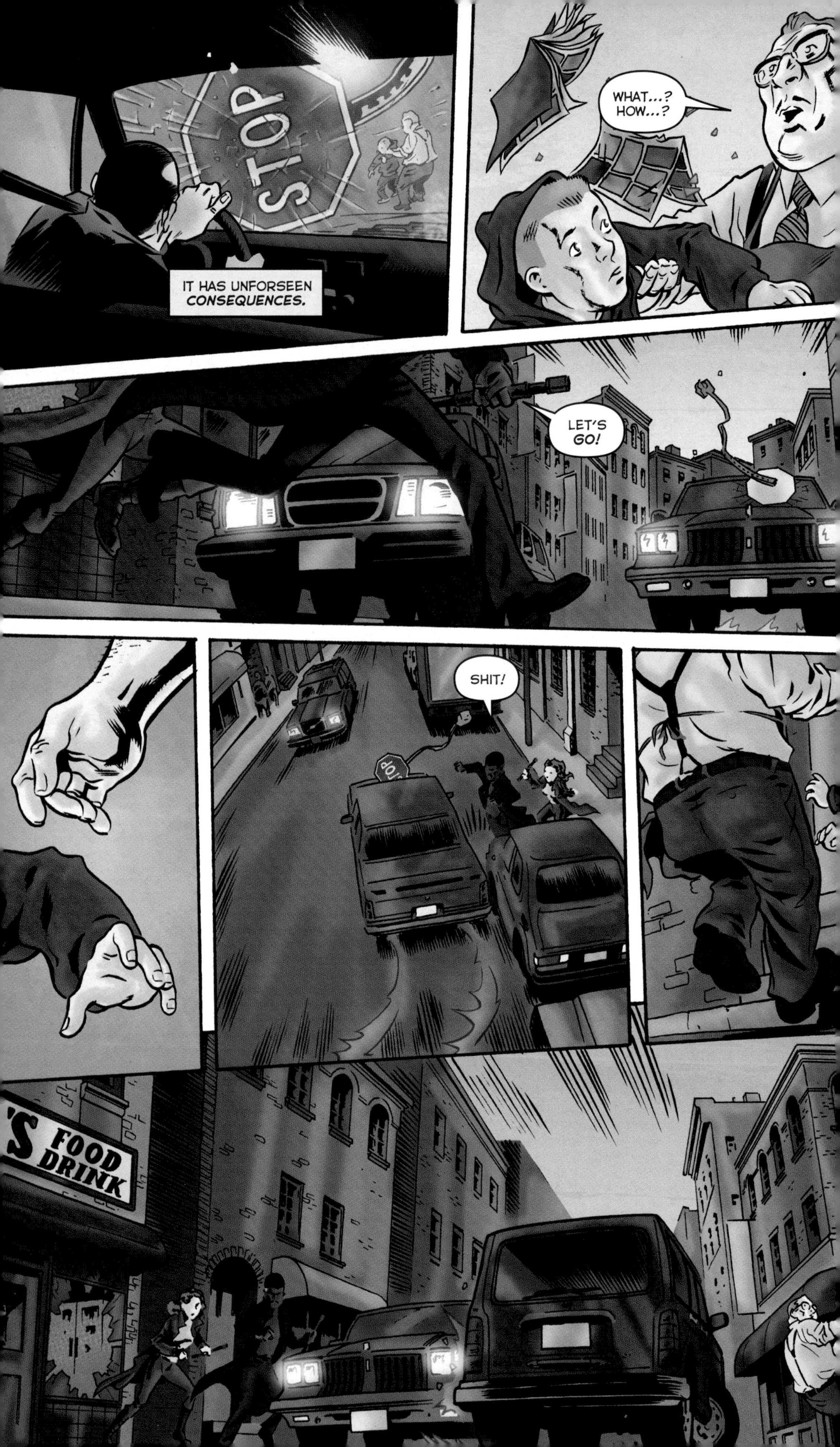

IT HAS UNFORSEEN CONSEQUENCES.
WHAT...? HOW...?
LET'S GO!
SHIT!
STOP
'S FOOD DRINK

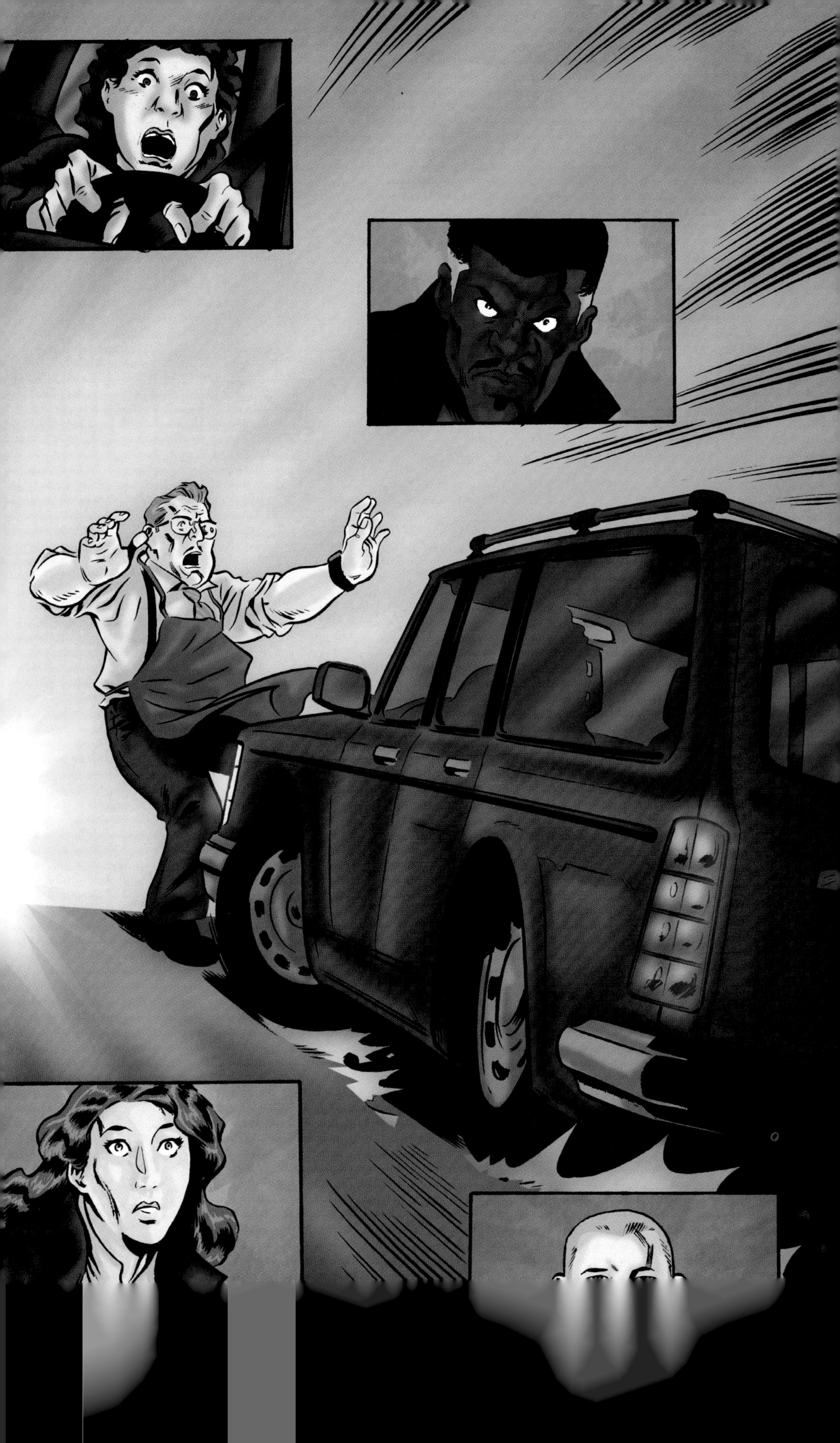

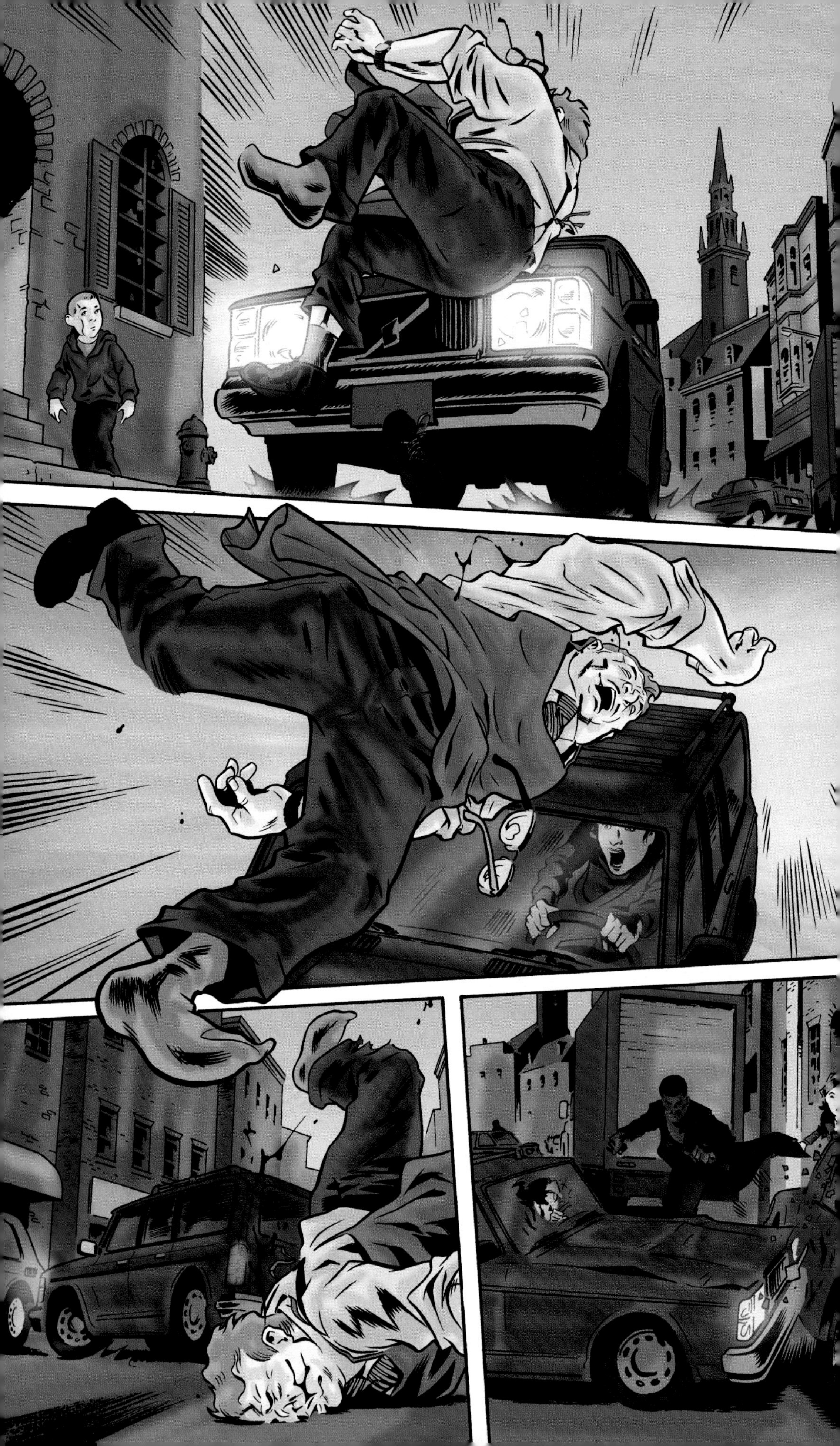

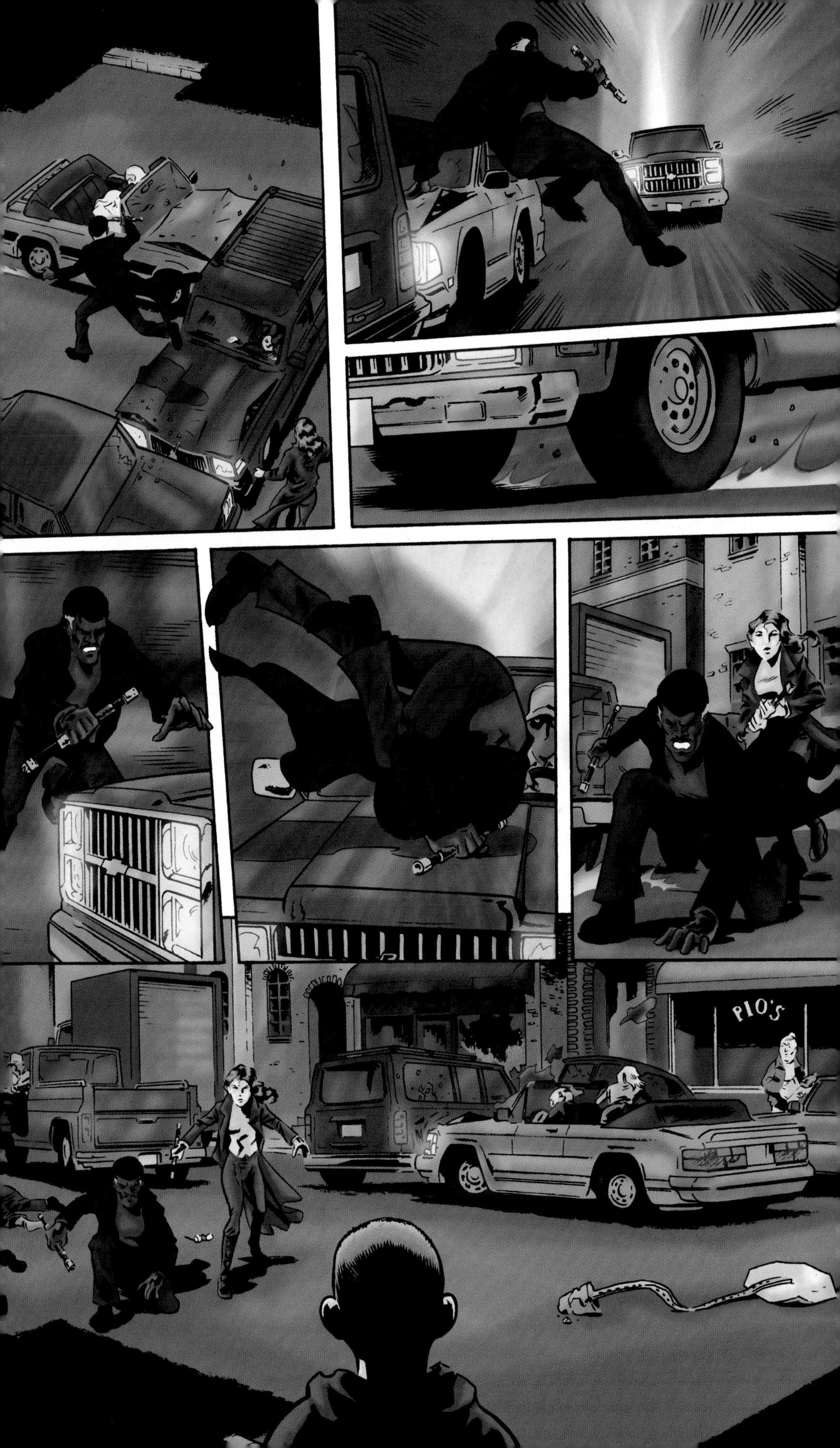
PIO'S

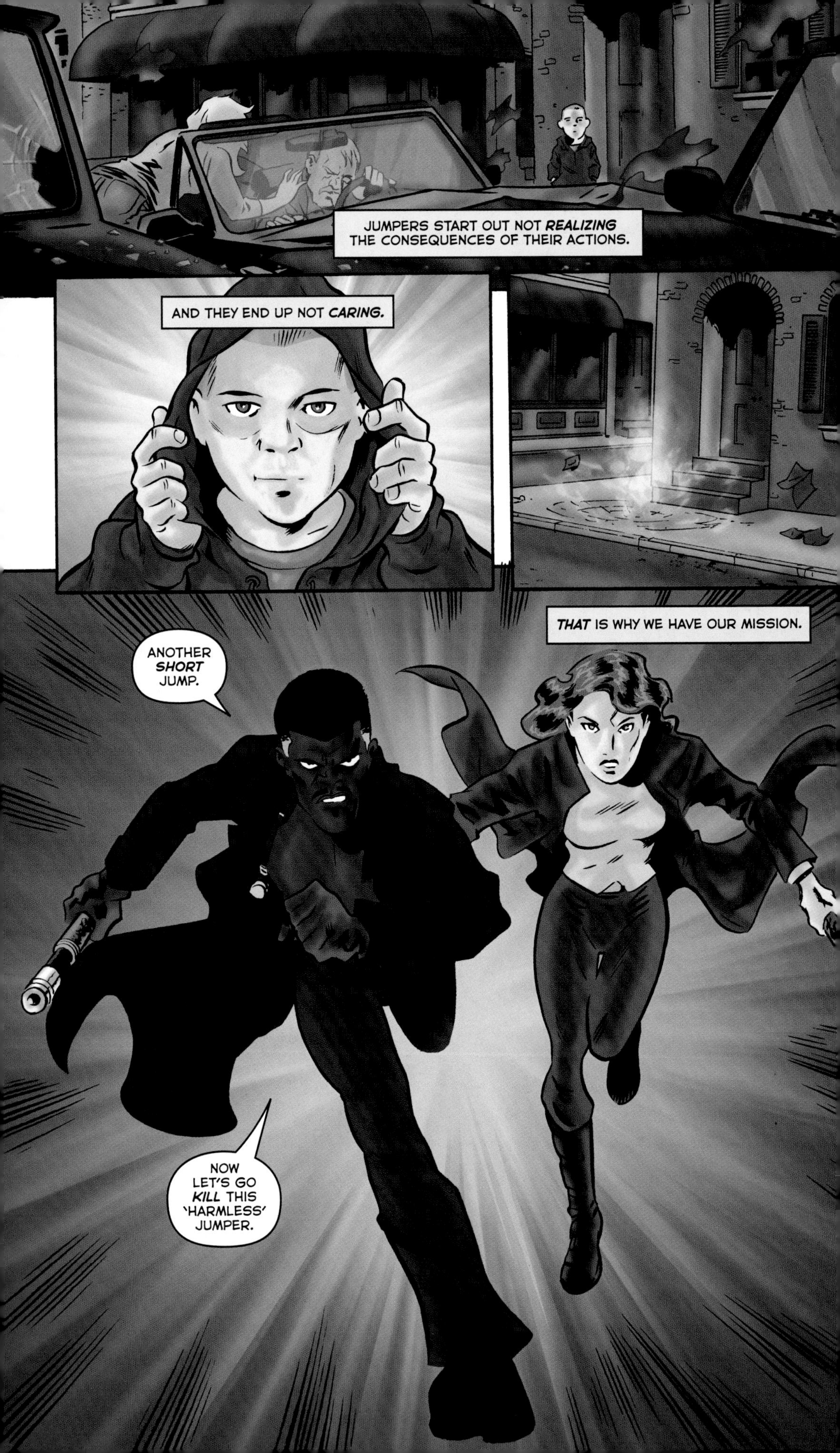
JUMPERS START OUT NOT *REALIZING* THE CONSEQUENCES OF THEIR ACTIONS.
AND THEY END UP NOT *CARING.*
THAT IS WHY WE HAVE OUR MISSION.
ANOTHER *SHORT* JUMP.
NOW LET'S GO *KILL* THIS 'HARMLESS' JUMPER.

CHAPTER 2

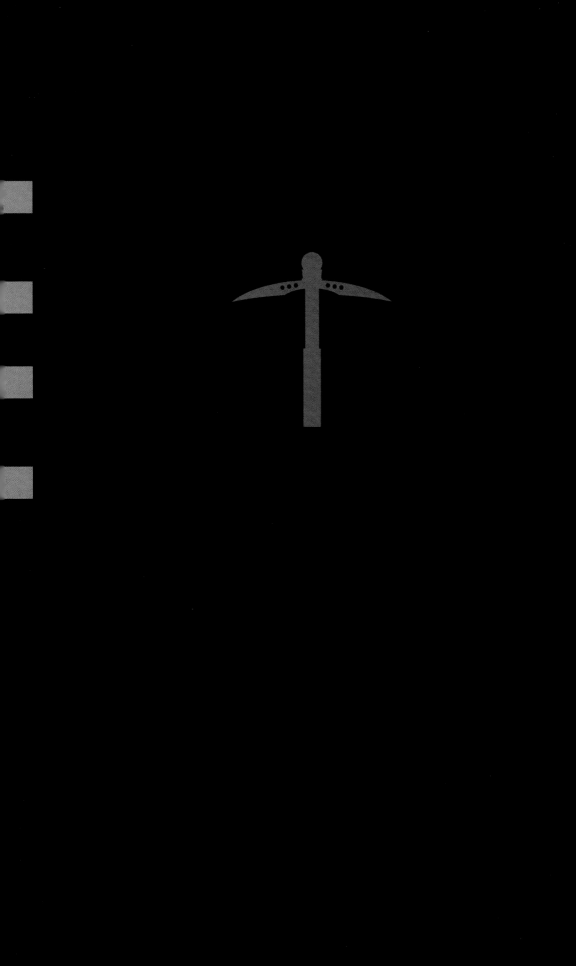

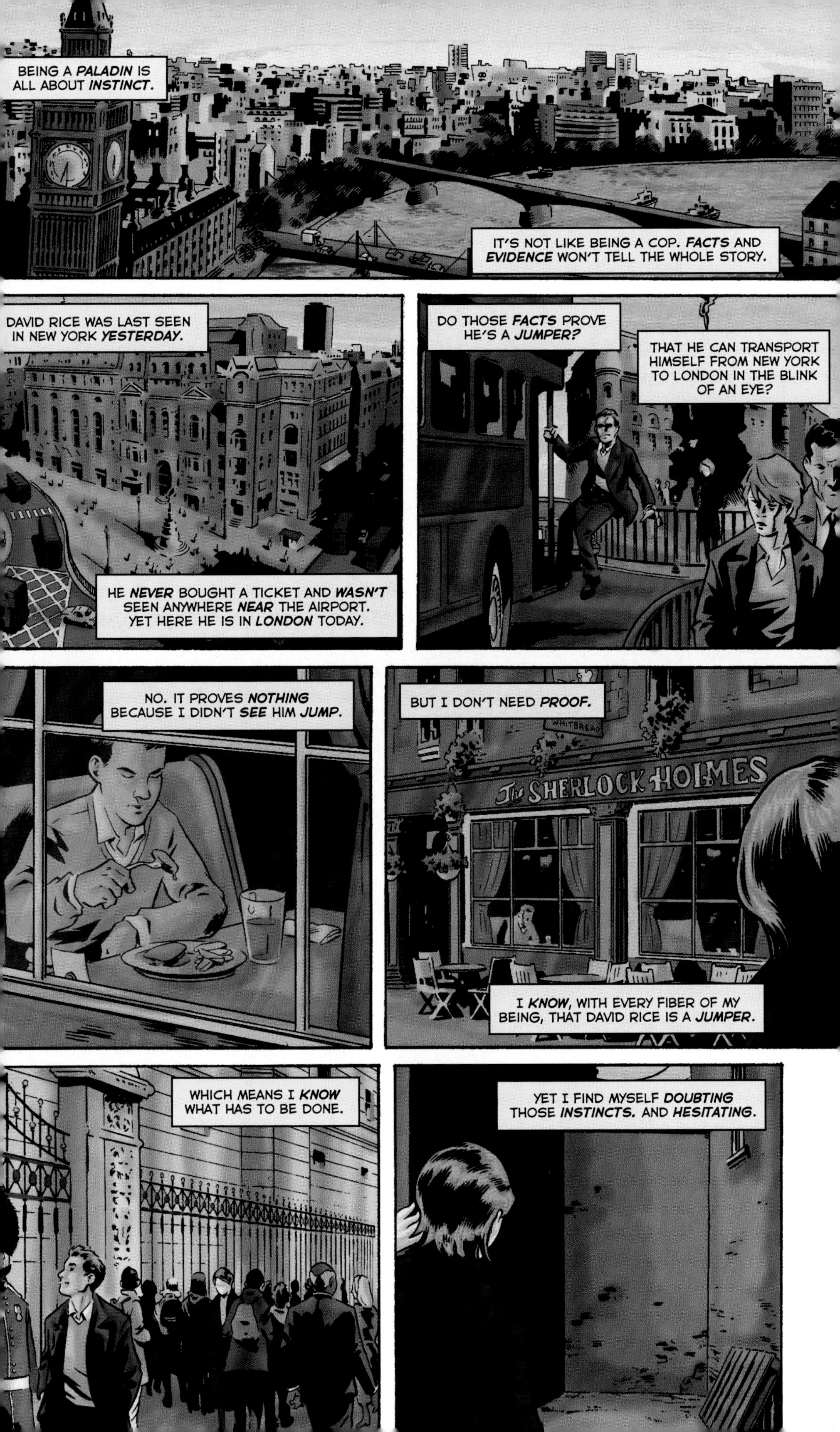
BEING A *PALADIN* IS ALL ABOUT *INSTINCT*.
IT'S NOT LIKE BEING A COP. *FACTS* AND *EVIDENCE* WON'T TELL THE WHOLE STORY.
DAVID RICE WAS LAST SEEN IN NEW YORK *YESTERDAY*.
HE *NEVER* BOUGHT A TICKET AND *WASN'T* SEEN ANYWHERE *NEAR* THE AIRPORT. YET HERE HE IS IN *LONDON* TODAY.
DO THOSE *FACTS* PROVE HE'S A *JUMPER?*
THAT HE CAN TRANSPORT HIMSELF FROM NEW YORK TO LONDON IN THE BLINK OF AN EYE?
NO. IT PROVES *NOTHING* BECAUSE I DIDN'T *SEE* HIM *JUMP*.
BUT I DON'T NEED *PROOF*.
WHITBREAD
The SHERLOCK HOLMES
I *KNOW*, WITH EVERY FIBER OF MY BEING, THAT DAVID RICE IS A *JUMPER*.
WHICH MEANS I *KNOW* WHAT HAS TO BE DONE.
YET I FIND MYSELF *DOUBTING* THOSE *INSTINCTS*. AND *HESITATING*.

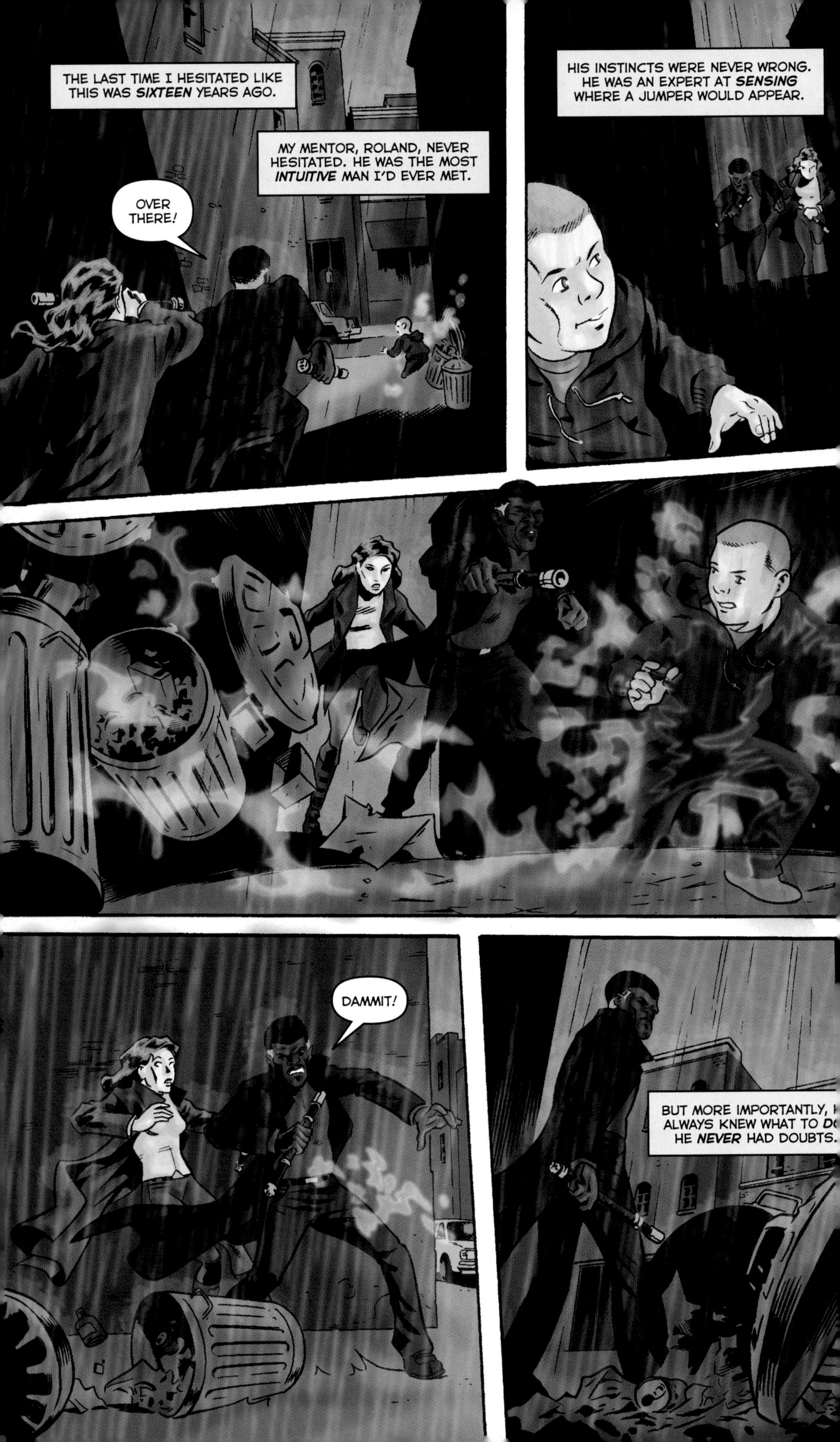
THE LAST TIME I HESITATED LIKE THIS WAS SIXTEEN YEARS AGO.
MY MENTOR, ROLAND, NEVER HESITATED. HE WAS THE MOST INTUITIVE MAN I'D EVER MET.
OVER THERE!
HIS INSTINCTS WERE NEVER WRONG. HE WAS AN EXPERT AT SENSING WHERE A JUMPER WOULD APPEAR.
DAMMIT!
BUT MORE IMPORTANTLY, H
ALWAYS KNEW WHAT TO DO
HE NEVER HAD DOUBTS.

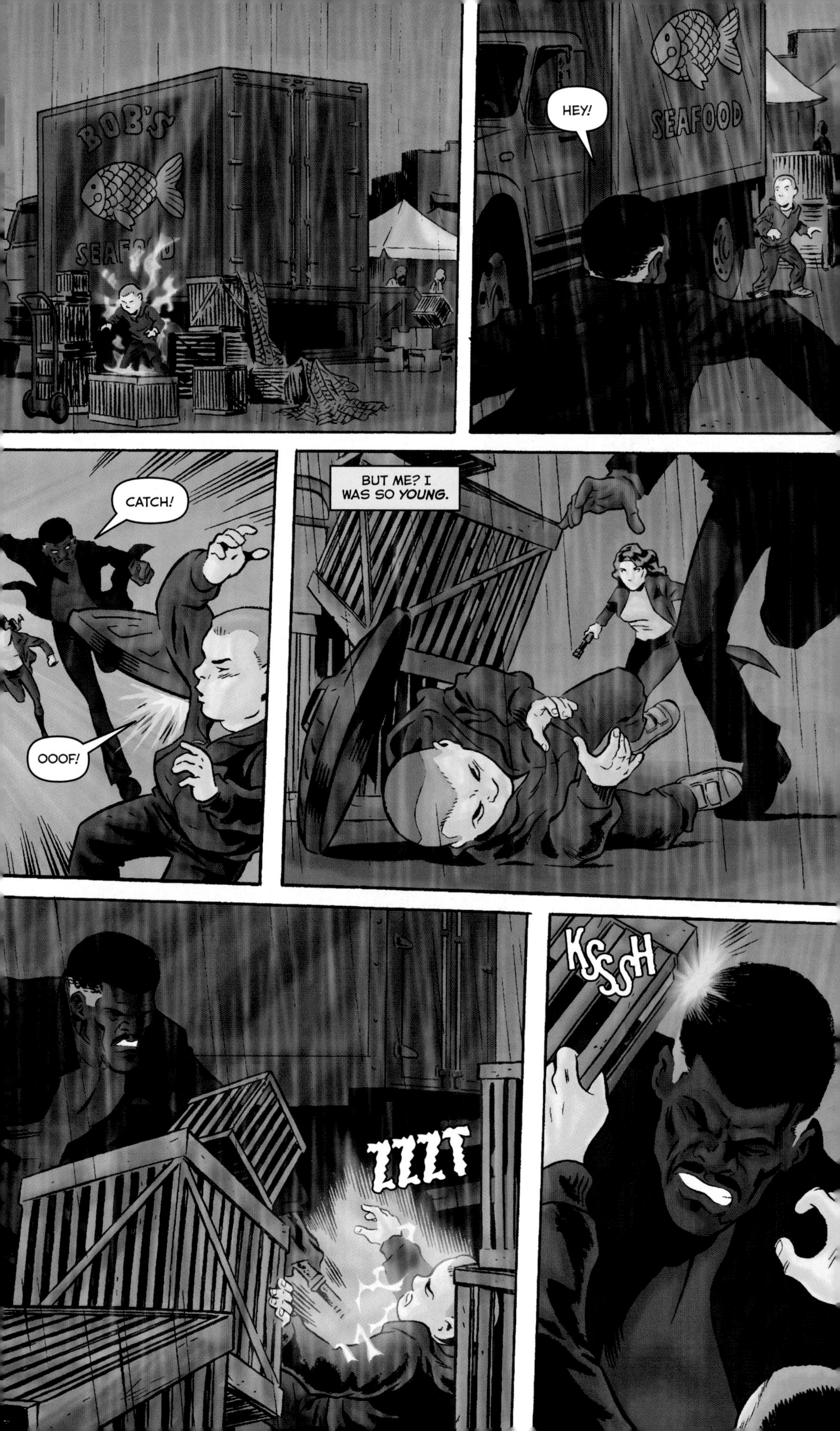
BOB'S
SEAFOOD
HEY!
SEAFOOD
CATCH!
OOOF!
BUT ME? I WAS SO YOUNG.
ZZZT
KSSSH

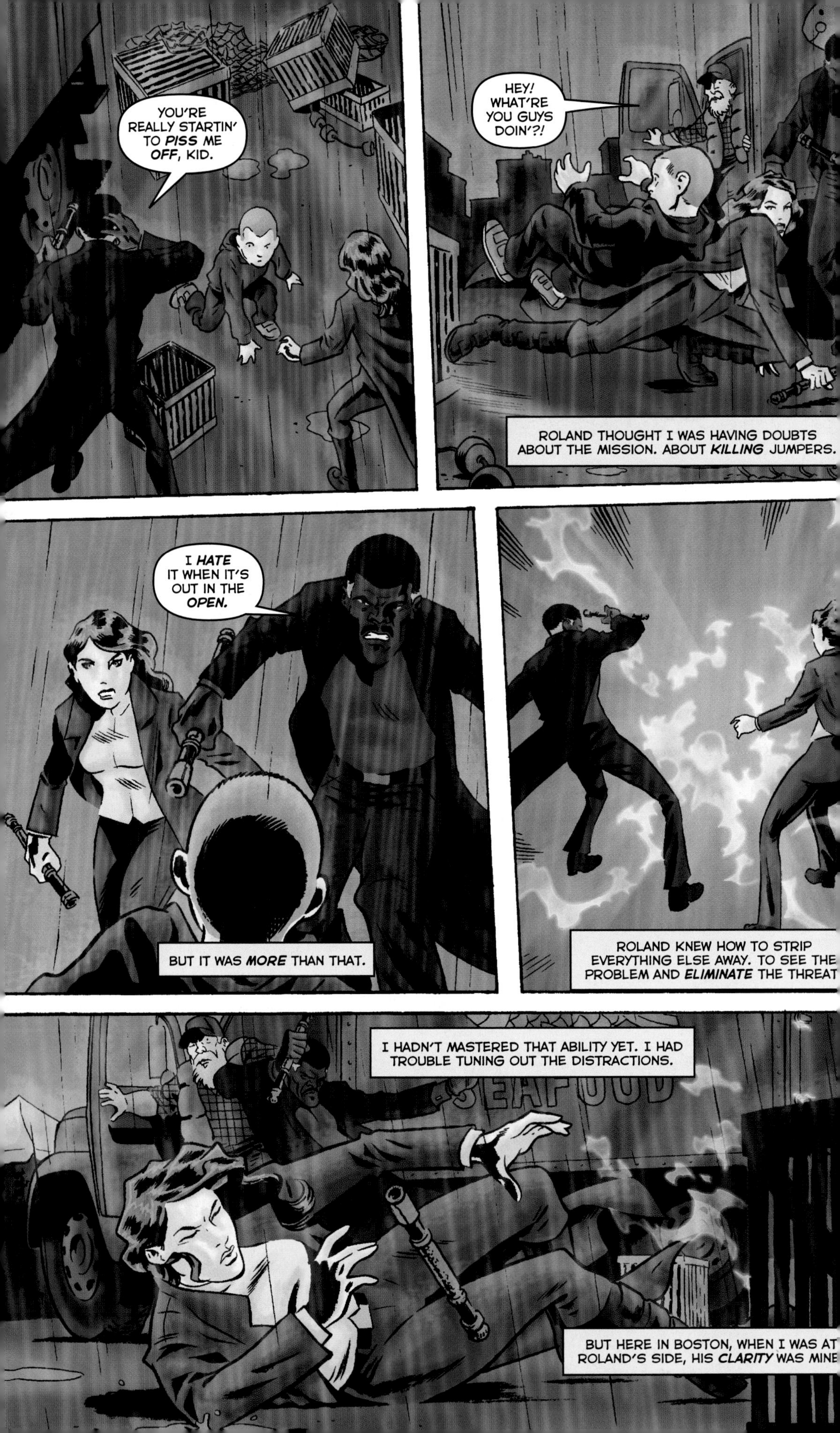
YOU'RE REALLY STARTIN' TO PISS ME OFF, KID.
HEY! WHAT'RE YOU GUYS DOIN'?!
ROLAND THOUGHT I WAS HAVING DOUBTS ABOUT THE MISSION. ABOUT KILLING JUMPERS.
I HATE IT WHEN IT'S OUT IN THE OPEN.
BUT IT WAS MORE THAN THAT.
ROLAND KNEW HOW TO STRIP EVERYTHING ELSE AWAY. TO SEE THE PROBLEM AND ELIMINATE THE THREAT
I HADN'T MASTERED THAT ABILITY YET. I HAD TROUBLE TUNING OUT THE DISTRACTIONS.
SEAFOOD
BUT HERE IN BOSTON, WHEN I WAS AT ROLAND'S SIDE, HIS CLARITY WAS MINE

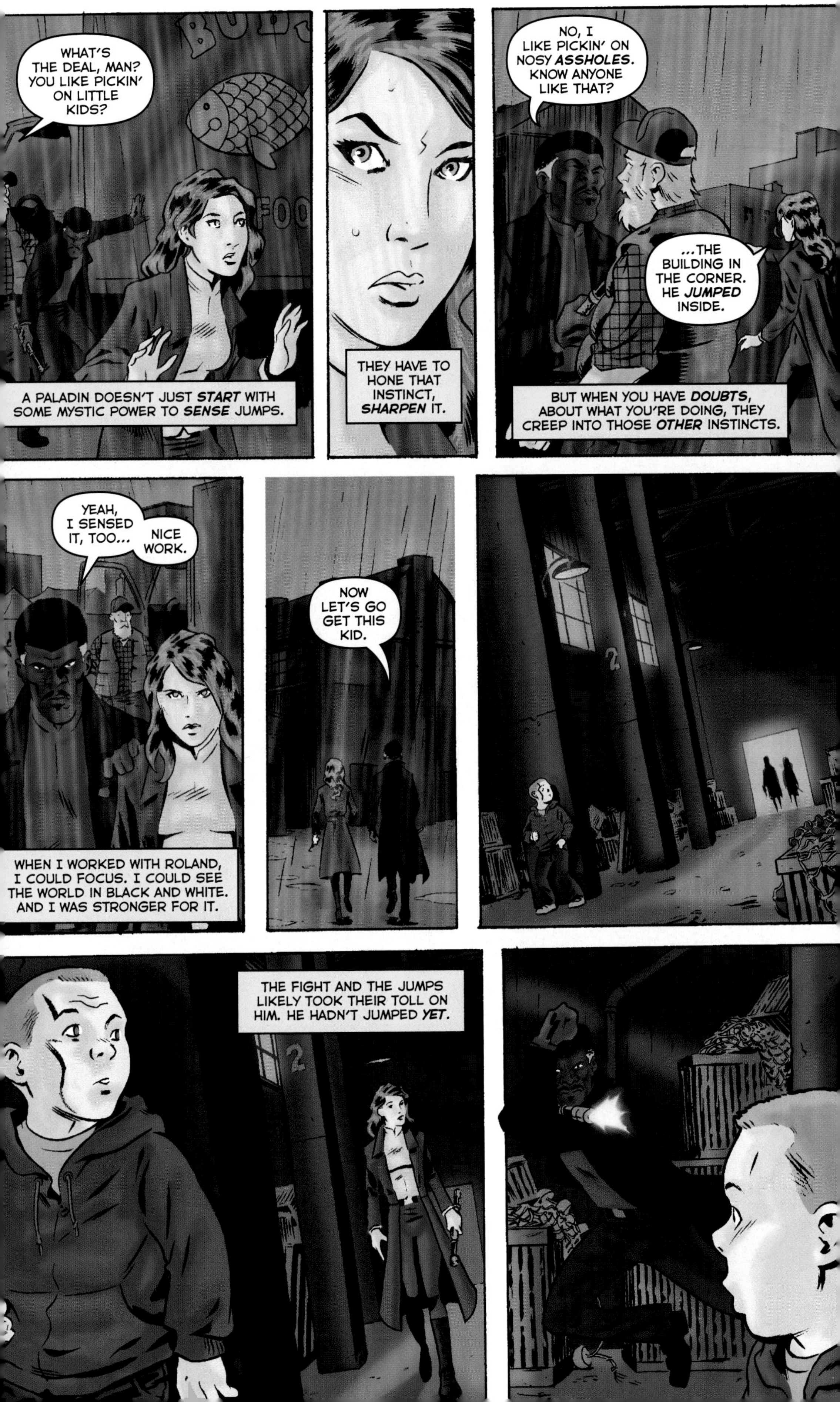
WHAT'S THE DEAL, MAN? YOU LIKE PICKIN' ON LITTLE KIDS?
A PALADIN DOESN'T JUST START WITH SOME MYSTIC POWER TO SENSE JUMPS.
THEY HAVE TO HONE THAT INSTINCT, SHARPEN IT.
NO, I LIKE PICKIN' ON NOSY ASSHOLES. KNOW ANYONE LIKE THAT?
...THE BUILDING IN THE CORNER. HE JUMPED INSIDE.
BUT WHEN YOU HAVE DOUBTS, ABOUT WHAT YOU'RE DOING, THEY CREEP INTO THOSE OTHER INSTINCTS.
YEAH, I SENSED IT, TOO...
NICE WORK.
WHEN I WORKED WITH ROLAND, I COULD FOCUS. I COULD SEE THE WORLD IN BLACK AND WHITE. AND I WAS STRONGER FOR IT.
NOW LET'S GO GET THIS KID.
THE FIGHT AND THE JUMPS LIKELY TOOK THEIR TOLL ON HIM. HE HADN'T JUMPED YET.

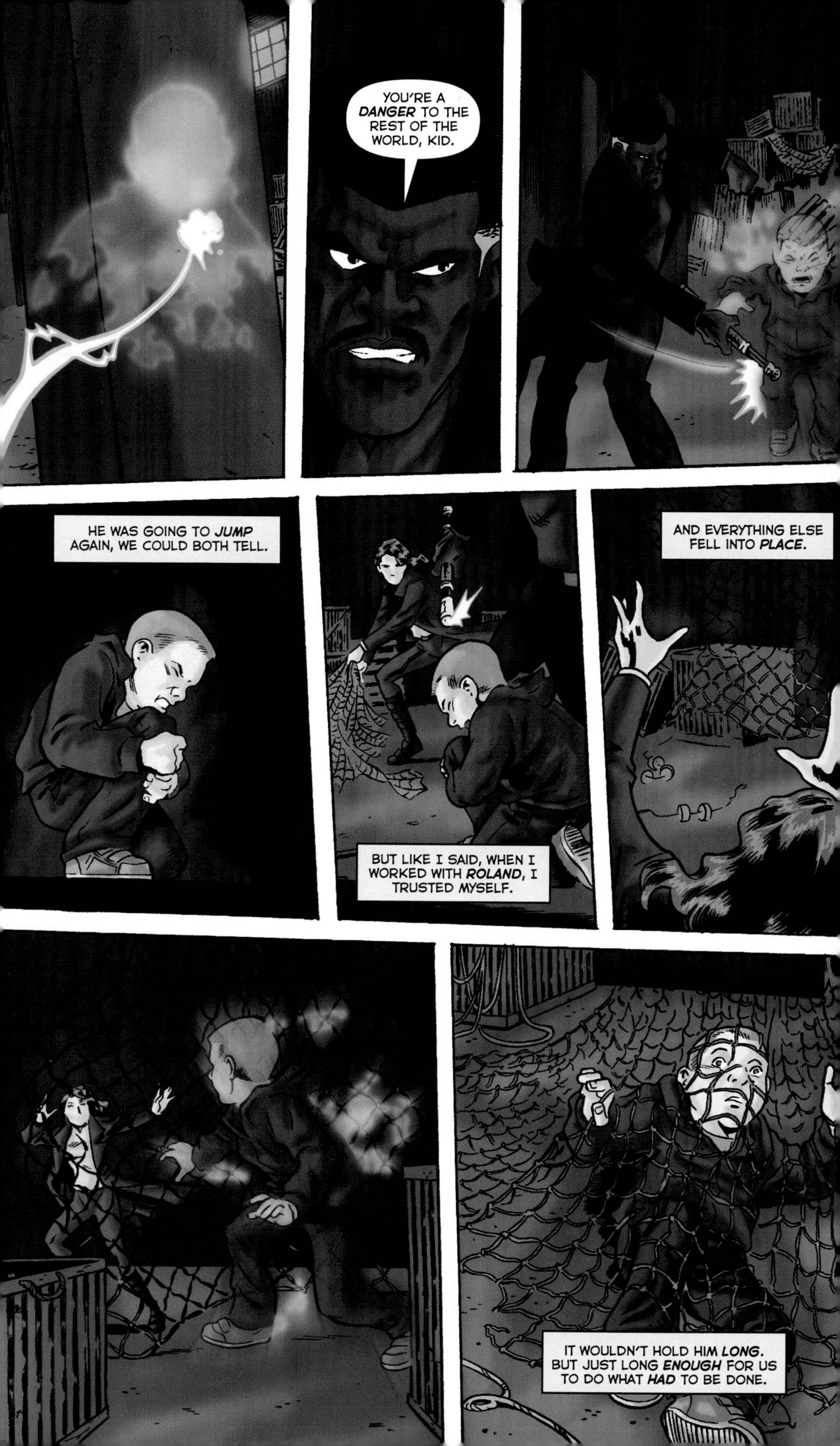
YOU'RE A DANGER TO THE REST OF THE WORLD, KID.
HE WAS GOING TO JUMP AGAIN, WE COULD BOTH TELL.
BUT LIKE I SAID, WHEN I WORKED WITH ROLAND, I TRUSTED MYSELF.
AND EVERYTHING ELSE FELL INTO PLACE.
IT WOULDN'T HOLD HIM LONG. BUT JUST LONG ENOUGH FOR US TO DO WHAT HAD TO BE DONE.

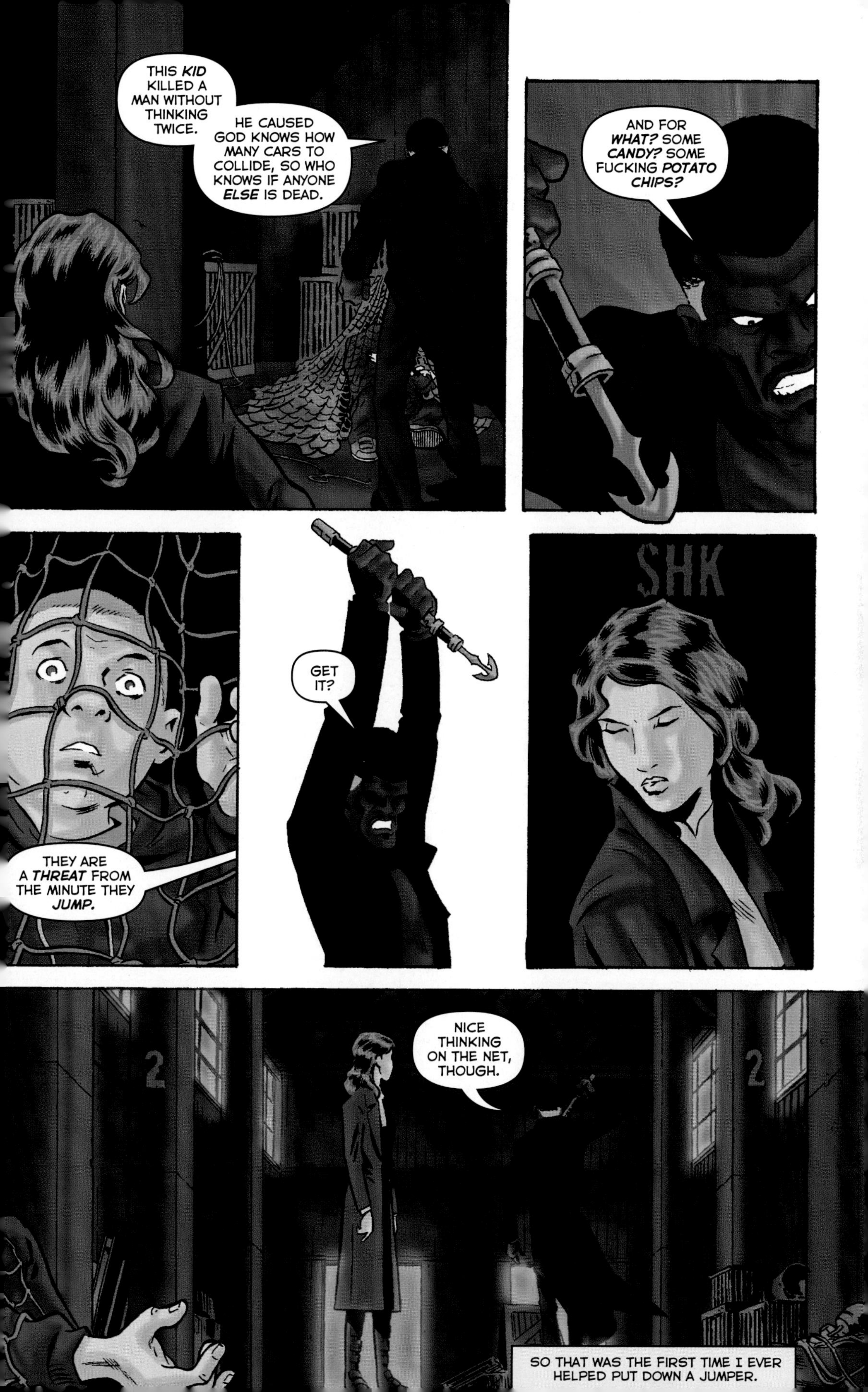
THIS KID KILLED A MAN WITHOUT THINKING TWICE.
HE CAUSED GOD KNOWS HOW MANY CARS TO COLLIDE, SO WHO KNOWS IF ANYONE ELSE IS DEAD.
AND FOR WHAT? SOME CANDY? SOME FUCKING POTATO CHIPS?
THEY ARE A THREAT FROM THE MINUTE THEY JUMP.
GET IT?
SHK
NICE THINKING ON THE NET, THOUGH.
SO THAT WAS THE FIRST TIME I EVER HELPED PUT DOWN A JUMPER.

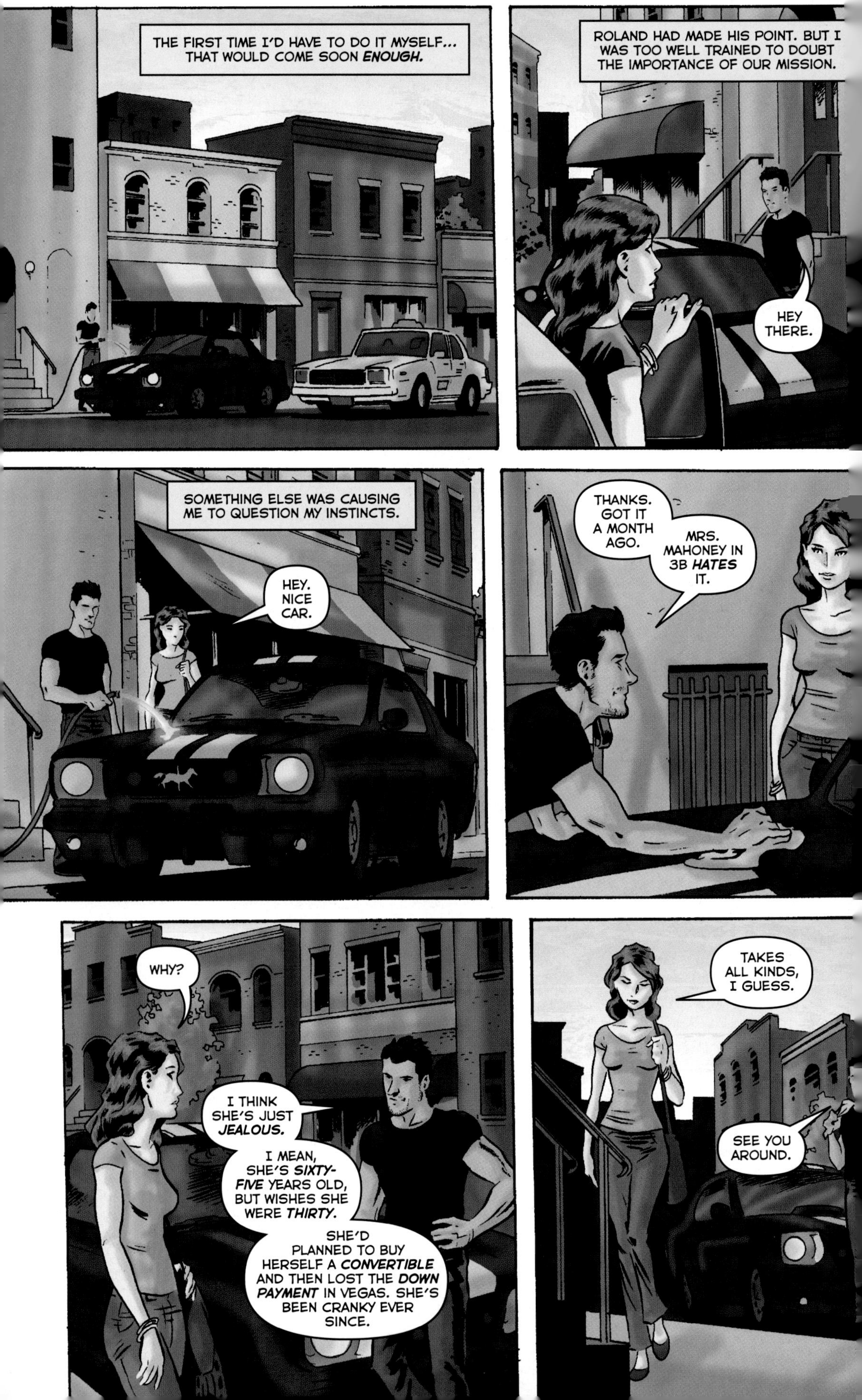
THE FIRST TIME I'D HAVE TO DO IT MYSELF... THAT WOULD COME SOON ENOUGH.
ROLAND HAD MADE HIS POINT. BUT I WAS TOO WELL TRAINED TO DOUBT THE IMPORTANCE OF OUR MISSION.
HEY THERE.
SOMETHING ELSE WAS CAUSING ME TO QUESTION MY INSTINCTS.
HEY. NICE CAR.
THANKS. GOT IT A MONTH AGO.
MRS. MAHONEY IN 3B HATES IT.
WHY?
I THINK SHE'S JUST JEALOUS.
I MEAN, SHE'S SIXTY-FIVE YEARS OLD, BUT WISHES SHE WERE THIRTY.
SHE'D PLANNED TO BUY HERSELF A CONVERTIBLE AND THEN LOST THE DOWN PAYMENT IN VEGAS. SHE'S BEEN CRANKY EVER SINCE.
TAKES ALL KINDS, I GUESS.
SEE YOU AROUND.

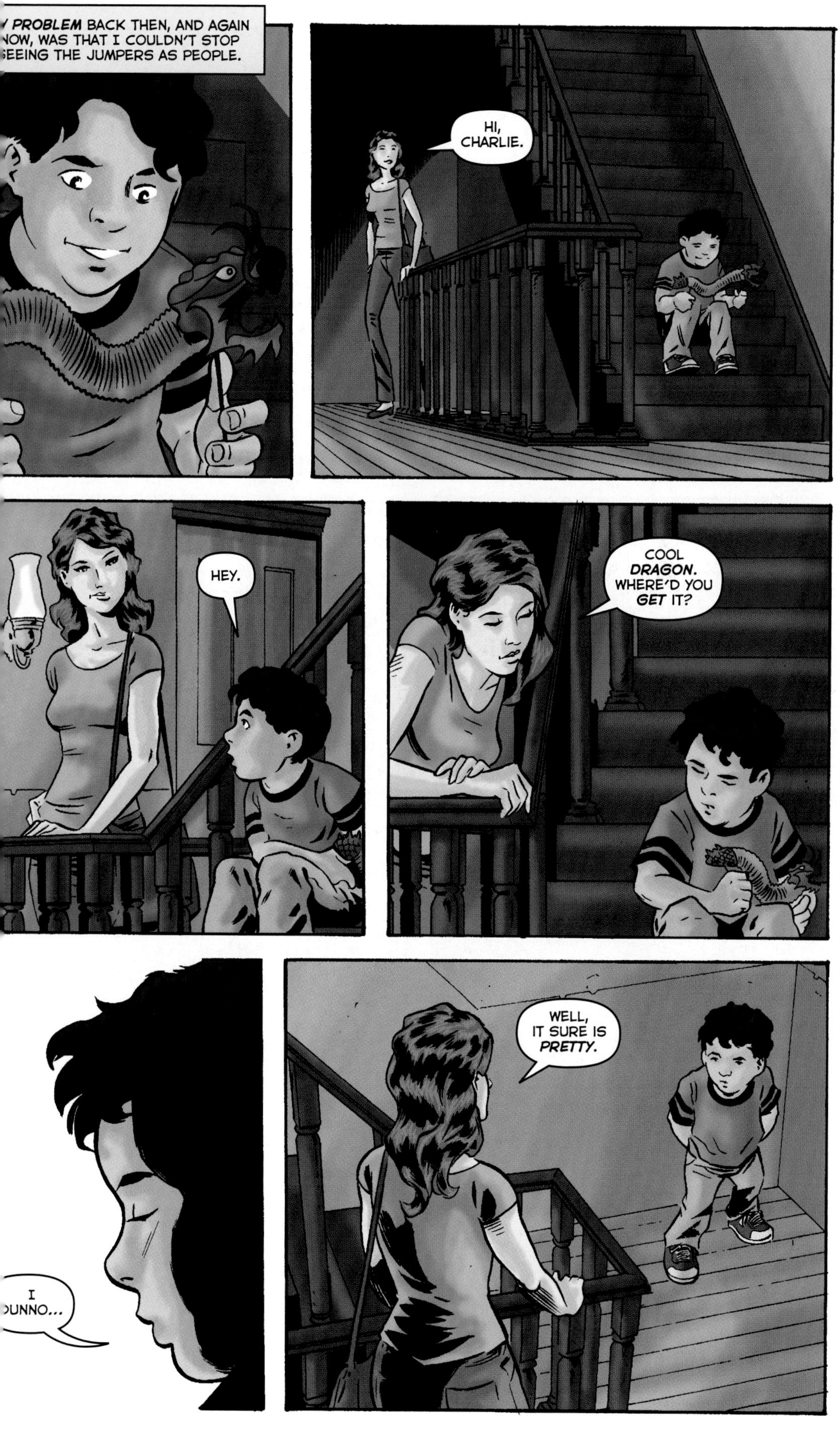

/ PROBLEM BACK THEN, AND AGAIN
NOW, WAS THAT I COULDN'T STOP
SEEING THE JUMPERS AS PEOPLE.
HI, CHARLIE.
HEY.
COOL DRAGON. WHERE'D YOU GET IT?
I DUNNO...
WELL, IT SURE IS PRETTY.

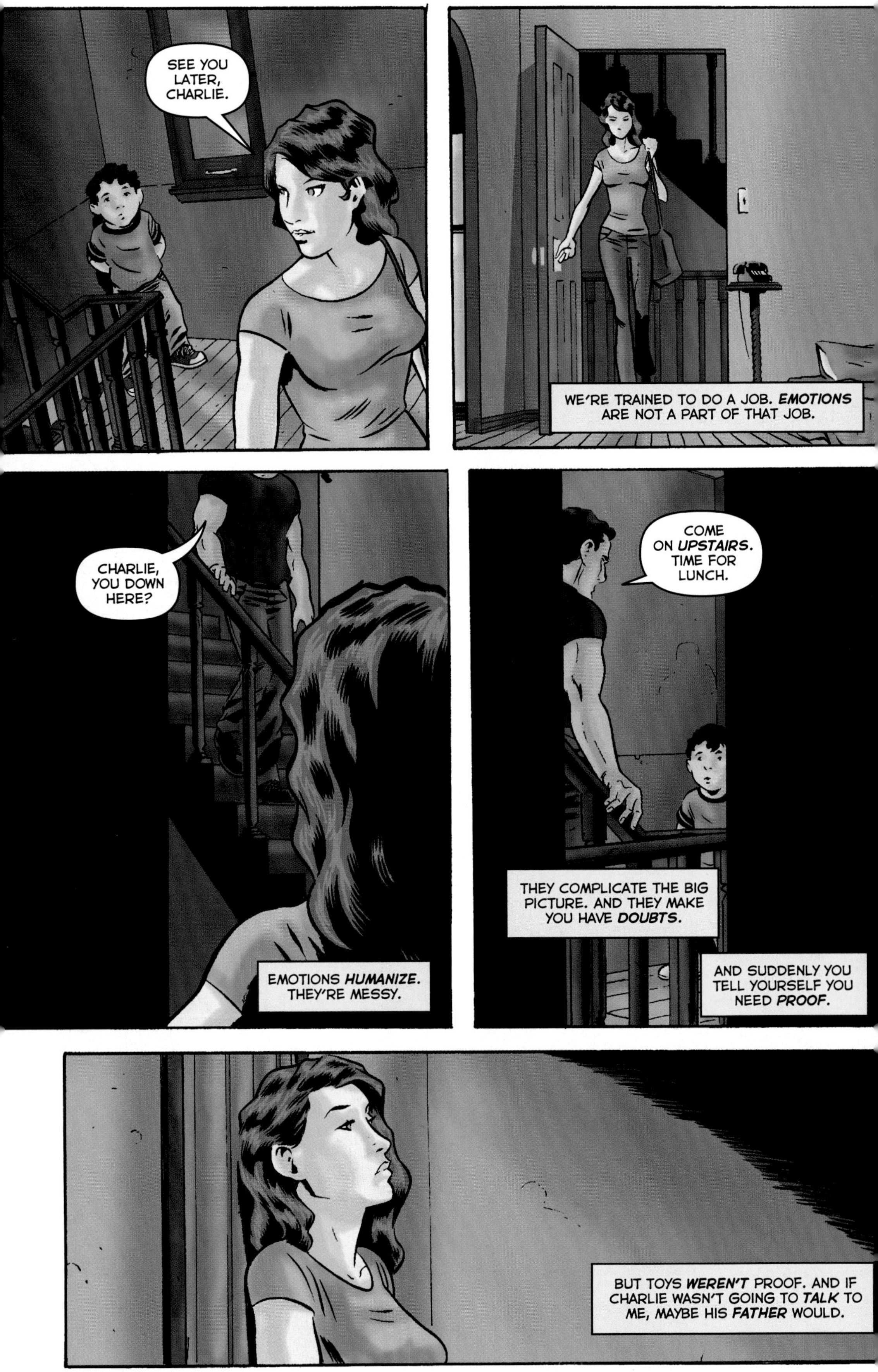
SEE YOU LATER, CHARLIE.
WE'RE TRAINED TO DO A JOB. EMOTIONS ARE NOT A PART OF THAT JOB.
CHARLIE, YOU DOWN HERE?
EMOTIONS HUMANIZE. THEY'RE MESSY.
COME ON UPSTAIRS. TIME FOR LUNCH.
THEY COMPLICATE THE BIG PICTURE. AND THEY MAKE YOU HAVE DOUBTS.
AND SUDDENLY YOU TELL YOURSELF YOU NEED PROOF.
BUT TOYS WEREN'T PROOF. AND IF CHARLIE WASN'T GOING TO TALK TO ME, MAYBE HIS FATHER WOULD.

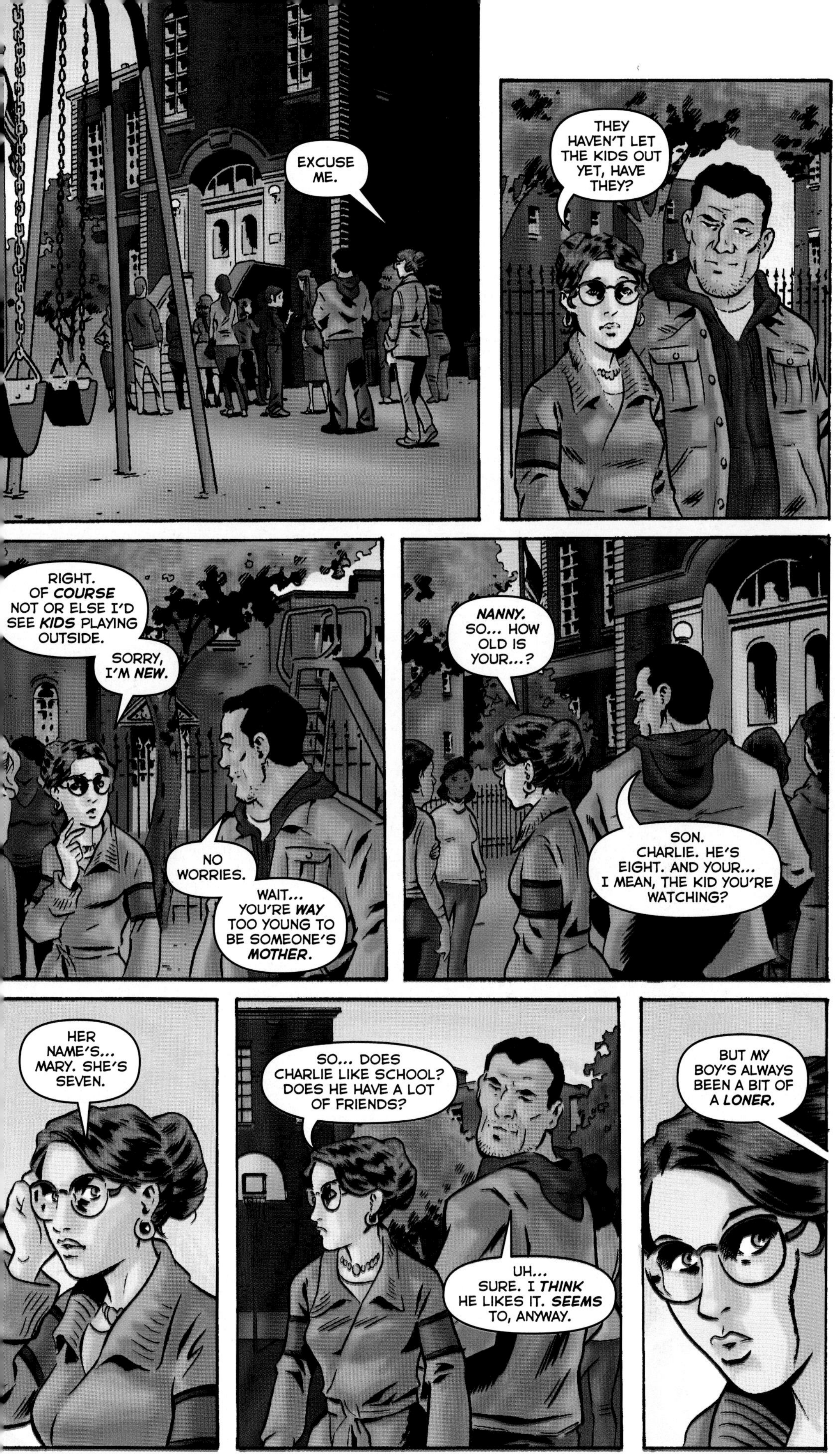

EXCUSE ME.
THEY HAVEN'T LET THE KIDS OUT YET, HAVE THEY?
RIGHT. OF COURSE NOT OR ELSE I'D SEE KIDS PLAYING OUTSIDE.
SORRY, I'M NEW.
NO WORRIES.
WAIT... YOU'RE WAY TOO YOUNG TO BE SOMEONE'S MOTHER.
NANNY. SO... HOW OLD IS YOUR...?
SON. CHARLIE. HE'S EIGHT. AND YOUR... I MEAN, THE KID YOU'RE WATCHING?
HER NAME'S... MARY. SHE'S SEVEN.
SO... DOES CHARLIE LIKE SCHOOL? DOES HE HAVE A LOT OF FRIENDS?
UH... SURE. I THINK HE LIKES IT. SEEMS TO, ANYWAY.
BUT MY BOY'S ALWAYS BEEN A BIT OF A LONER.

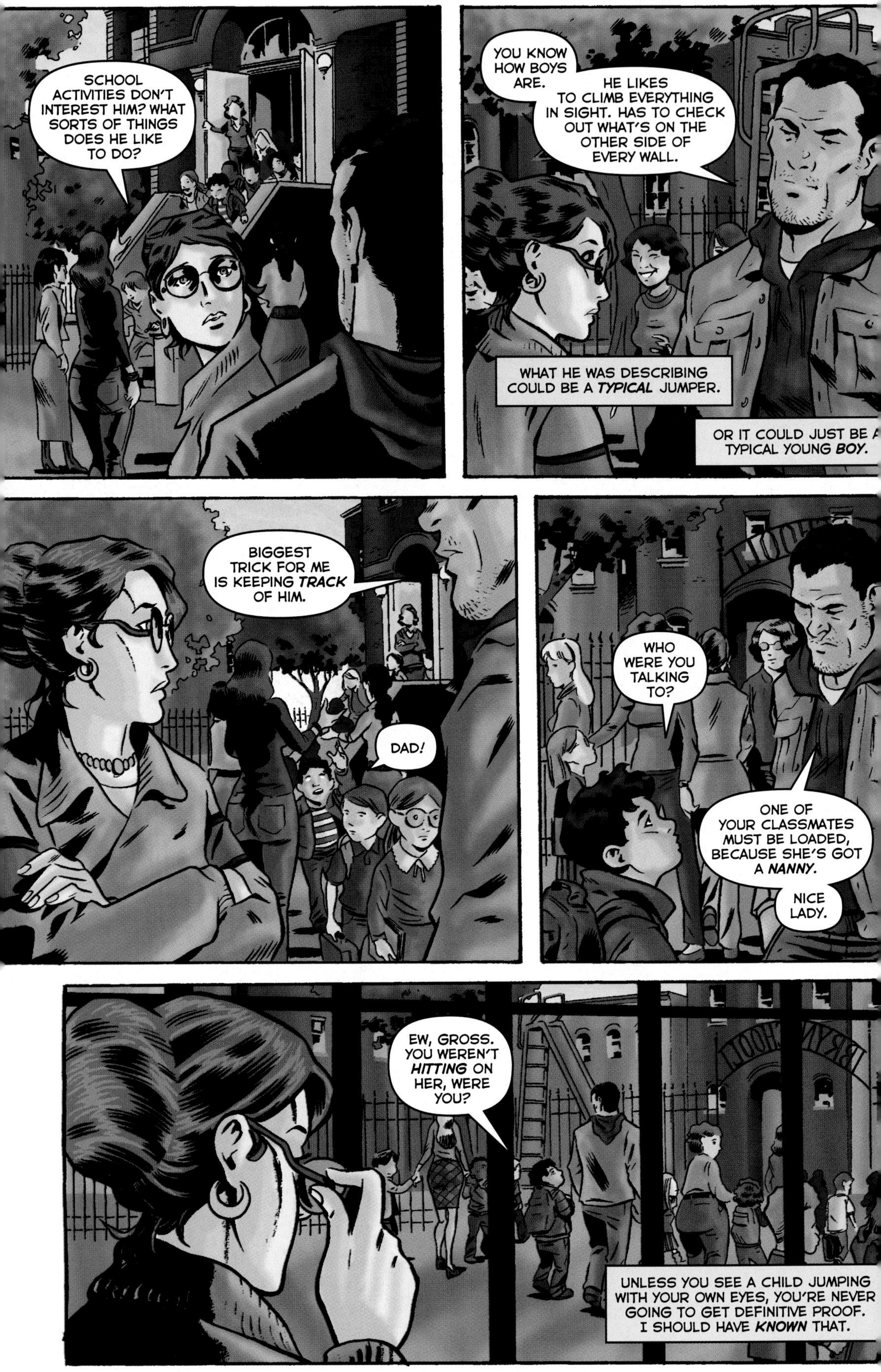
SCHOOL ACTIVITIES DON'T INTEREST HIM? WHAT SORTS OF THINGS DOES HE LIKE TO DO?
YOU KNOW HOW BOYS ARE.
HE LIKES TO CLIMB EVERYTHING IN SIGHT. HAS TO CHECK OUT WHAT'S ON THE OTHER SIDE OF EVERY WALL.
WHAT HE WAS DESCRIBING COULD BE A *TYPICAL* JUMPER.
OR IT COULD JUST BE A TYPICAL YOUNG *BOY*.
BIGGEST TRICK FOR ME IS KEEPING *TRACK* OF HIM.
DAD!
WHO WERE YOU TALKING TO?
ONE OF YOUR CLASSMATES MUST BE LOADED, BECAUSE SHE'S GOT A *NANNY*.
NICE LADY.
EW, GROSS. YOU WEREN'T *HITTING* ON HER, WERE YOU?
UNLESS YOU SEE A CHILD JUMPING WITH YOUR OWN EYES, YOU'RE NEVER GOING TO GET DEFINITIVE PROOF. I SHOULD HAVE *KNOWN* THAT.

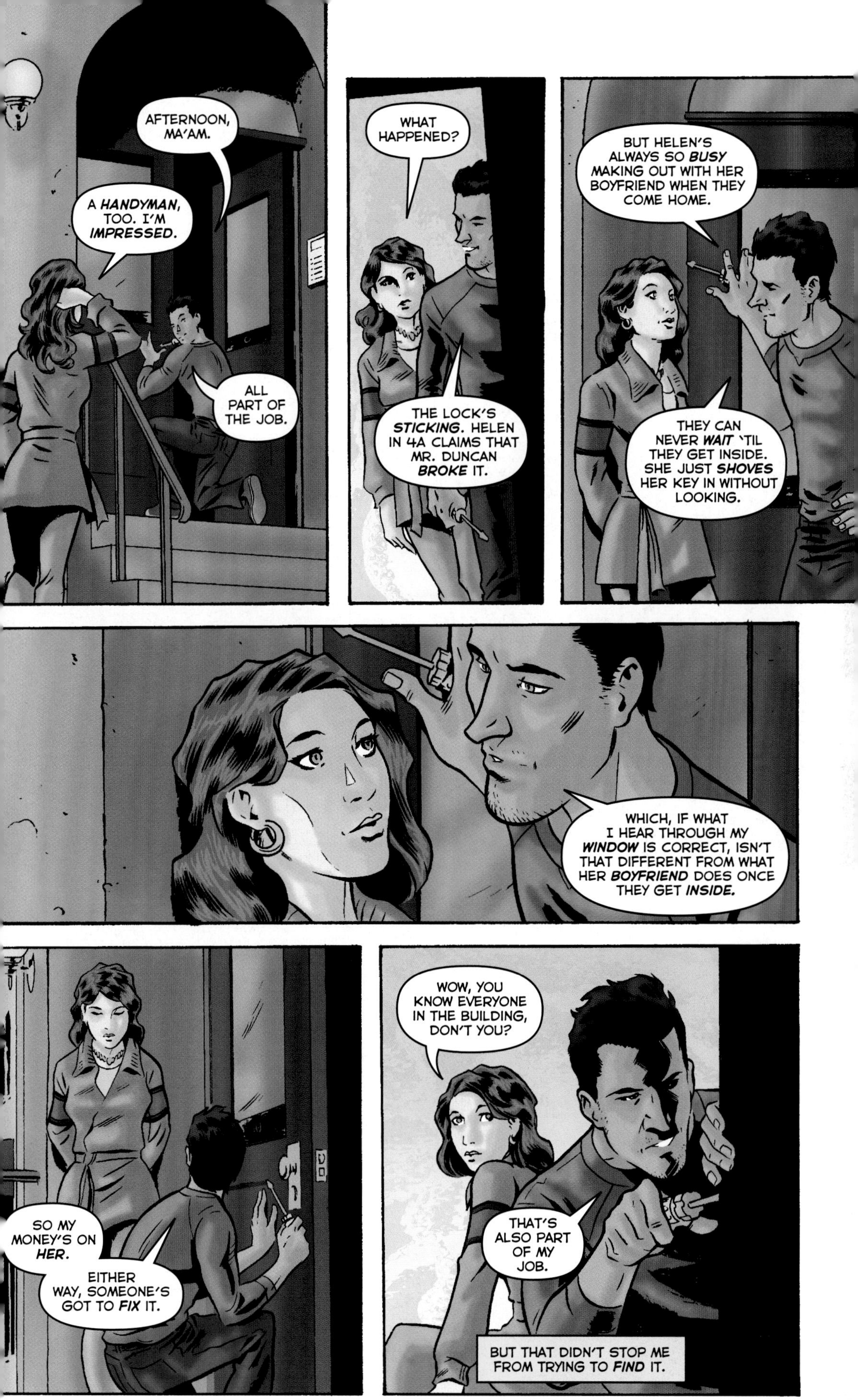
AFTERNOON, MA'AM.
A *HANDYMAN*, TOO. I'M *IMPRESSED*.
ALL PART OF THE JOB.
WHAT HAPPENED?
THE LOCK'S *STICKING*. HELEN IN 4A CLAIMS THAT MR. DUNCAN *BROKE* IT.
BUT HELEN'S ALWAYS SO *BUSY* MAKING OUT WITH HER BOYFRIEND WHEN THEY COME HOME.
THEY CAN NEVER *WAIT* 'TIL THEY GET INSIDE. SHE JUST *SHOVES* HER KEY IN WITHOUT LOOKING.
WHICH, IF WHAT I HEAR THROUGH MY *WINDOW* IS CORRECT, ISN'T THAT DIFFERENT FROM WHAT HER *BOYFRIEND* DOES ONCE THEY GET *INSIDE.*
SO MY MONEY'S ON *HER*.
EITHER WAY, SOMEONE'S GOT TO *FIX* IT.
WOW, YOU KNOW EVERYONE IN THE BUILDING, DON'T YOU?
THAT'S ALSO PART OF MY JOB.
BUT THAT DIDN'T STOP ME FROM TRYING TO *FIND* IT.

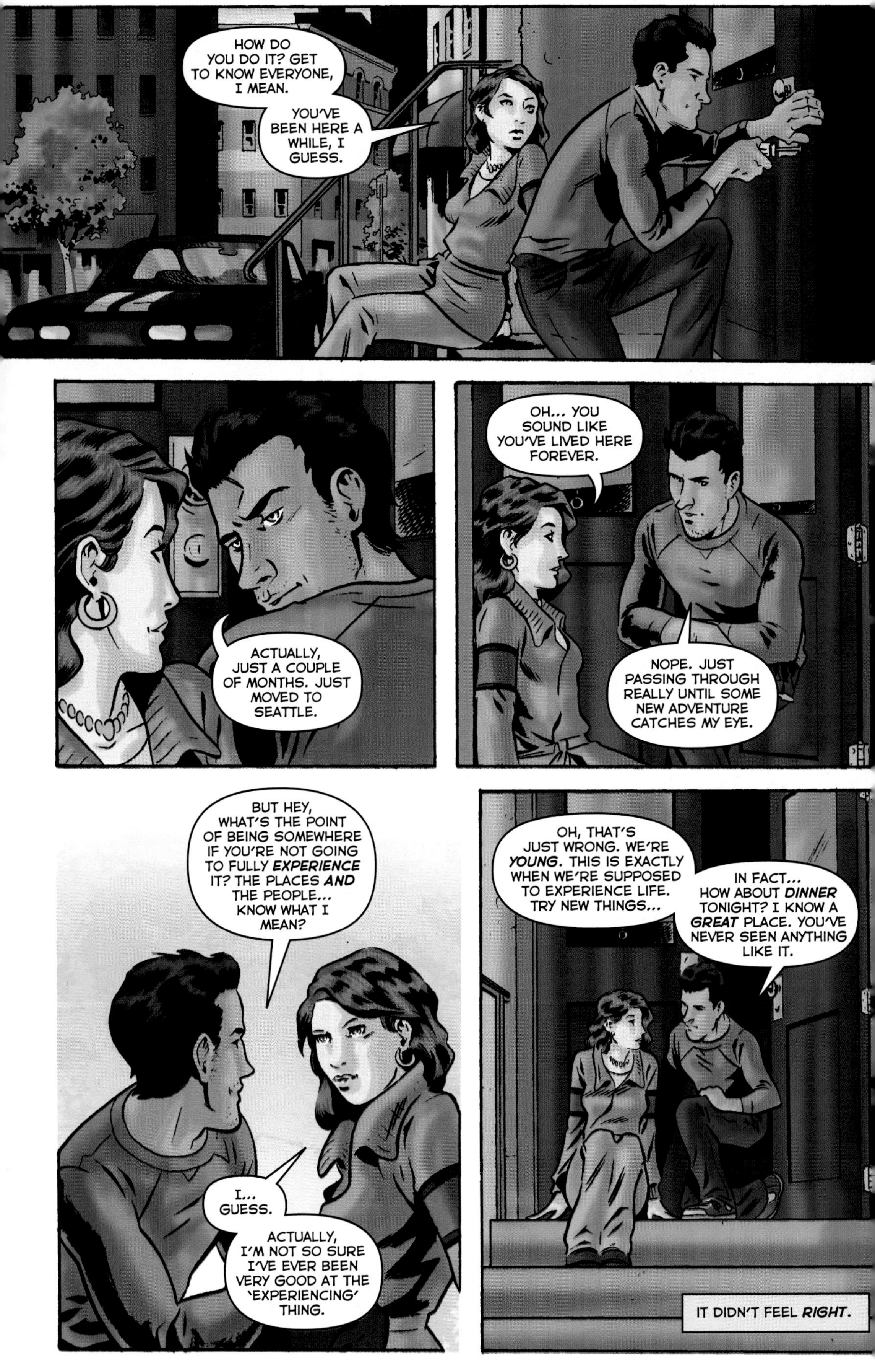
HOW DO YOU DO IT? GET TO KNOW EVERYONE, I MEAN.
YOU'VE BEEN HERE A WHILE, I GUESS.
ACTUALLY, JUST A COUPLE OF MONTHS. JUST MOVED TO SEATTLE.
OH... YOU SOUND LIKE YOU'VE LIVED HERE FOREVER.
NOPE. JUST PASSING THROUGH REALLY UNTIL SOME NEW ADVENTURE CATCHES MY EYE.
BUT HEY, WHAT'S THE POINT OF BEING SOMEWHERE IF YOU'RE NOT GOING TO FULLY ***EXPERIENCE*** IT? THE PLACES ***AND*** THE PEOPLE... KNOW WHAT I MEAN?
I... GUESS.
ACTUALLY, I'M NOT SO SURE I'VE EVER BEEN VERY GOOD AT THE 'EXPERIENCING' THING.
OH, THAT'S JUST WRONG. WE'RE ***YOUNG***. THIS IS EXACTLY WHEN WE'RE SUPPOSED TO EXPERIENCE LIFE. TRY NEW THINGS...
IN FACT... HOW ABOUT ***DINNER*** TONIGHT? I KNOW A ***GREAT*** PLACE. YOU'VE NEVER SEEN ANYTHING LIKE IT.
IT DIDN'T FEEL ***RIGHT***.

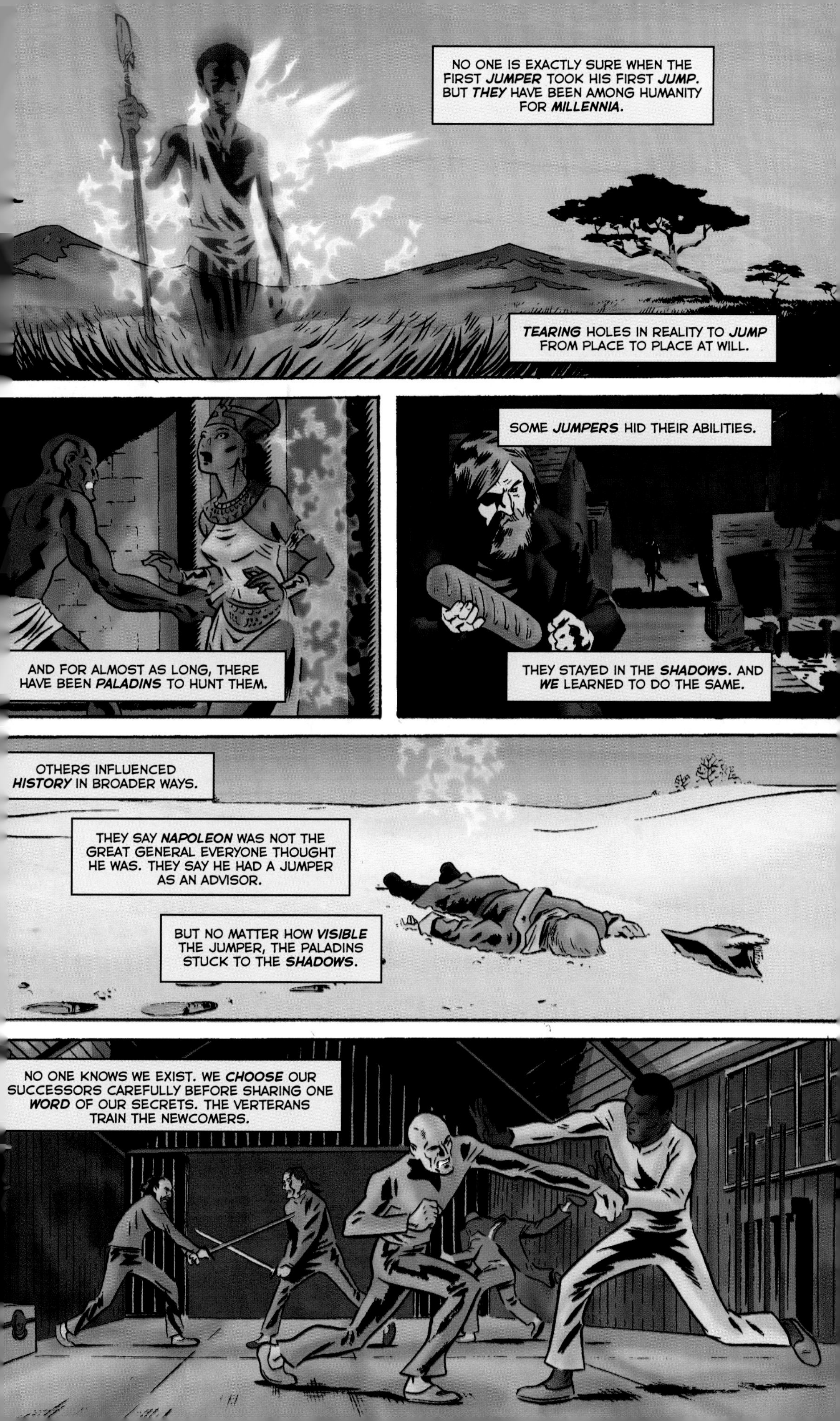

NO ONE IS EXACTLY SURE WHEN THE FIRST JUMPER TOOK HIS FIRST JUMP. BUT THEY HAVE BEEN AMONG HUMANITY FOR MILLENNIA.
TEARING HOLES IN REALITY TO JUMP FROM PLACE TO PLACE AT WILL.
AND FOR ALMOST AS LONG, THERE HAVE BEEN PALADINS TO HUNT THEM.
SOME JUMPERS HID THEIR ABILITIES.
THEY STAYED IN THE SHADOWS. AND WE LEARNED TO DO THE SAME.
OTHERS INFLUENCED HISTORY IN BROADER WAYS.
THEY SAY NAPOLEON WAS NOT THE GREAT GENERAL EVERYONE THOUGHT HE WAS. THEY SAY HE HAD A JUMPER AS AN ADVISOR.
BUT NO MATTER HOW VISIBLE THE JUMPER, THE PALADINS STUCK TO THE SHADOWS.
NO ONE KNOWS WE EXIST. WE CHOOSE OUR SUCCESSORS CAREFULLY BEFORE SHARING ONE WORD OF OUR SECRETS. THE VERTERANS TRAIN THE NEWCOMERS.

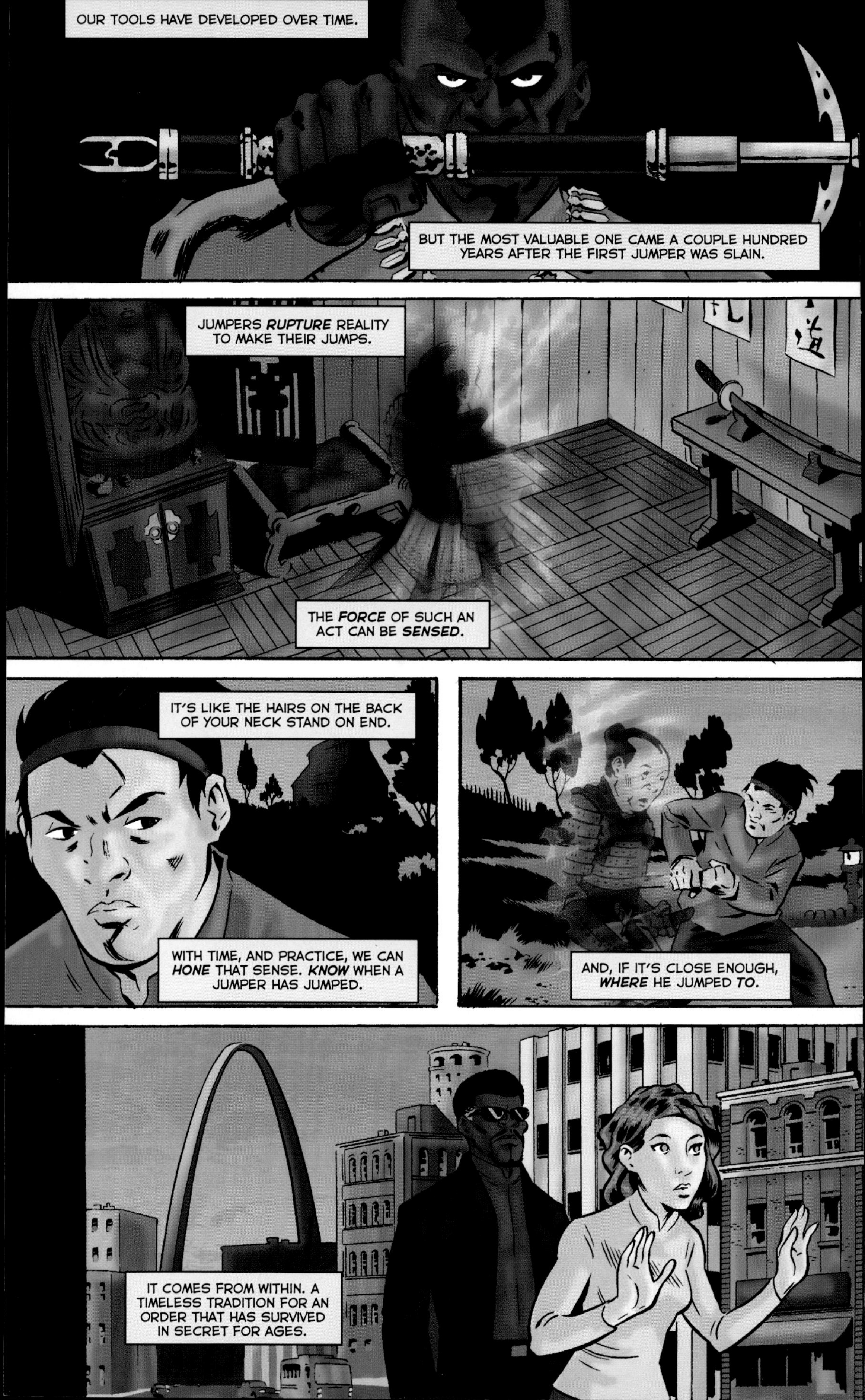
OUR TOOLS HAVE DEVELOPED OVER TIME.
BUT THE MOST VALUABLE ONE CAME A COUPLE HUNDRED YEARS AFTER THE FIRST JUMPER WAS SLAIN.
JUMPERS *RUPTURE* REALITY TO MAKE THEIR JUMPS.
THE *FORCE* OF SUCH AN ACT CAN BE *SENSED.*
IT'S LIKE THE HAIRS ON THE BACK OF YOUR NECK STAND ON END.
WITH TIME, AND PRACTICE, WE CAN *HONE* THAT SENSE. *KNOW* WHEN A JUMPER HAS JUMPED.
AND, IF IT'S CLOSE ENOUGH, *WHERE* HE JUMPED *TO.*
IT COMES FROM WITHIN. A TIMELESS TRADITION FOR AN ORDER THAT HAS SURVIVED IN SECRET FOR AGES.

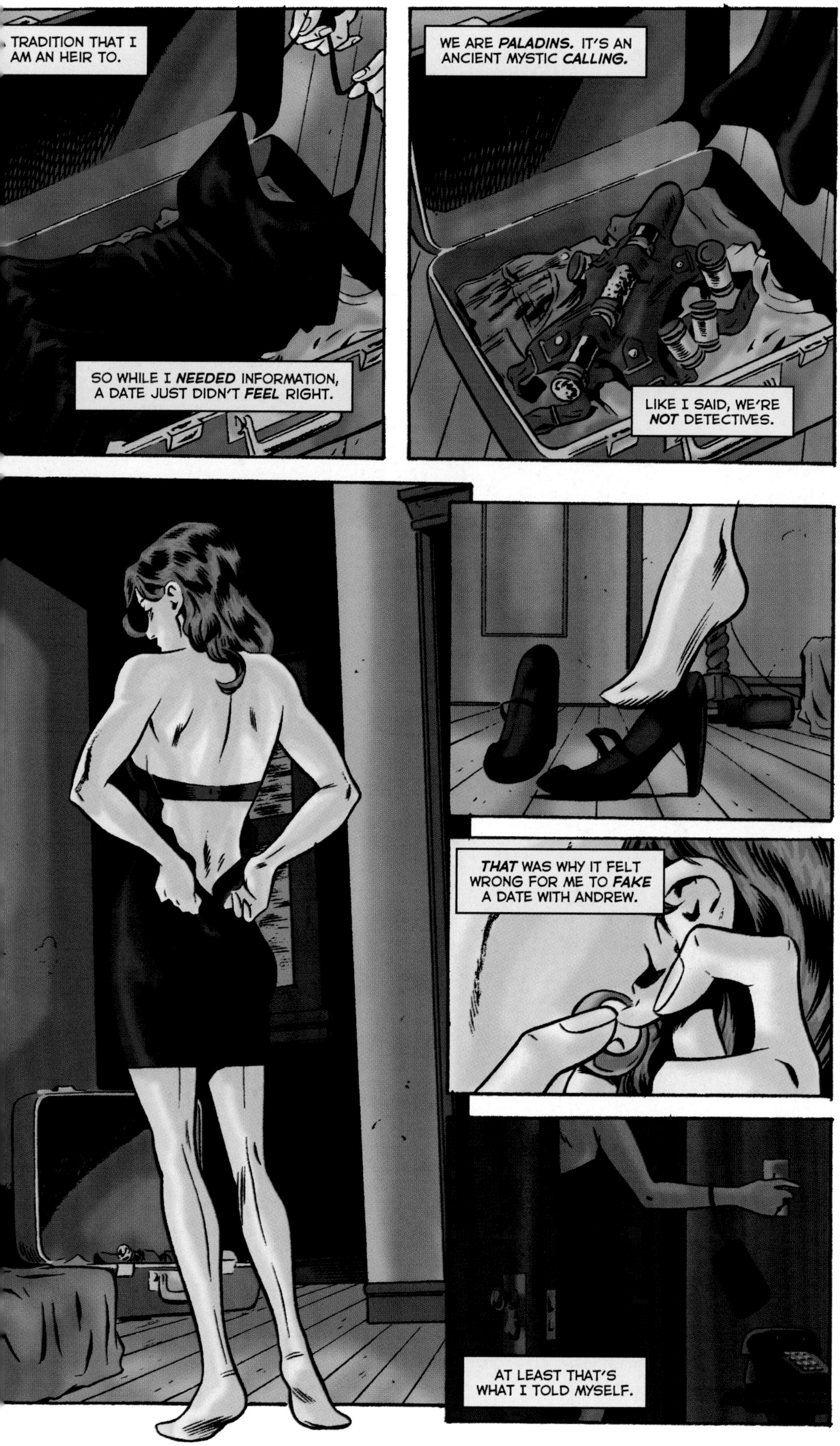
TRADITION THAT I AM AN HEIR TO.
SO WHILE I *NEEDED* INFORMATION, A DATE JUST DIDN'T *FEEL* RIGHT.
WE ARE *PALADINS.* IT'S AN ANCIENT MYSTIC *CALLING.*
LIKE I SAID, WE'RE *NOT* DETECTIVES.
THAT WAS WHY IT FELT WRONG FOR ME TO *FAKE* A DATE WITH ANDREW.
AT LEAST THAT'S WHAT I TOLD MYSELF.

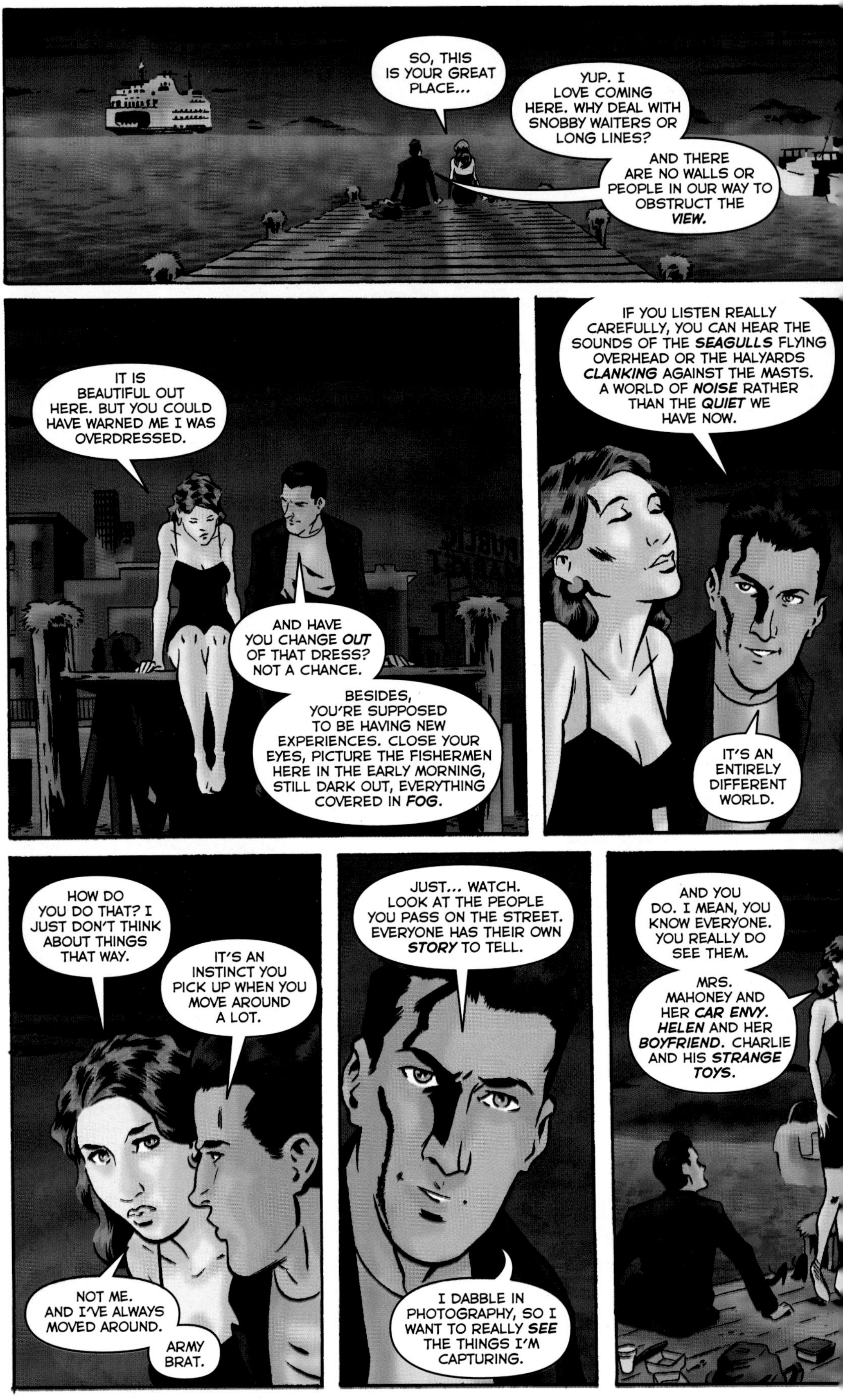
SO, THIS IS YOUR GREAT PLACE...
YUP. I LOVE COMING HERE. WHY DEAL WITH SNOBBY WAITERS OR LONG LINES?
AND THERE ARE NO WALLS OR PEOPLE IN OUR WAY TO OBSTRUCT THE *VIEW.*
IT IS BEAUTIFUL OUT HERE. BUT YOU COULD HAVE WARNED ME I WAS OVERDRESSED.
AND HAVE YOU CHANGE *OUT* OF THAT DRESS? NOT A CHANCE.
BESIDES, YOU'RE SUPPOSED TO BE HAVING NEW EXPERIENCES. CLOSE YOUR EYES, PICTURE THE FISHERMEN HERE IN THE EARLY MORNING, STILL DARK OUT, EVERYTHING COVERED IN *FOG*.
IF YOU LISTEN REALLY CAREFULLY, YOU CAN HEAR THE SOUNDS OF THE *SEAGULLS* FLYING OVERHEAD OR THE HALYARDS *CLANKING* AGAINST THE MASTS. A WORLD OF *NOISE* RATHER THAN THE *QUIET* WE HAVE NOW.
IT'S AN ENTIRELY DIFFERENT WORLD.
HOW DO YOU DO THAT? I JUST DON'T THINK ABOUT THINGS THAT WAY.
IT'S AN INSTINCT YOU PICK UP WHEN YOU MOVE AROUND A LOT.
NOT ME. AND I'VE ALWAYS MOVED AROUND.
ARMY BRAT.
JUST... WATCH. LOOK AT THE PEOPLE YOU PASS ON THE STREET. EVERYONE HAS THEIR OWN *STORY* TO TELL.
I DABBLE IN PHOTOGRAPHY, SO I WANT TO REALLY *SEE* THE THINGS I'M CAPTURING.
AND YOU DO. I MEAN, YOU KNOW EVERYONE. YOU REALLY DO SEE THEM.
MRS. MAHONEY AND HER *CAR ENVY. HELEN* AND HER *BOYFRIEND*. CHARLIE AND HIS *STRANGE TOYS.*

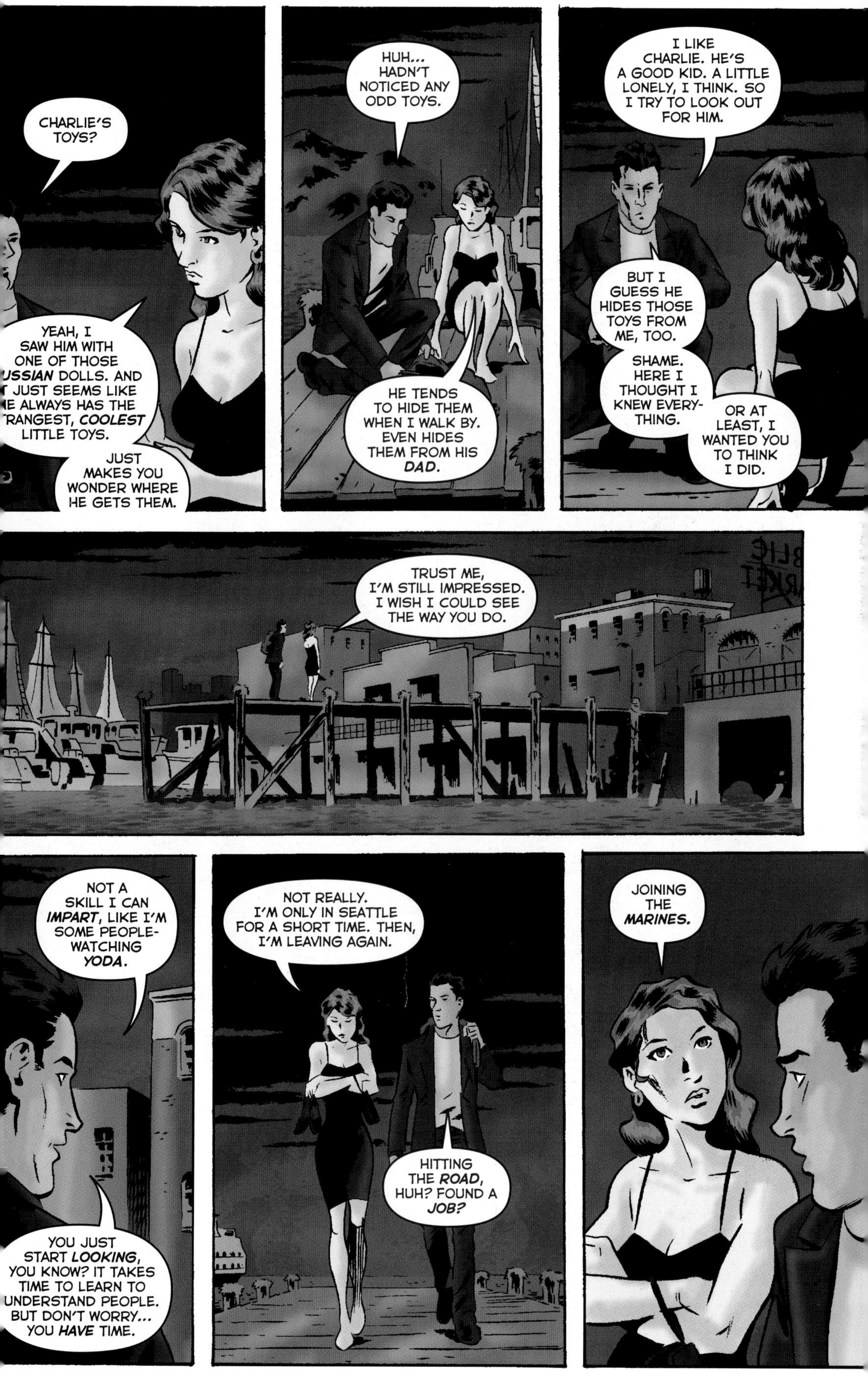
CHARLIE'S TOYS?
YEAH, I SAW HIM WITH ONE OF THOSE USSIAN DOLLS. AND T JUST SEEMS LIKE E ALWAYS HAS THE RANGEST, COOLEST LITTLE TOYS.
JUST MAKES YOU WONDER WHERE HE GETS THEM.
HUH... HADN'T NOTICED ANY ODD TOYS.
HE TENDS TO HIDE THEM WHEN I WALK BY. EVEN HIDES THEM FROM HIS DAD.
I LIKE CHARLIE. HE'S A GOOD KID. A LITTLE LONELY, I THINK. SO I TRY TO LOOK OUT FOR HIM.
BUT I GUESS HE HIDES THOSE TOYS FROM ME, TOO.
SHAME. HERE I THOUGHT I KNEW EVERY-THING.
OR AT LEAST, I WANTED YOU TO THINK I DID.
TRUST ME, I'M STILL IMPRESSED. I WISH I COULD SEE THE WAY YOU DO.
NOT A SKILL I CAN IMPART, LIKE I'M SOME PEOPLE-WATCHING YODA.
YOU JUST START LOOKING, YOU KNOW? IT TAKES TIME TO LEARN TO UNDERSTAND PEOPLE. BUT DON'T WORRY... YOU HAVE TIME.
NOT REALLY. I'M ONLY IN SEATTLE FOR A SHORT TIME. THEN, I'M LEAVING AGAIN.
HITTING THE ROAD, HUH? FOUND A JOB?
JOINING THE MARINES.

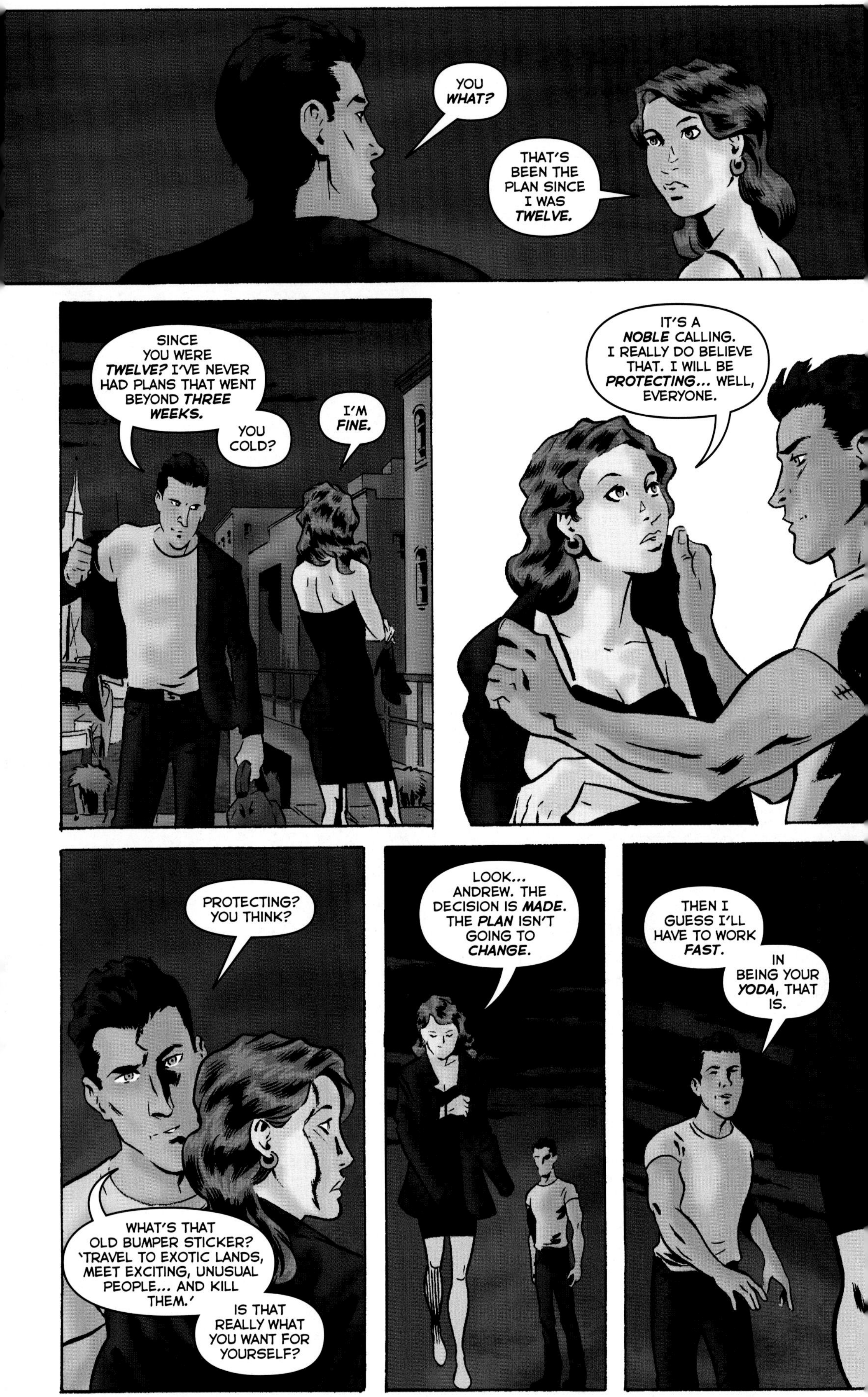
YOU *WHAT?*
THAT'S BEEN THE PLAN SINCE I WAS *TWELVE.*
SINCE YOU WERE *TWELVE?* I'VE NEVER HAD PLANS THAT WENT BEYOND *THREE WEEKS.*
YOU COLD?
I'M *FINE.*
IT'S A *NOBLE* CALLING. I REALLY DO BELIEVE THAT. I WILL BE *PROTECTING...* WELL, EVERYONE.
PROTECTING? YOU THINK?
WHAT'S THAT OLD BUMPER STICKER? 'TRAVEL TO EXOTIC LANDS, MEET EXCITING, UNUSUAL PEOPLE... AND KILL THEM.'
IS THAT REALLY WHAT YOU WANT FOR YOURSELF?
LOOK... ANDREW. THE DECISION IS *MADE.* THE *PLAN* ISN'T GOING TO *CHANGE.*
THEN I GUESS I'LL HAVE TO WORK *FAST.*
IN BEING YOUR *YODA,* THAT IS.

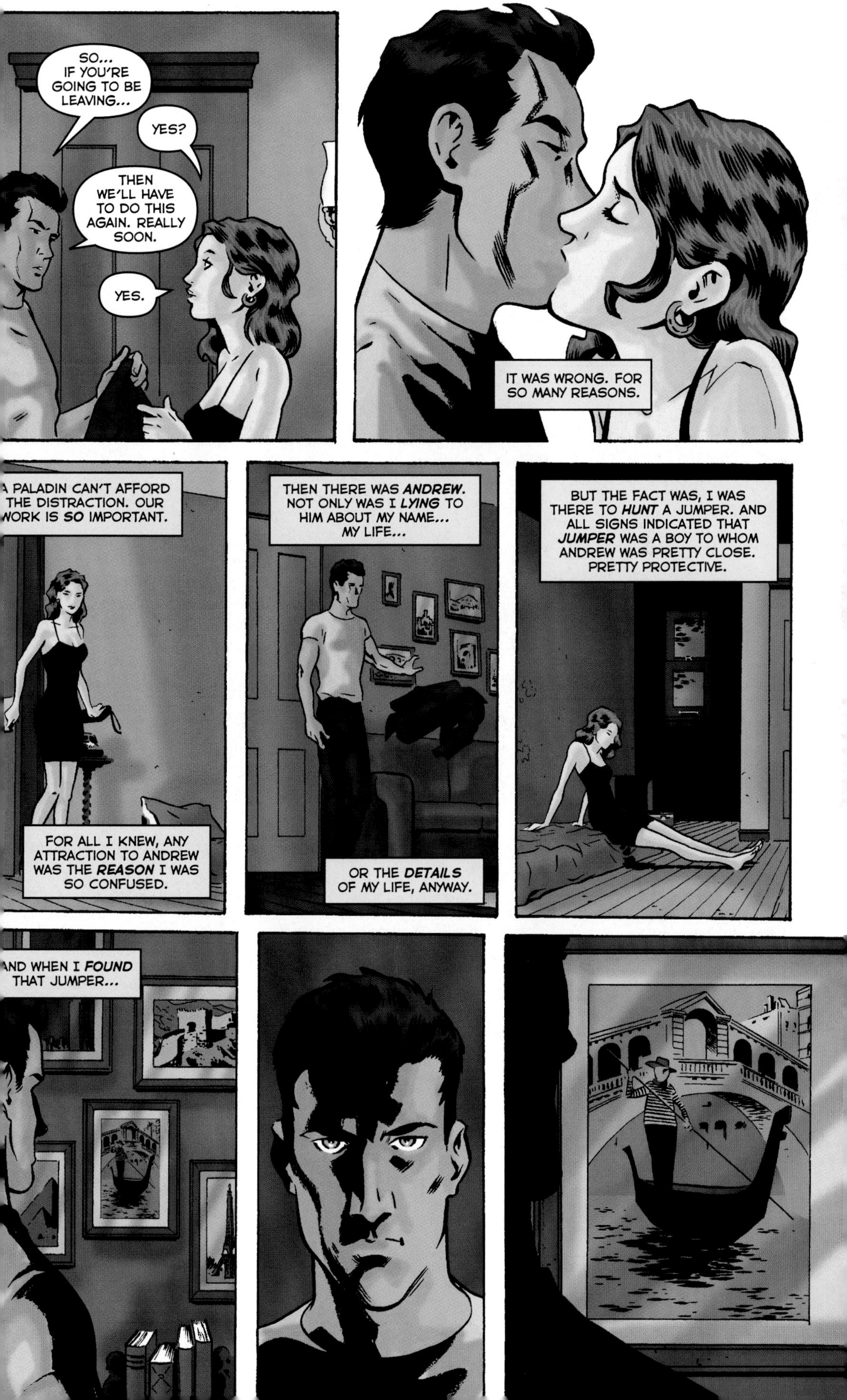

SO... IF YOU'RE GOING TO BE LEAVING...
YES?
THEN WE'LL HAVE TO DO THIS AGAIN. REALLY SOON.
YES.
IT WAS WRONG. FOR SO MANY REASONS.
A PALADIN CAN'T AFFORD THE DISTRACTION. OUR WORK IS SO IMPORTANT.
FOR ALL I KNEW, ANY ATTRACTION TO ANDREW WAS THE REASON I WAS SO CONFUSED.
THEN THERE WAS ANDREW. NOT ONLY WAS I LYING TO HIM ABOUT MY NAME... MY LIFE...
OR THE DETAILS OF MY LIFE, ANYWAY.
BUT THE FACT WAS, I WAS THERE TO HUNT A JUMPER. AND ALL SIGNS INDICATED THAT JUMPER WAS A BOY TO WHOM ANDREW WAS PRETTY CLOSE. PRETTY PROTECTIVE.
AND WHEN I FOUND THAT JUMPER...

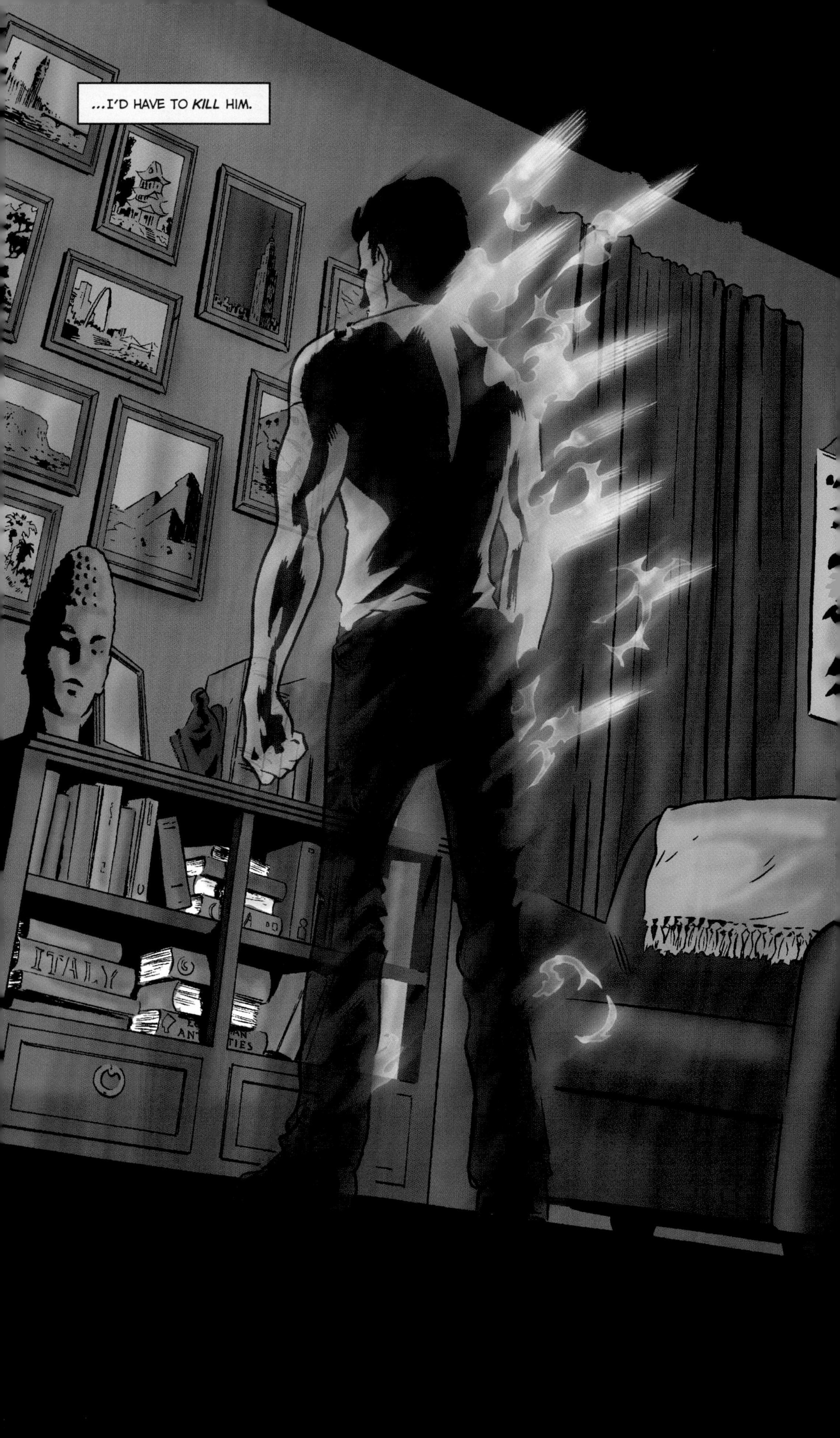
...I'D HAVE TO *KILL* HIM.
ITALY

CHAPTER 3

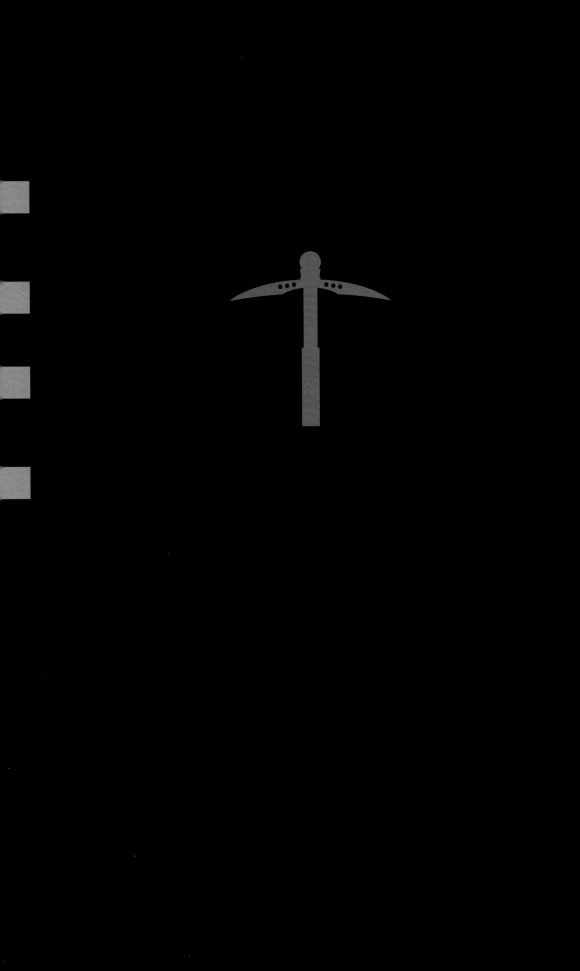

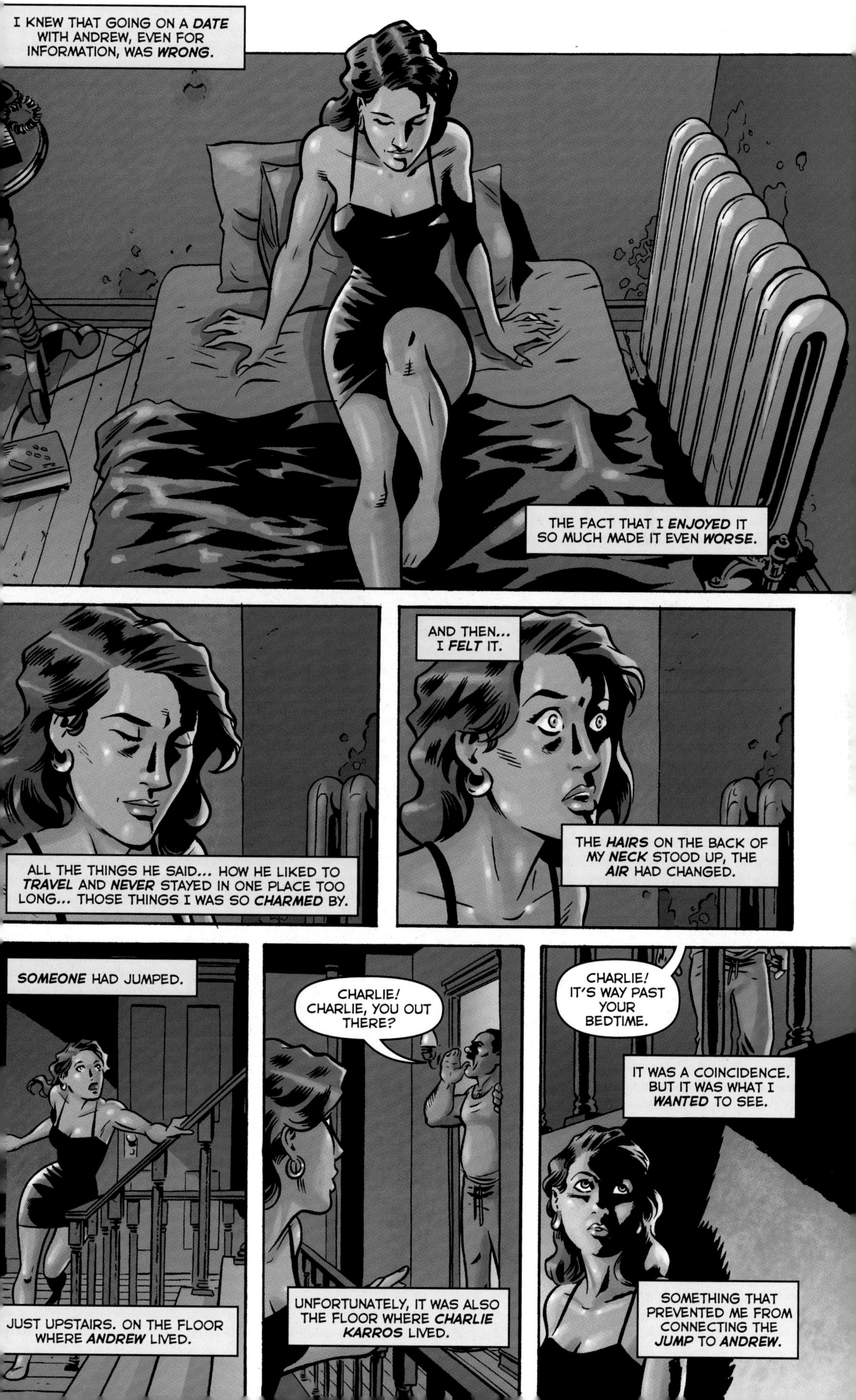
I KNEW THAT GOING ON A DATE WITH ANDREW, EVEN FOR INFORMATION, WAS WRONG.
THE FACT THAT I ENJOYED IT SO MUCH MADE IT EVEN WORSE.
ALL THE THINGS HE SAID... HOW HE LIKED TO TRAVEL AND NEVER STAYED IN ONE PLACE TOO LONG... THOSE THINGS I WAS SO CHARMED BY.
AND THEN... I FELT IT.
THE HAIRS ON THE BACK OF MY NECK STOOD UP, THE AIR HAD CHANGED.
SOMEONE HAD JUMPED.
JUST UPSTAIRS. ON THE FLOOR WHERE ANDREW LIVED.
CHARLIE! CHARLIE, YOU OUT THERE?
UNFORTUNATELY, IT WAS ALSO THE FLOOR WHERE CHARLIE KARROS LIVED.
CHARLIE! IT'S WAY PAST YOUR BEDTIME.
IT WAS A COINCIDENCE. BUT IT WAS WHAT I WANTED TO SEE.
SOMETHING THAT PREVENTED ME FROM CONNECTING THE JUMP TO ANDREW.

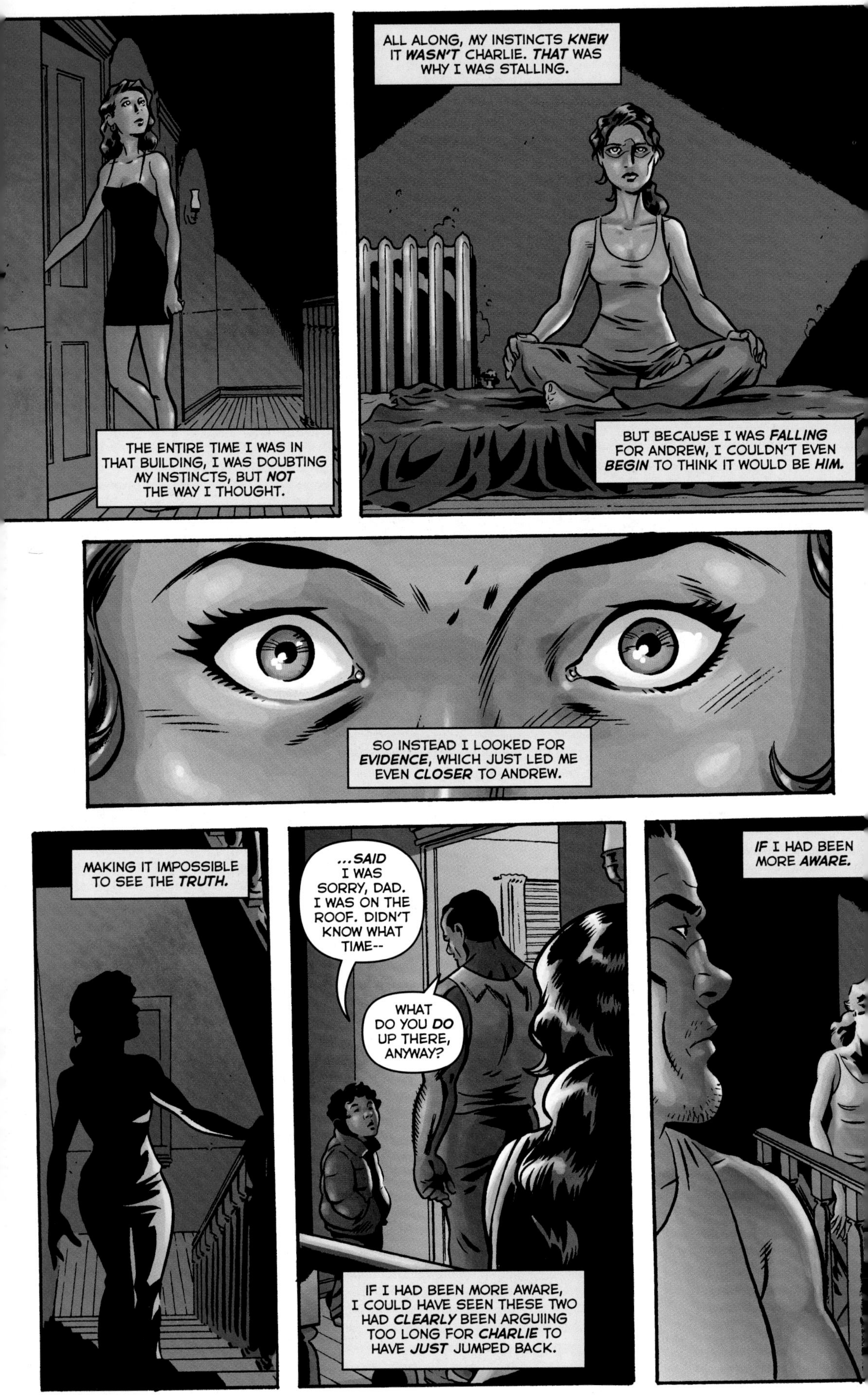
THE ENTIRE TIME I WAS IN THAT BUILDING, I WAS DOUBTING MY INSTINCTS, BUT NOT THE WAY I THOUGHT.
ALL ALONG, MY INSTINCTS KNEW IT WASN'T CHARLIE. THAT WAS WHY I WAS STALLING.
BUT BECAUSE I WAS FALLING FOR ANDREW, I COULDN'T EVEN BEGIN TO THINK IT WOULD BE HIM.
SO INSTEAD I LOOKED FOR EVIDENCE, WHICH JUST LED ME EVEN CLOSER TO ANDREW.
MAKING IT IMPOSSIBLE TO SEE THE TRUTH.
...SAID I WAS SORRY, DAD. I WAS ON THE ROOF. DIDN'T KNOW WHAT TIME--
WHAT DO YOU DO UP THERE, ANYWAY?
IF I HAD BEEN MORE AWARE, I COULD HAVE SEEN THESE TWO HAD CLEARLY BEEN ARGUIING TOO LONG FOR CHARLIE TO HAVE JUST JUMPED BACK.
IF I HAD BEEN MORE AWARE.

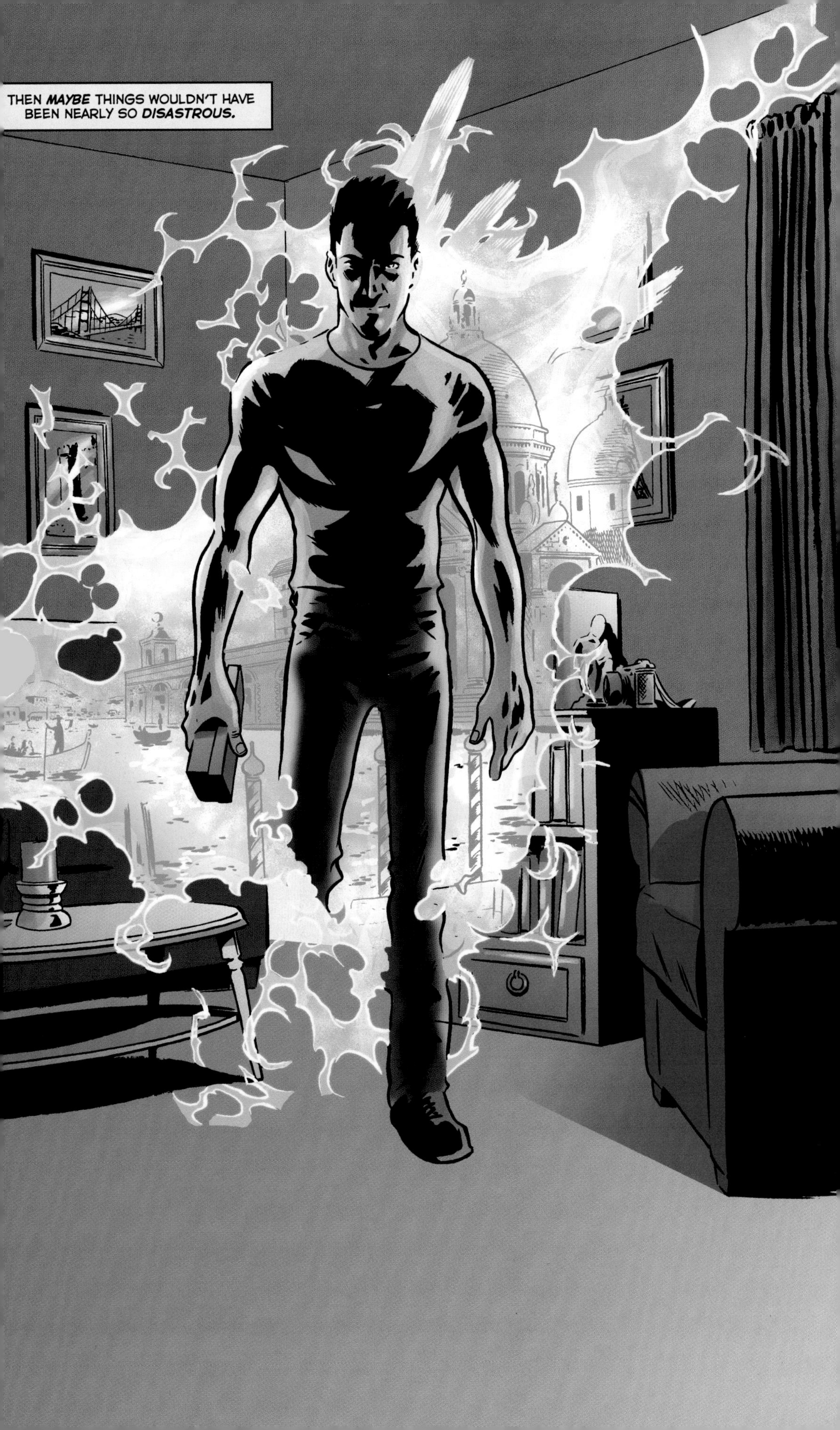
THEN *MAYBE* THINGS WOULDN'T HAVE BEEN NEARLY SO *DISASTROUS.*

YOU WANTED TO SEE ME?

WE'RE HEADING WEST. *KEMP* IS *DEAD.* KILLED BY A *JUMPER.*

THEY'RE GETTING *BOLDER.*

THEY *ARE.* THAT'S THE PROBLEM IF WE LET THEM GET TOO MUCH *EXPERIENCE.*

THAT'S WHY I NEED YOU TO TAKE CARE OF THIS *BANK* SITUATION. *FIND* THE JUMPER. *FINISH* THIS.

WE HAVEN'T SENSED A *JUMP* IN A WHILE. HE MAY HAVE MOVED ON.

I HATE *LYING* TO ROLAND. I HAVEN'T DONE IT SINCE ALL THOSE YEARS AGO IN SEATTLE.

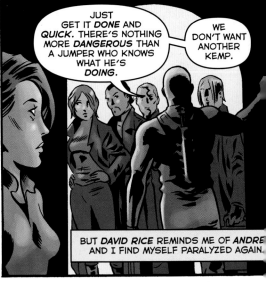

JUST GET IT *DONE* AND *QUICK.* THERE'S NOTHING MORE *DANGEROUS* THAN A JUMPER WHO KNOWS WHAT HE'S *DOING.*

WE DON'T WANT ANOTHER KEMP.

BUT *DAVID RICE* REMINDS ME OF *ANDRE* AND I FIND MYSELF PARALYZED AGAIN.

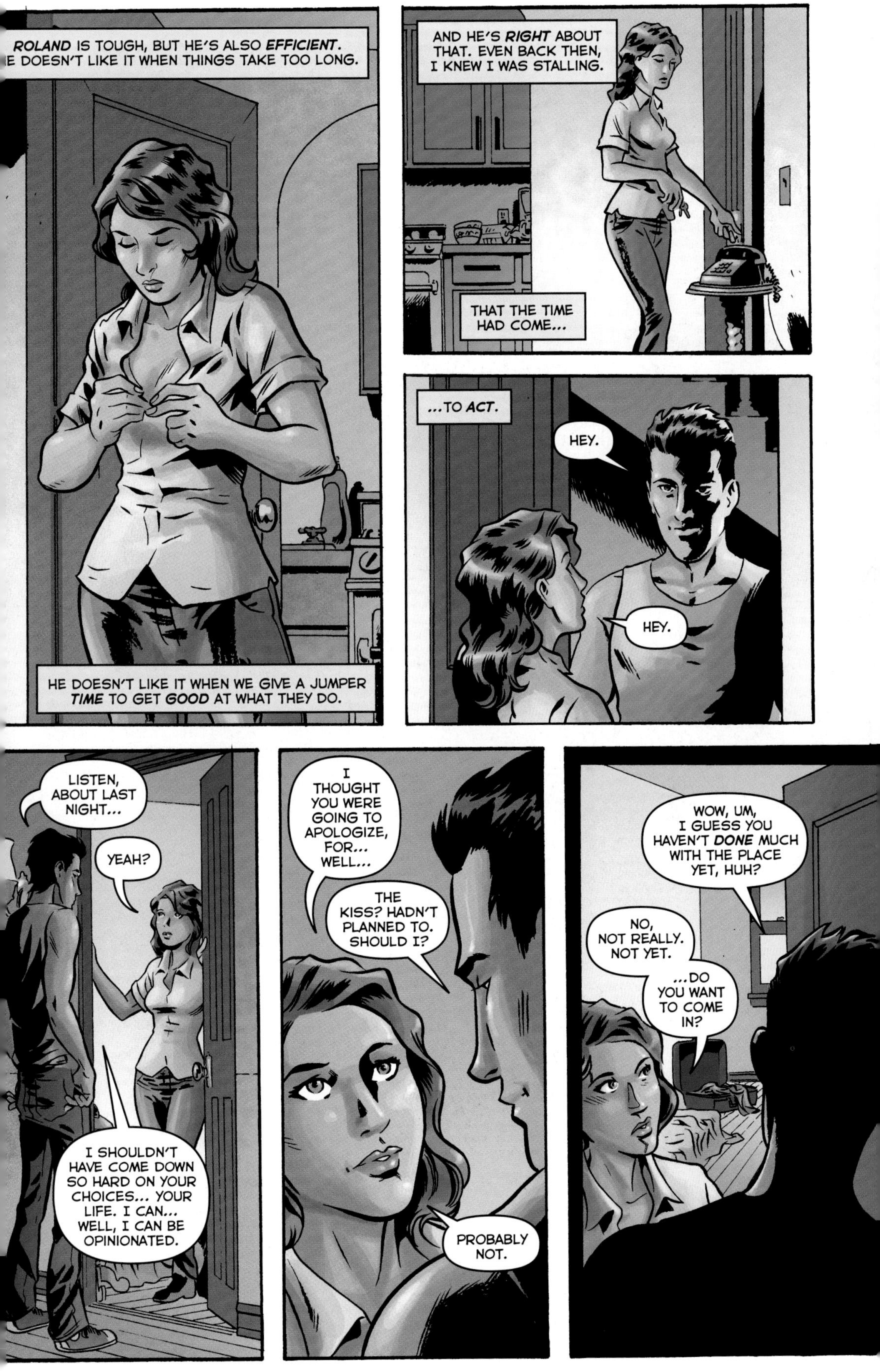
ROLAND IS TOUGH, BUT HE'S ALSO EFFICIENT.
E DOESN'T LIKE IT WHEN THINGS TAKE TOO LONG.
HE DOESN'T LIKE IT WHEN WE GIVE A JUMPER TIME TO GET GOOD AT WHAT THEY DO.
AND HE'S RIGHT ABOUT THAT. EVEN BACK THEN, I KNEW I WAS STALLING.
THAT THE TIME HAD COME...
...TO ACT.
HEY.
HEY.
LISTEN, ABOUT LAST NIGHT...
YEAH?
I SHOULDN'T HAVE COME DOWN SO HARD ON YOUR CHOICES... YOUR LIFE. I CAN... WELL, I CAN BE OPINIONATED.
I THOUGHT YOU WERE GOING TO APOLOGIZE, FOR... WELL...
THE KISS? HADN'T PLANNED TO. SHOULD I?
PROBABLY NOT.
WOW, UM, I GUESS YOU HAVEN'T DONE MUCH WITH THE PLACE YET, HUH?
NO, NOT REALLY. NOT YET.
...DO YOU WANT TO COME IN?

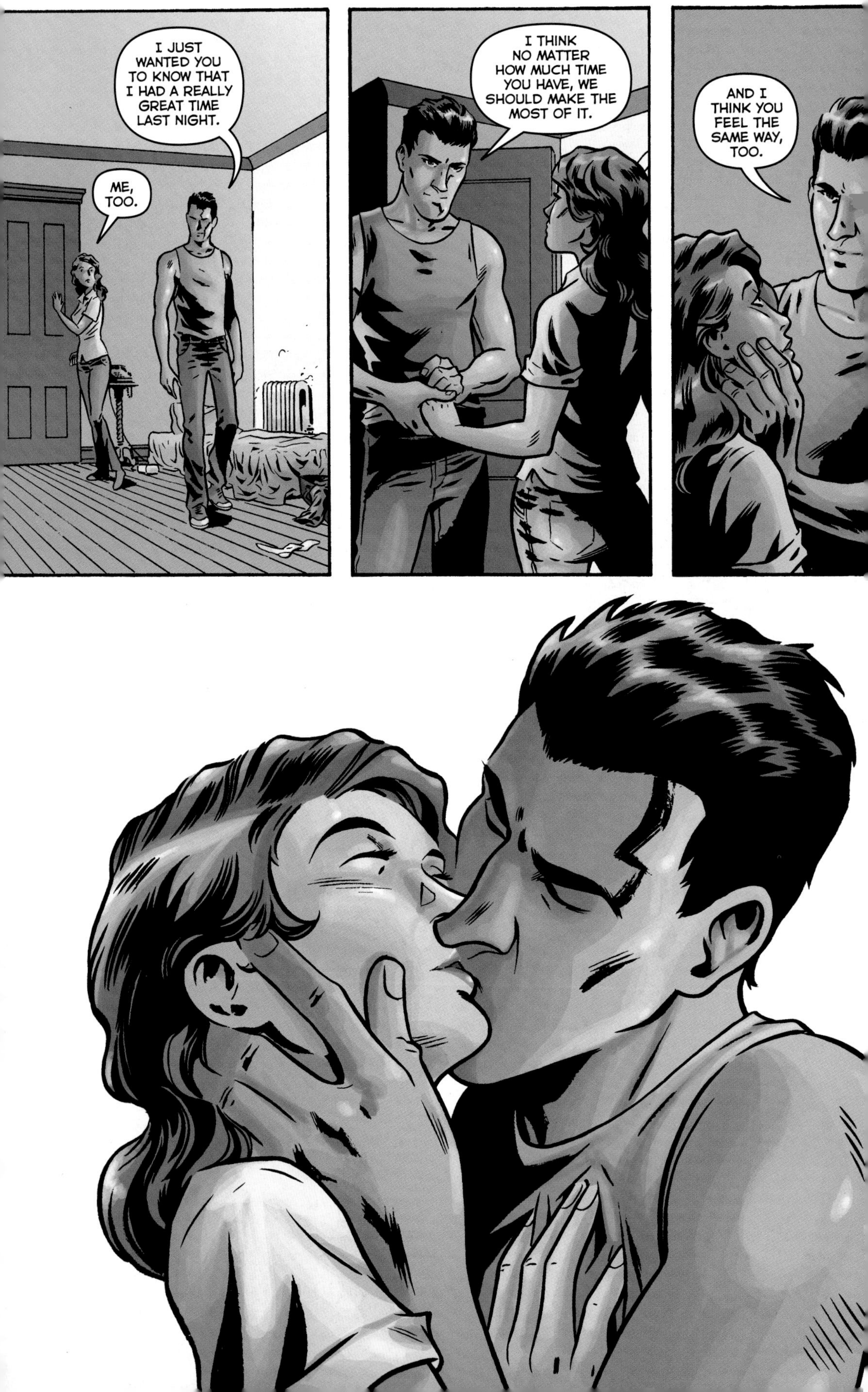
I JUST WANTED YOU TO KNOW THAT I HAD A REALLY GREAT TIME LAST NIGHT.
ME, TOO.
I THINK NO MATTER HOW MUCH TIME YOU HAVE, WE SHOULD MAKE THE MOST OF IT.
AND I THINK YOU FEEL THE SAME WAY, TOO.

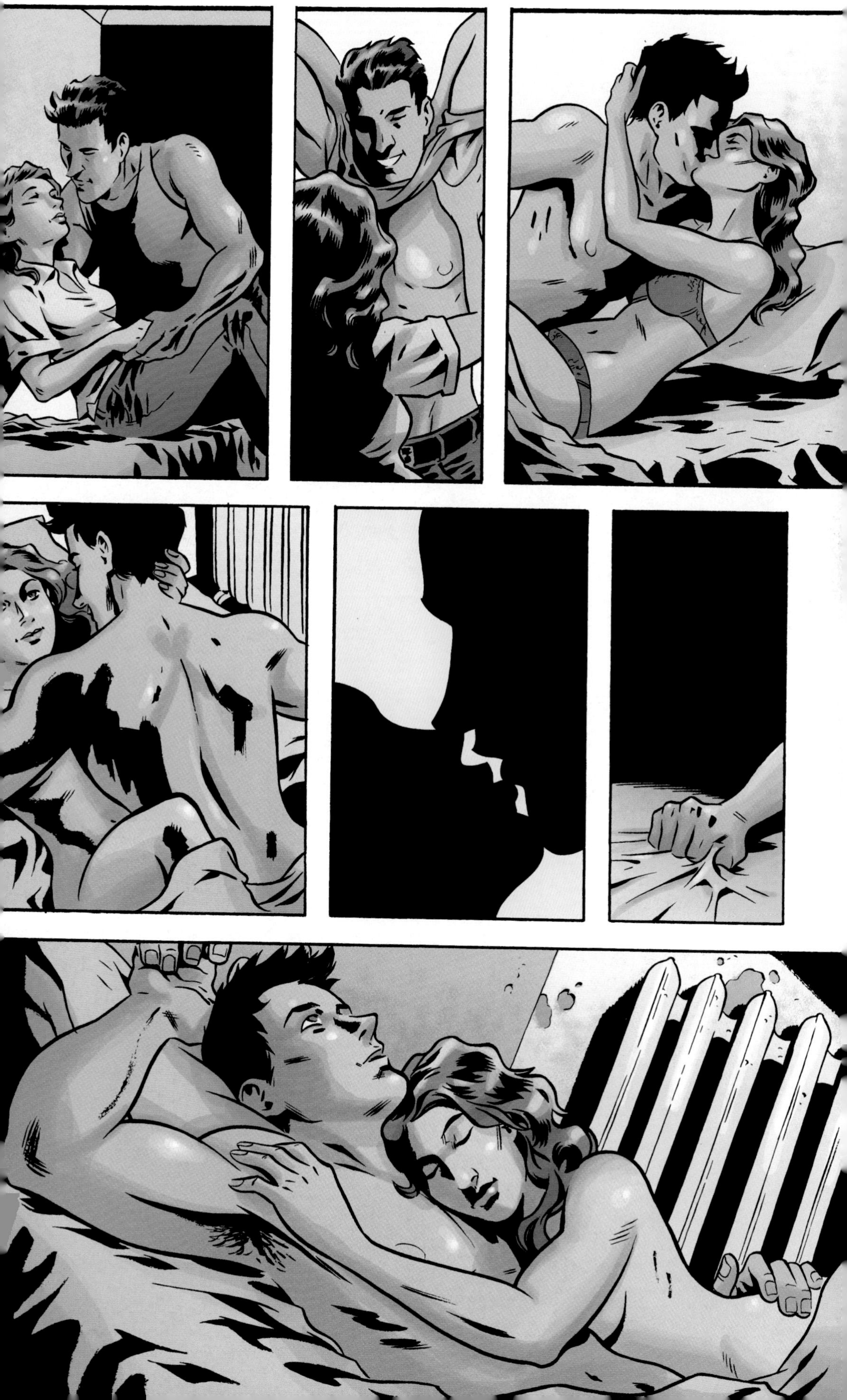

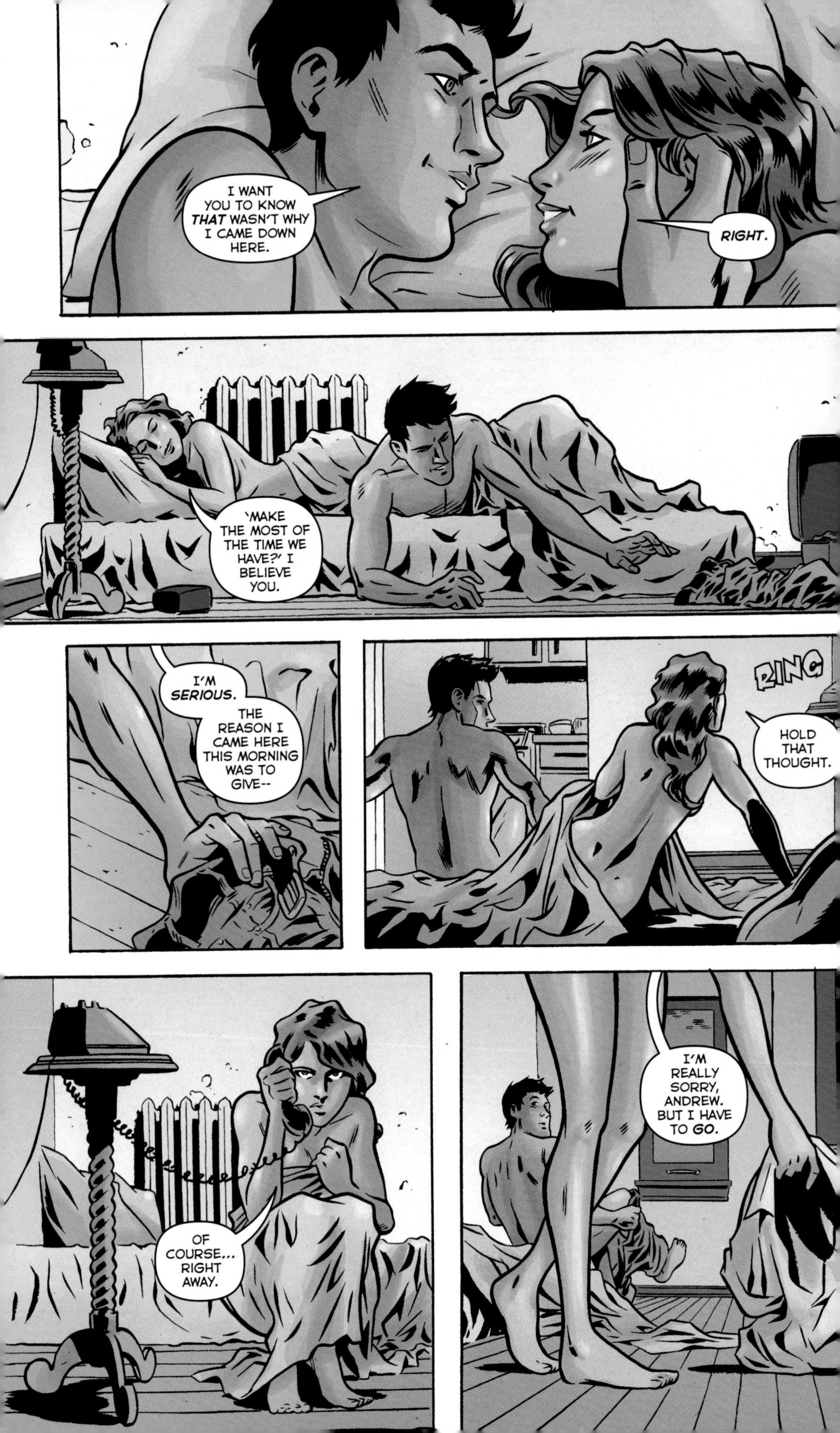
I WANT YOU TO KNOW THAT WASN'T WHY I CAME DOWN HERE.
RIGHT.
'MAKE THE MOST OF THE TIME WE HAVE?' I BELIEVE YOU.
I'M SERIOUS.
THE REASON I CAME HERE THIS MORNING WAS TO GIVE--
RING
HOLD THAT THOUGHT.
OF COURSE... RIGHT AWAY.
I'M REALLY SORRY, ANDREW. BUT I HAVE TO GO.

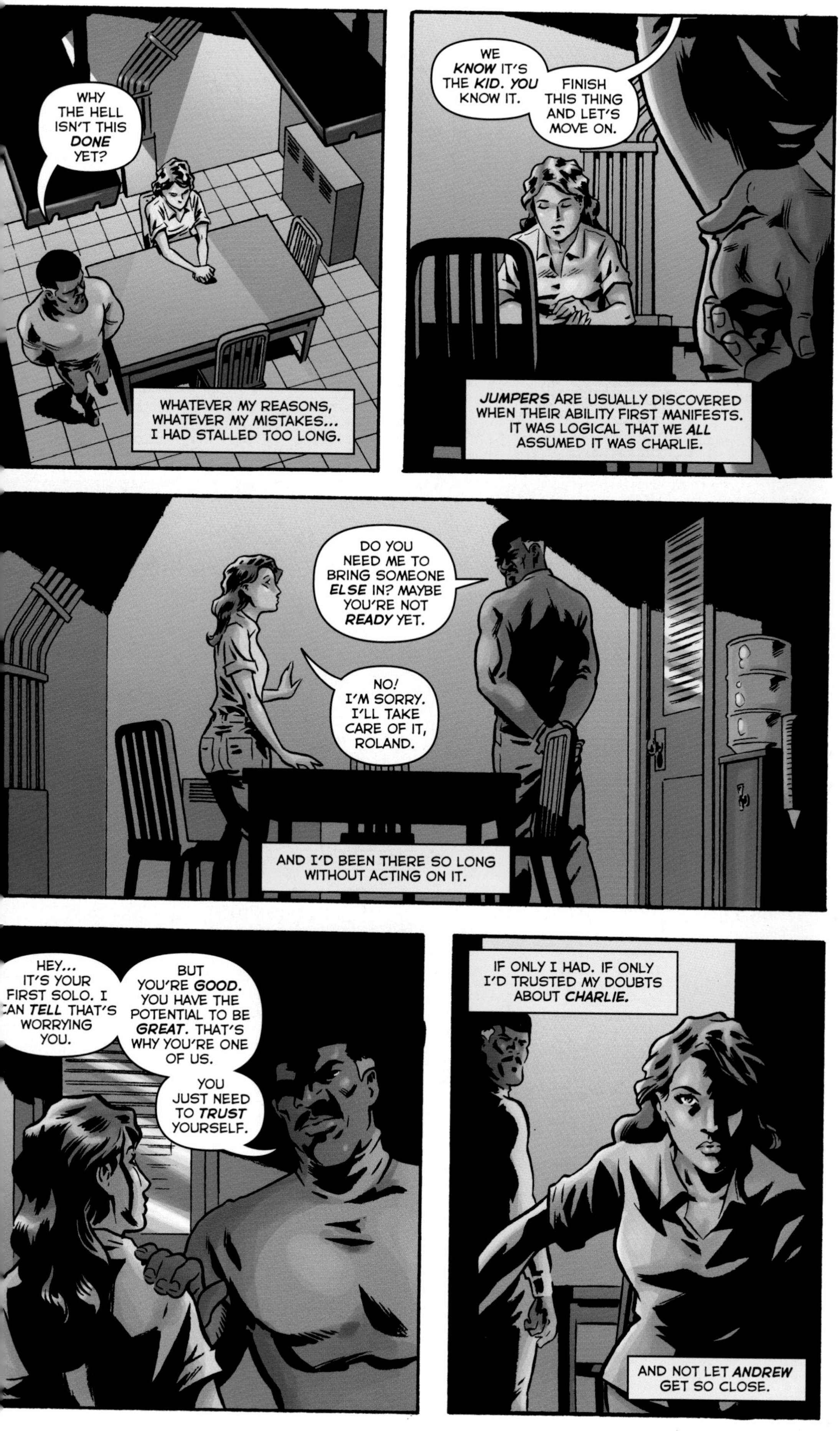
WHY THE HELL ISN'T THIS DONE YET?
WHATEVER MY REASONS, WHATEVER MY MISTAKES... I HAD STALLED TOO LONG.
WE KNOW IT'S THE KID. YOU KNOW IT.
FINISH THIS THING AND LET'S MOVE ON.
JUMPERS ARE USUALLY DISCOVERED WHEN THEIR ABILITY FIRST MANIFESTS. IT WAS LOGICAL THAT WE ALL ASSUMED IT WAS CHARLIE.
DO YOU NEED ME TO BRING SOMEONE ELSE IN? MAYBE YOU'RE NOT READY YET.
NO! I'M SORRY. I'LL TAKE CARE OF IT, ROLAND.
AND I'D BEEN THERE SO LONG WITHOUT ACTING ON IT.
HEY... IT'S YOUR FIRST SOLO. I CAN TELL THAT'S WORRYING YOU.
BUT YOU'RE GOOD. YOU HAVE THE POTENTIAL TO BE GREAT. THAT'S WHY YOU'RE ONE OF US.
YOU JUST NEED TO TRUST YOURSELF.
IF ONLY I HAD. IF ONLY I'D TRUSTED MY DOUBTS ABOUT CHARLIE.
AND NOT LET ANDREW GET SO CLOSE.

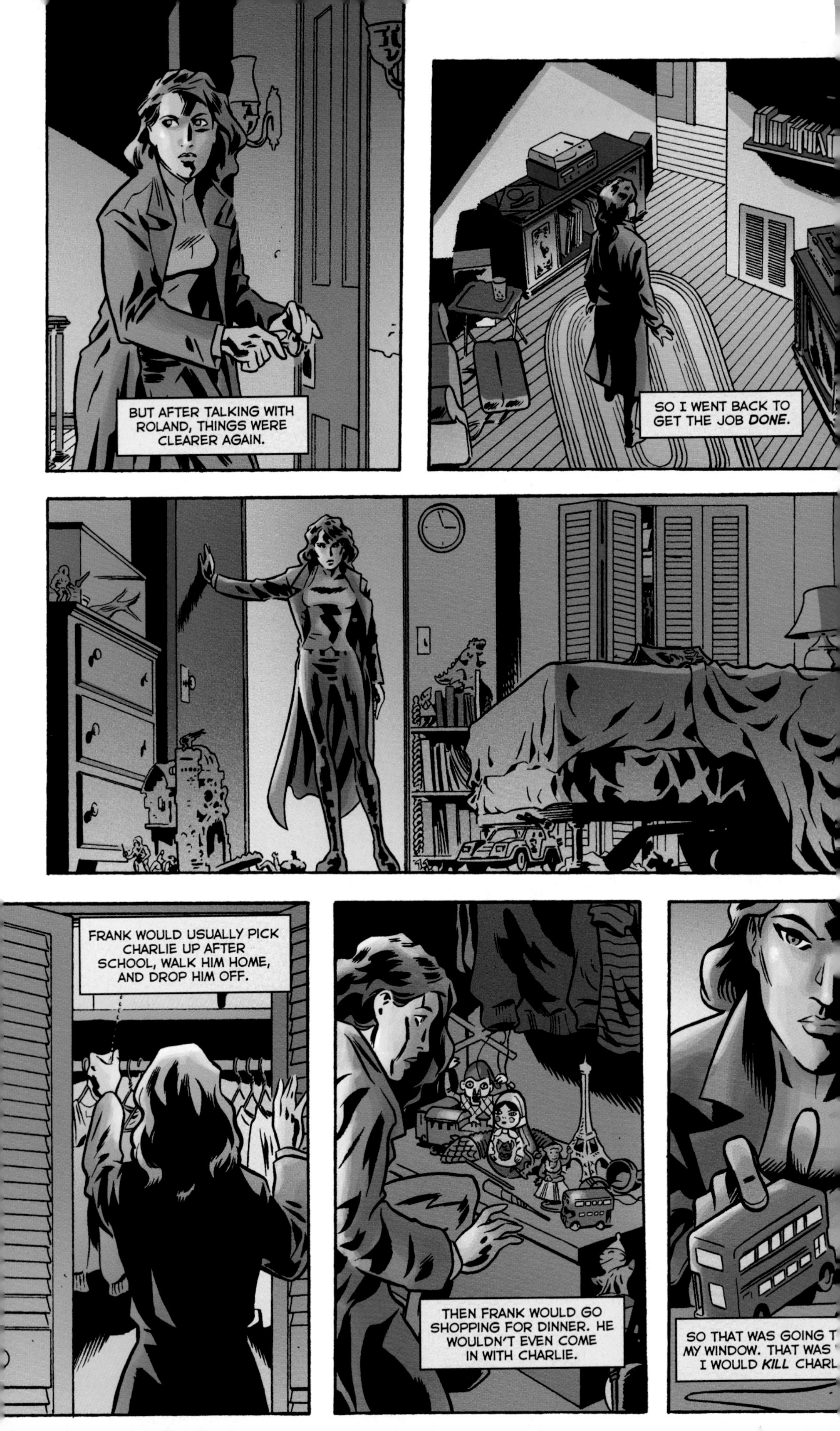

BUT AFTER TALKING WITH ROLAND, THINGS WERE CLEARER AGAIN.
SO I WENT BACK TO GET THE JOB DONE.
FRANK WOULD USUALLY PICK CHARLIE UP AFTER SCHOOL, WALK HIM HOME, AND DROP HIM OFF.
THEN FRANK WOULD GO SHOPPING FOR DINNER. HE WOULDN'T EVEN COME IN WITH CHARLIE.
SO THAT WAS GOING T
MY WINDOW. THAT WAS
I WOULD KILL CHARL

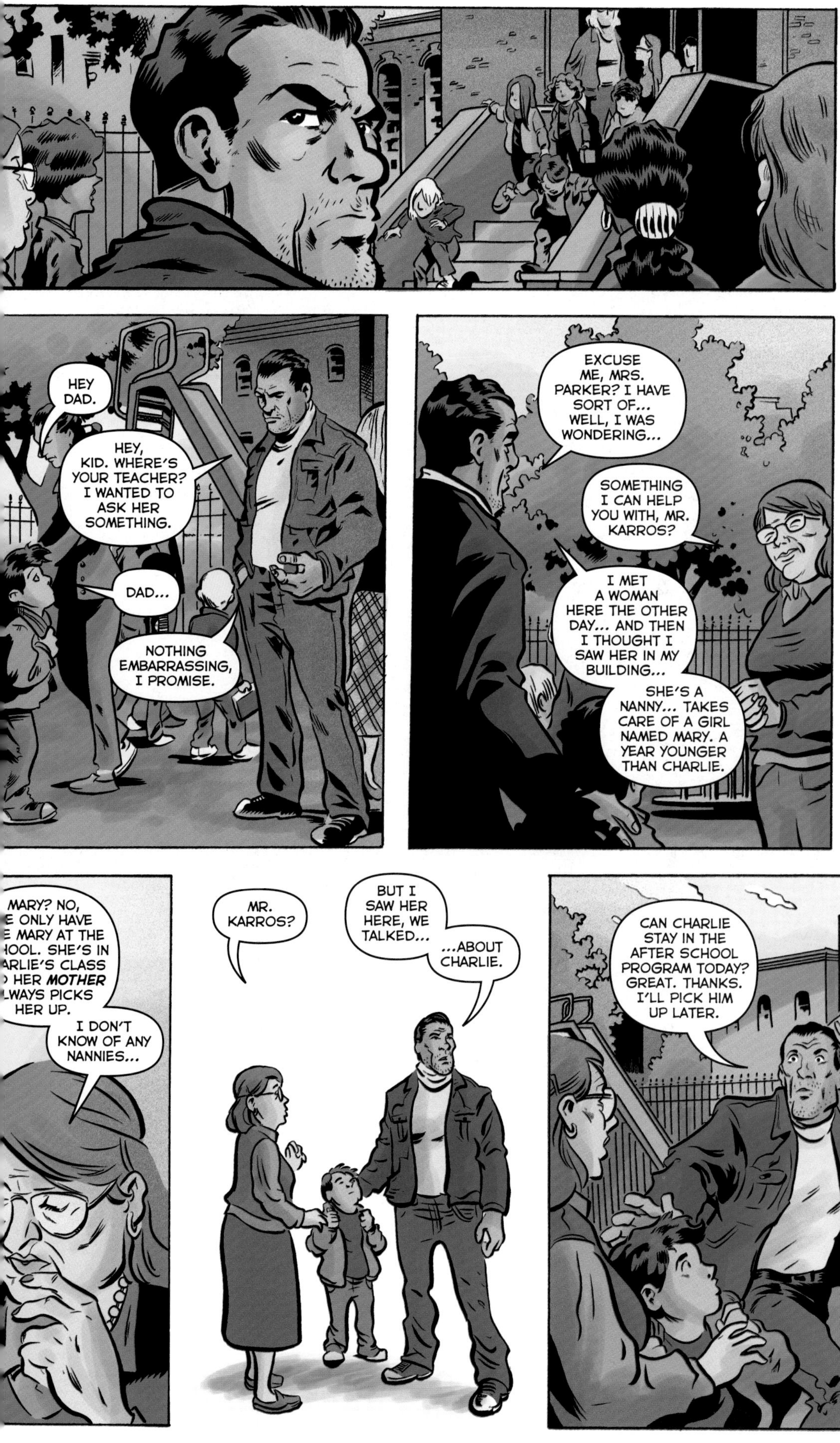
HEY DAD.
HEY, KID. WHERE'S YOUR TEACHER? I WANTED TO ASK HER SOMETHING.
DAD...
NOTHING EMBARRASSING, I PROMISE.
EXCUSE ME, MRS. PARKER? I HAVE SORT OF... WELL, I WAS WONDERING...
SOMETHING I CAN HELP YOU WITH, MR. KARROS?
I MET A WOMAN HERE THE OTHER DAY... AND THEN I THOUGHT I SAW HER IN MY BUILDING...
SHE'S A NANNY... TAKES CARE OF A GIRL NAMED MARY. A YEAR YOUNGER THAN CHARLIE.
MARY? NO, E ONLY HAVE E MARY AT THE HOOL. SHE'S IN ARLIE'S CLASS D HER MOTHER LWAYS PICKS HER UP.
I DON'T KNOW OF ANY NANNIES...
MR. KARROS?
BUT I SAW HER HERE, WE TALKED...
...ABOUT CHARLIE.
CAN CHARLIE STAY IN THE AFTER SCHOOL PROGRAM TODAY? GREAT. THANKS. I'LL PICK HIM UP LATER.

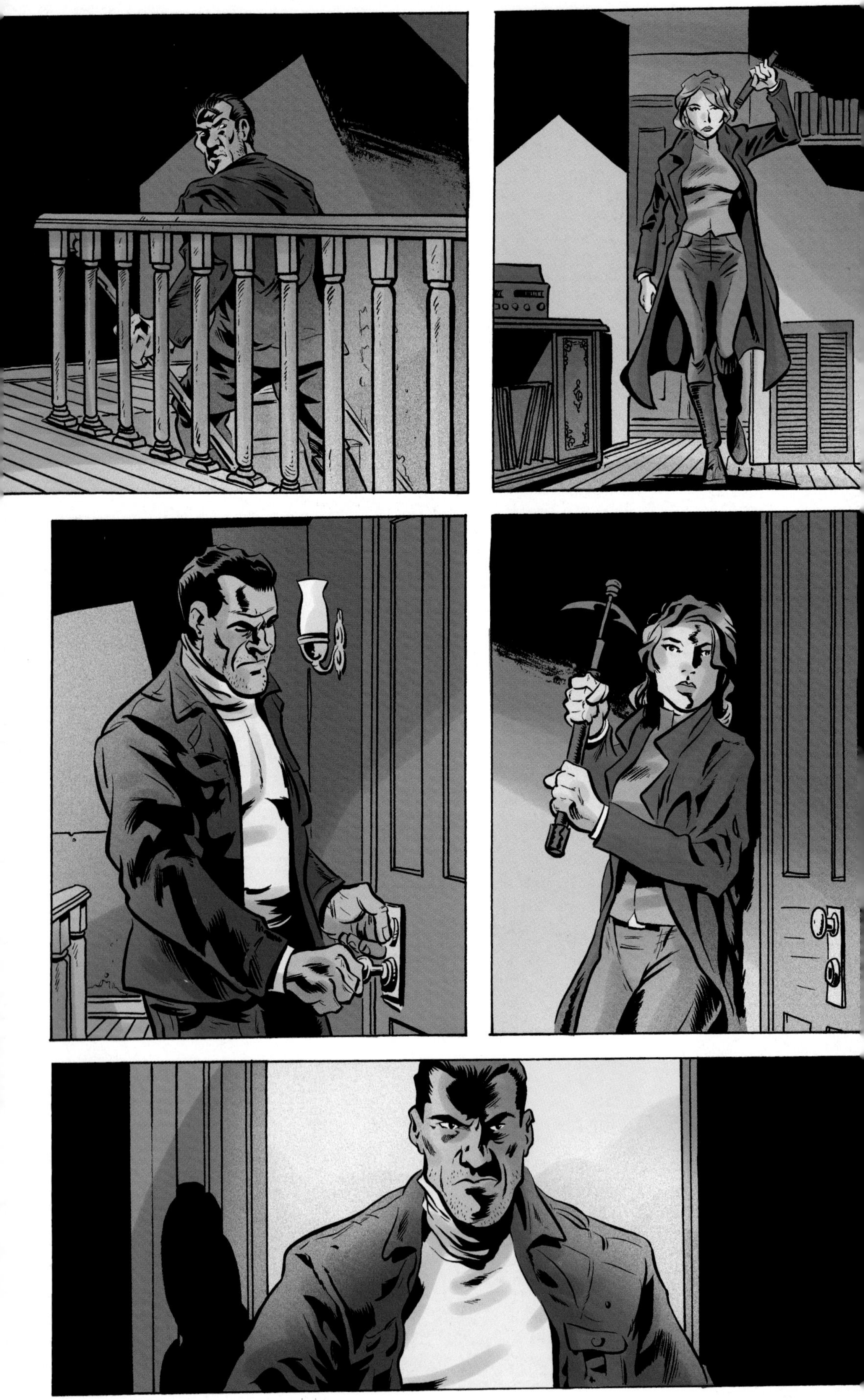

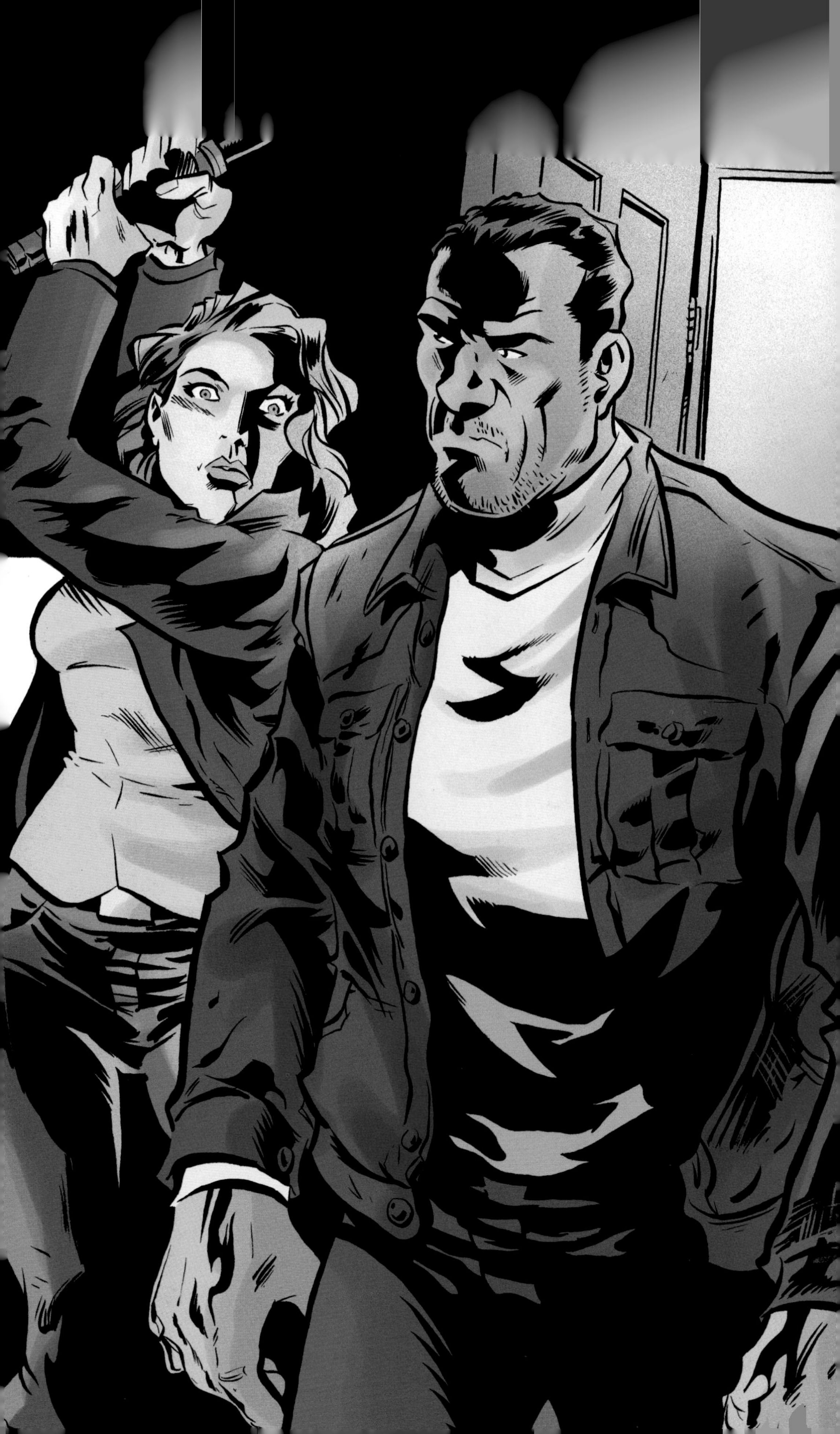

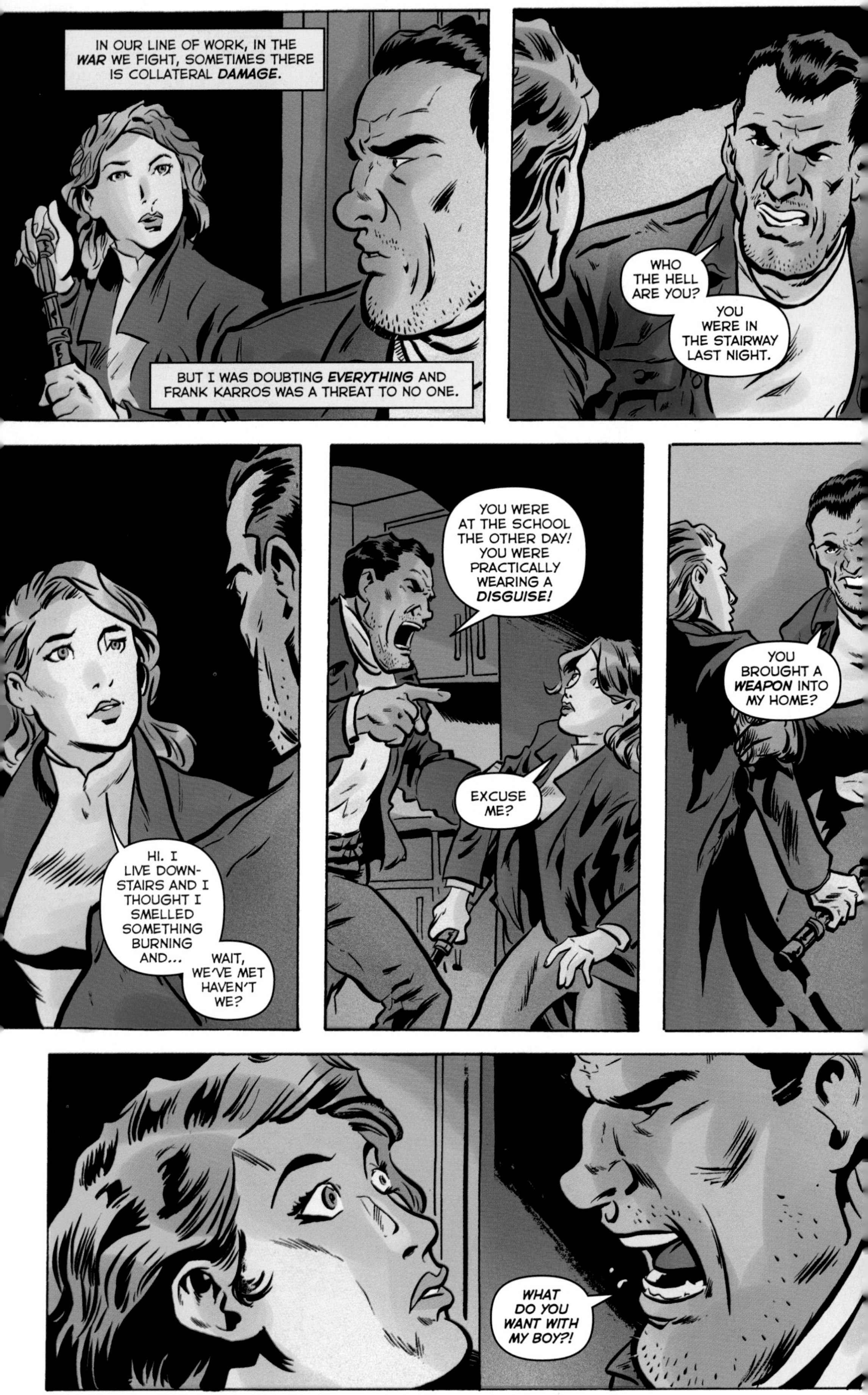
IN OUR LINE OF WORK, IN THE WAR WE FIGHT, SOMETIMES THERE IS COLLATERAL DAMAGE.
BUT I WAS DOUBTING EVERYTHING AND FRANK KARROS WAS A THREAT TO NO ONE.
WHO THE HELL ARE YOU?
YOU WERE IN THE STAIRWAY LAST NIGHT.
HI. I LIVE DOWN-STAIRS AND I THOUGHT I SMELLED SOMETHING BURNING AND...
WAIT, WE'VE MET HAVEN'T WE?
YOU WERE AT THE SCHOOL THE OTHER DAY! YOU WERE PRACTICALLY WEARING A DISGUISE!
EXCUSE ME?
YOU BROUGHT A WEAPON INTO MY HOME?
WHAT DO YOU WANT WITH MY BOY?!

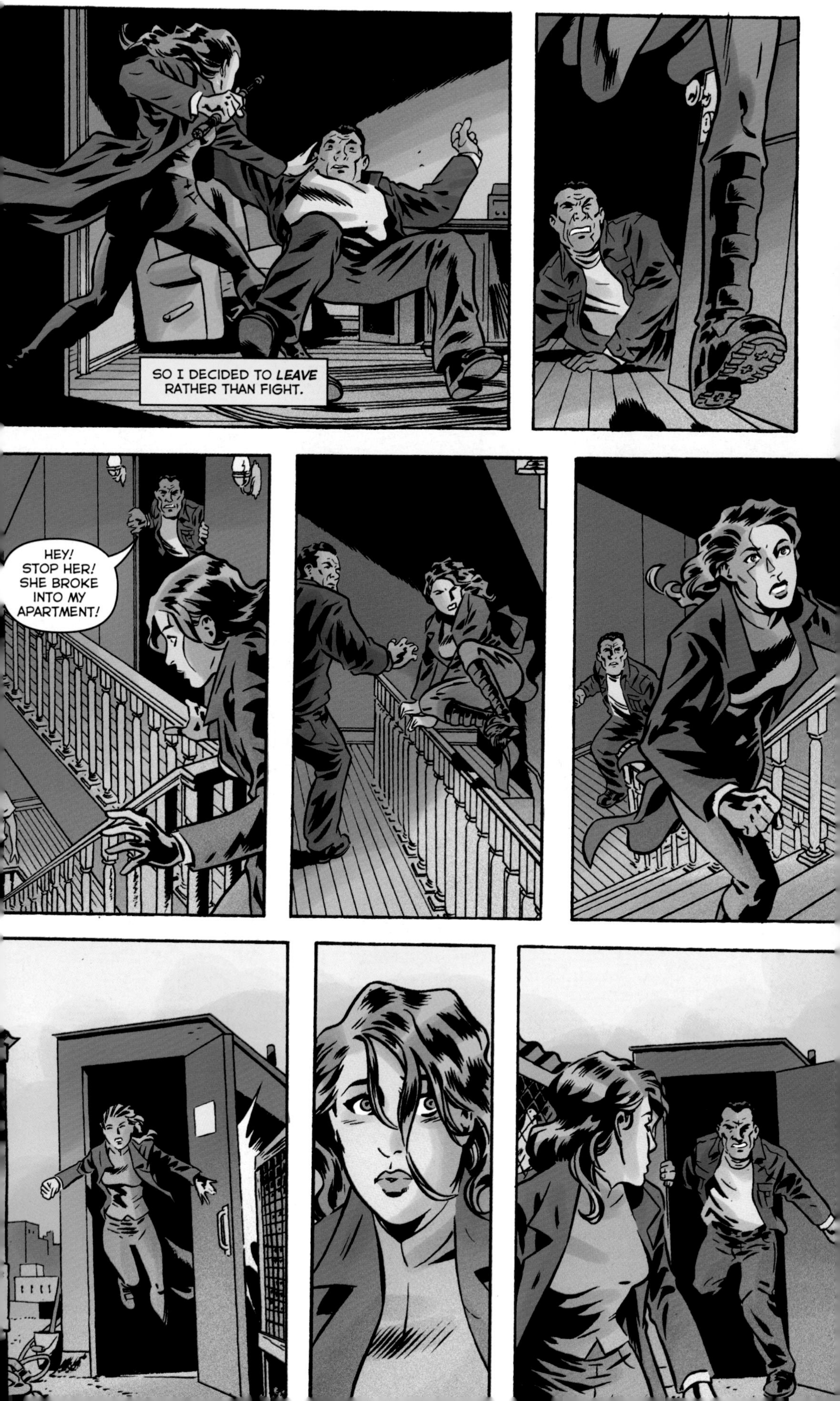

SO I DECIDED TO *LEAVE* RATHER THAN FIGHT.
HEY! STOP HER! SHE BROKE INTO MY APARTMENT!

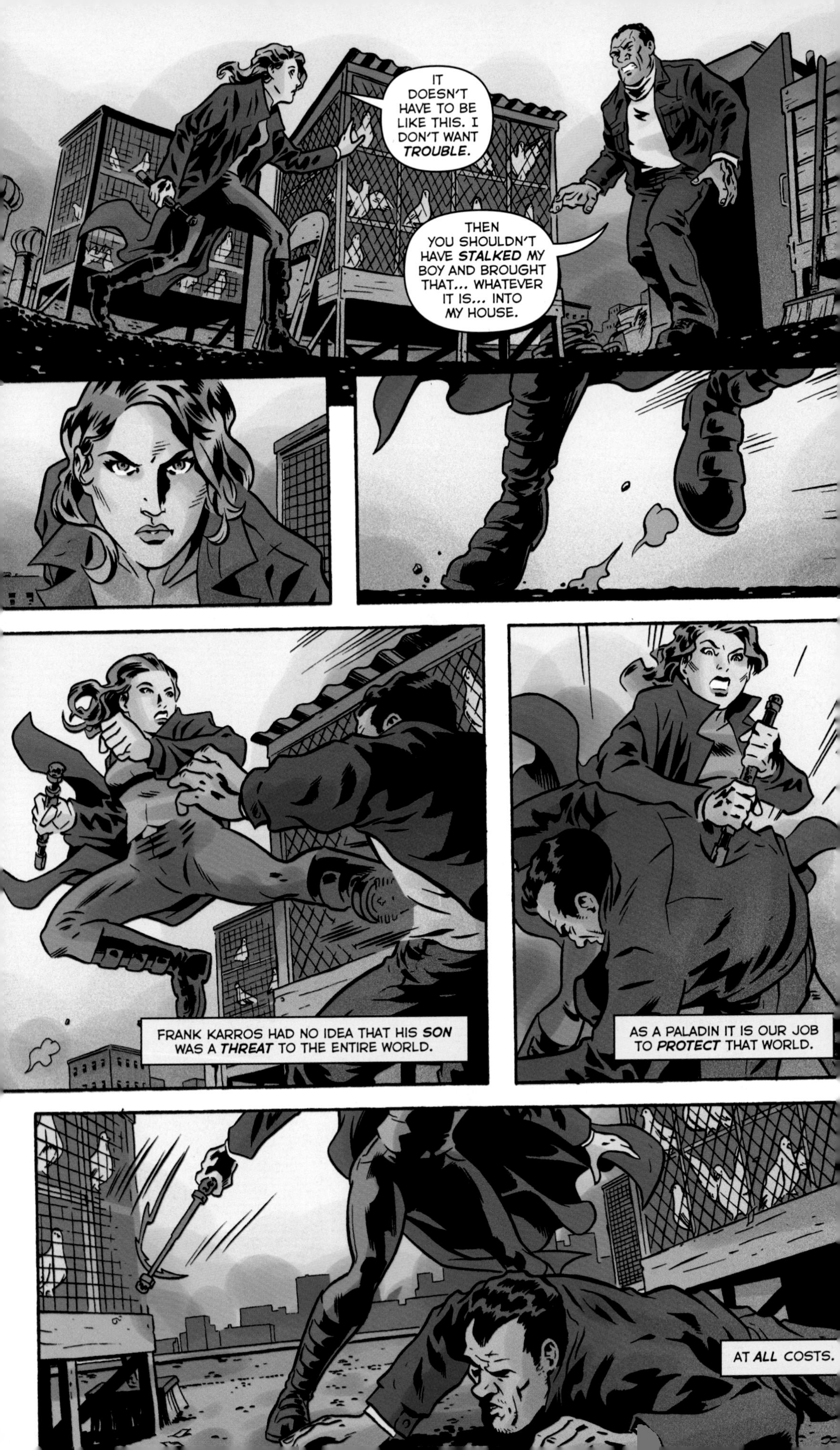
IT DOESN'T HAVE TO BE LIKE THIS. I DON'T WANT TROUBLE.
THEN YOU SHOULDN'T HAVE STALKED MY BOY AND BROUGHT THAT... WHATEVER IT IS... INTO MY HOUSE.
FRANK KARROS HAD NO IDEA THAT HIS SON WAS A THREAT TO THE ENTIRE WORLD.
AS A PALADIN IT IS OUR JOB TO PROTECT THAT WORLD.
AT ALL COSTS.

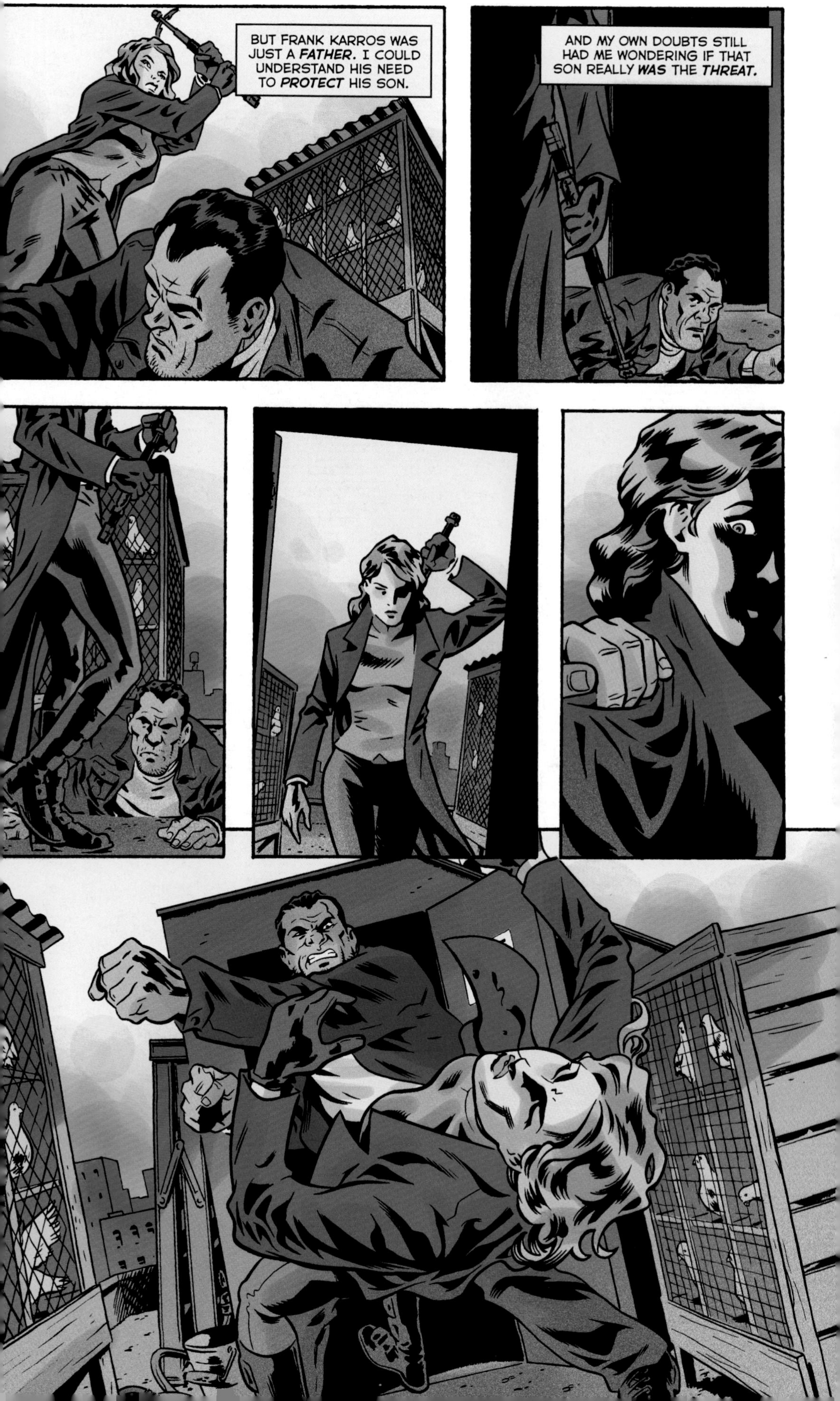
BUT FRANK KARROS WAS JUST A FATHER. I COULD UNDERSTAND HIS NEED TO PROTECT HIS SON.
AND MY OWN DOUBTS STILL HAD ME WONDERING IF THAT SON REALLY WAS THE THREAT.

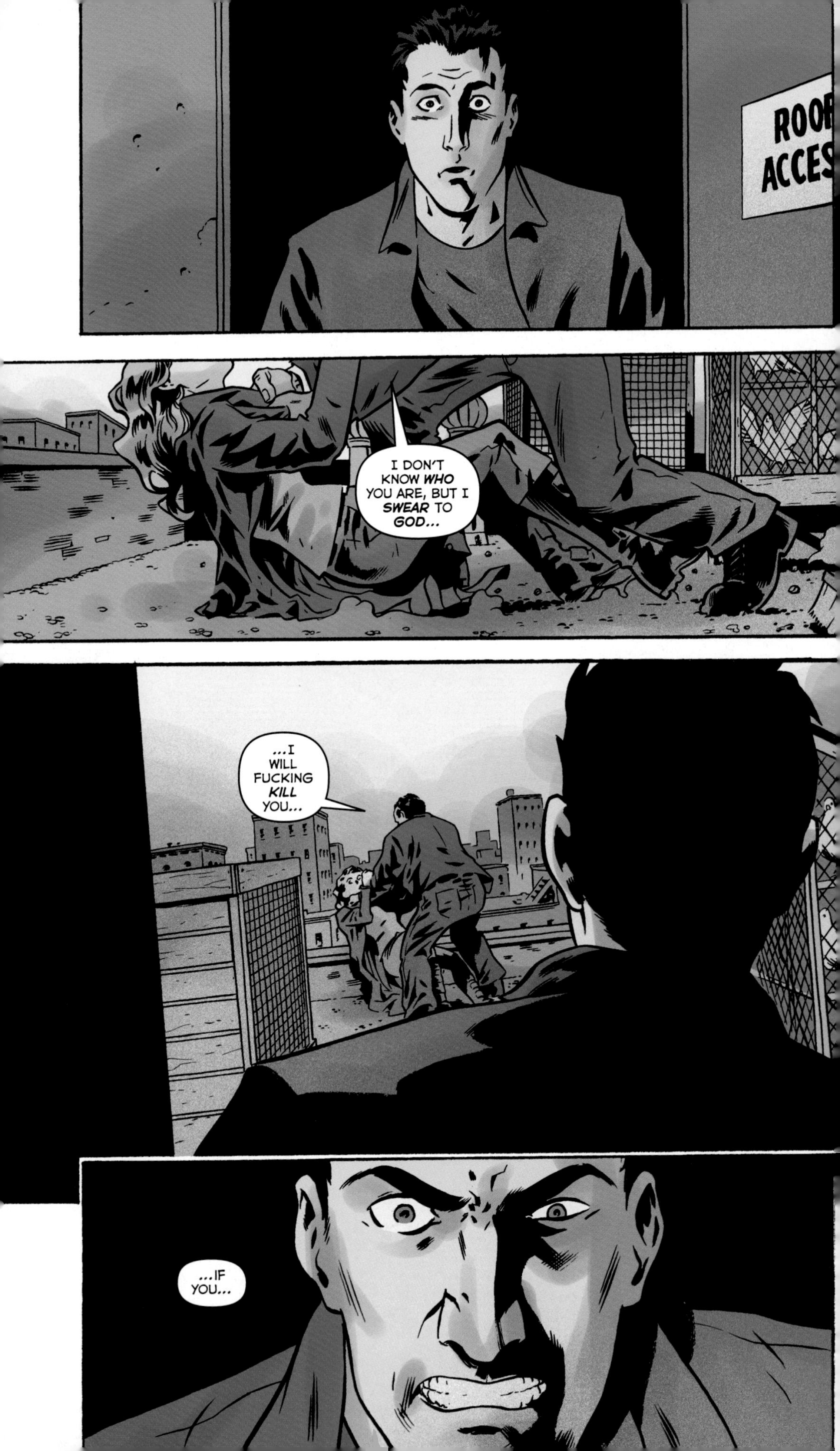
ROOF
ACCES
I DON'T KNOW WHO YOU ARE, BUT I SWEAR TO GOD...
...I WILL FUCKING KILL YOU...
...IF YOU...

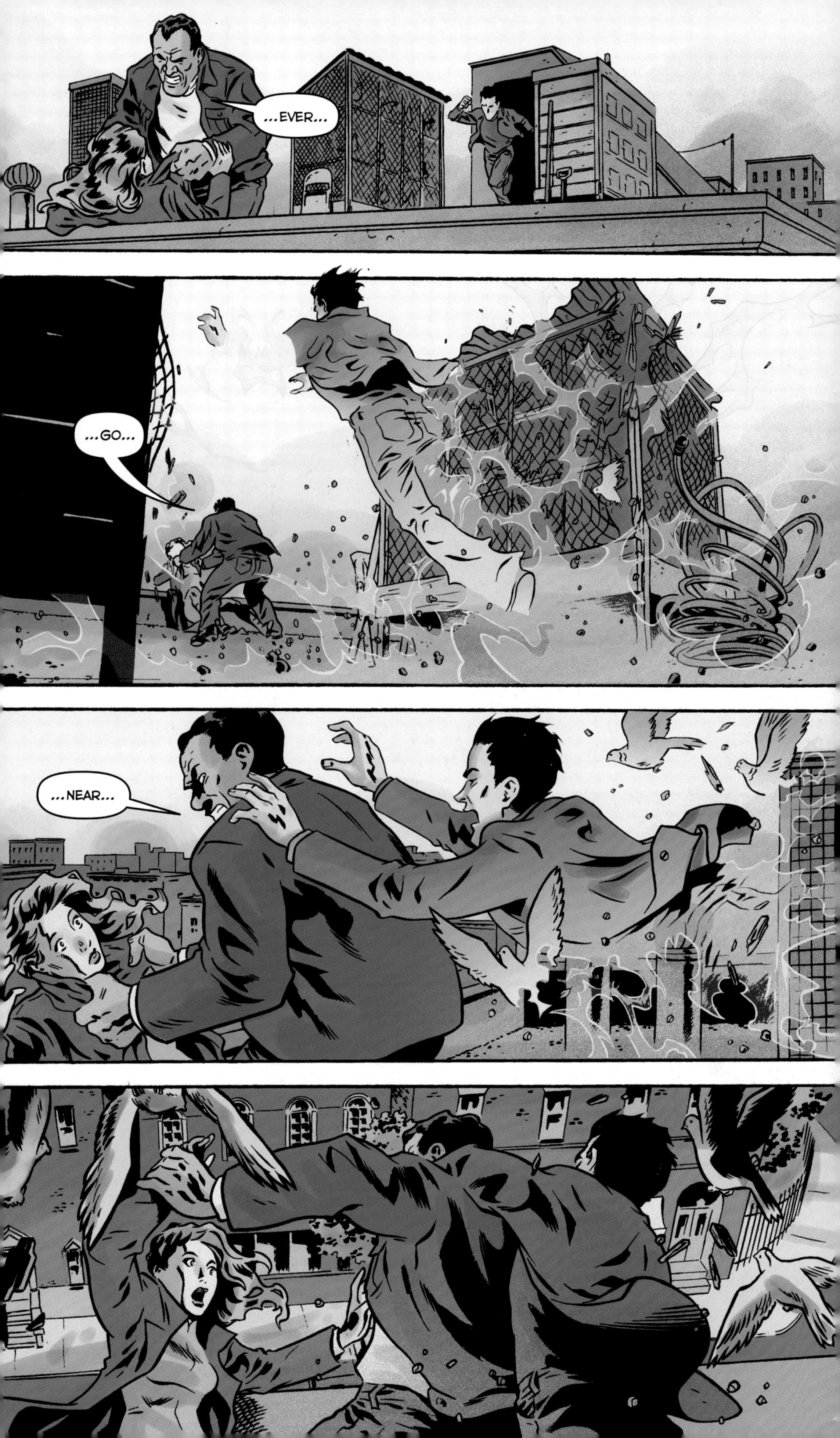
...EVER...
...GO...
...NEAR...

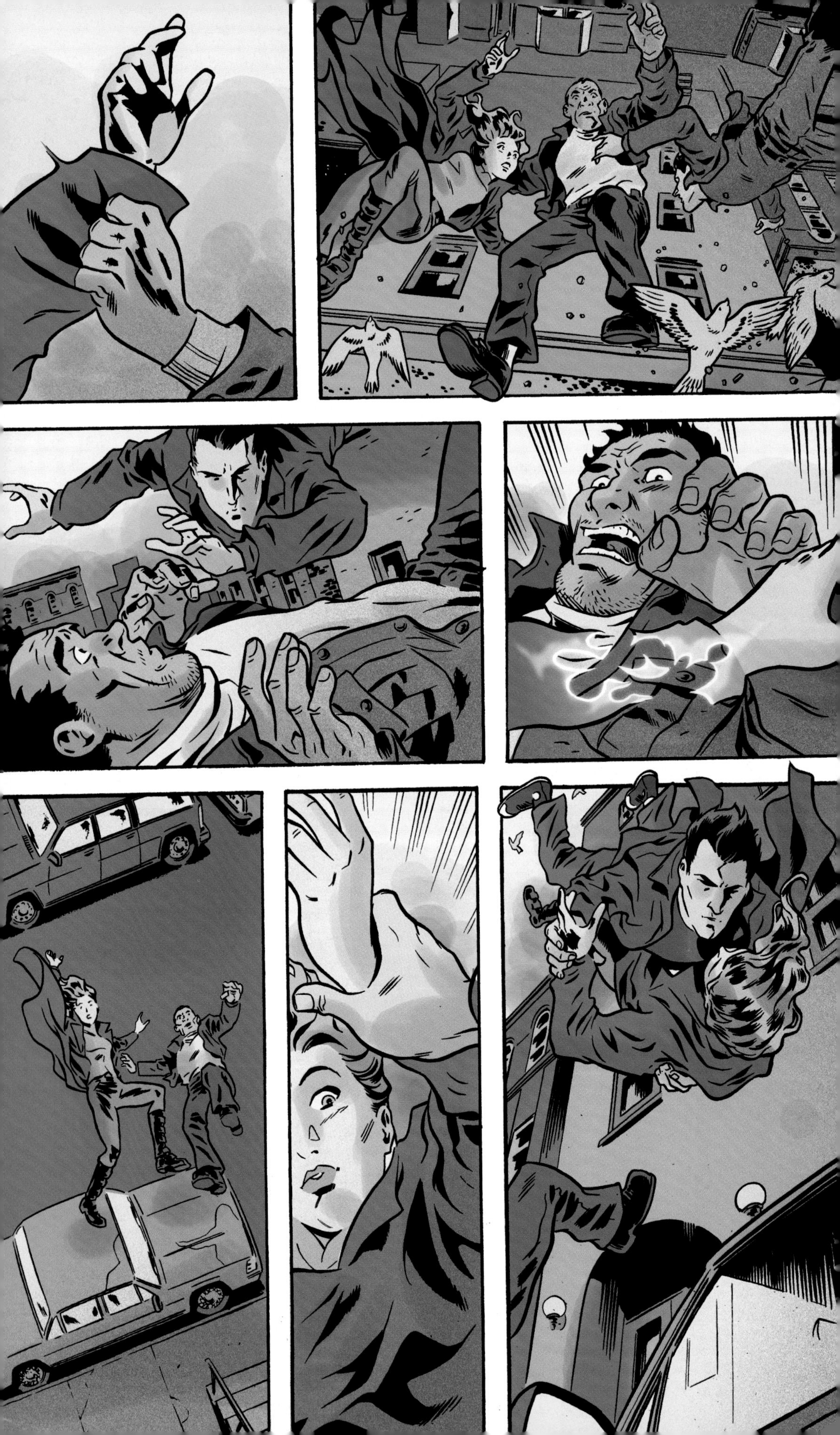

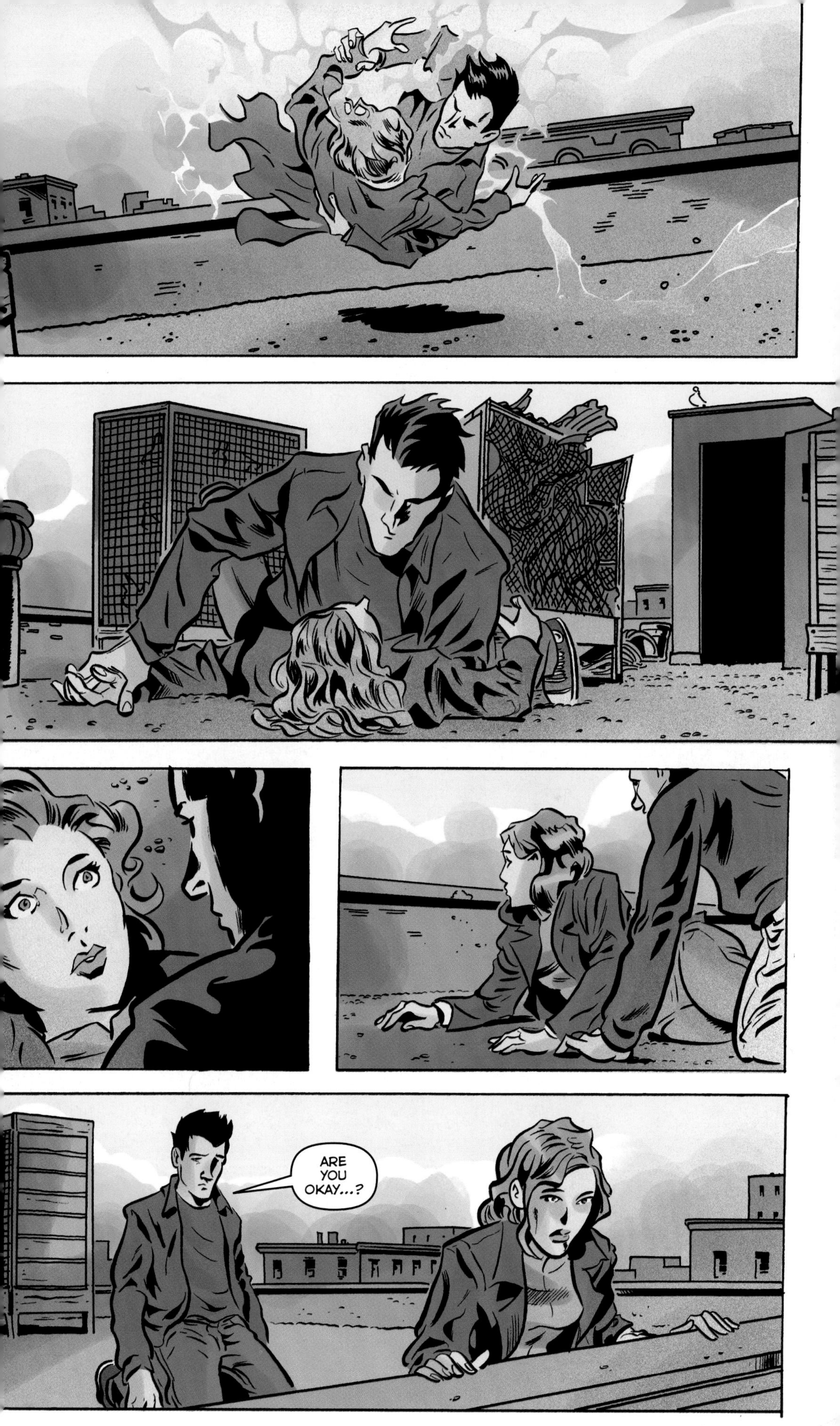
ARE YOU OKAY...?

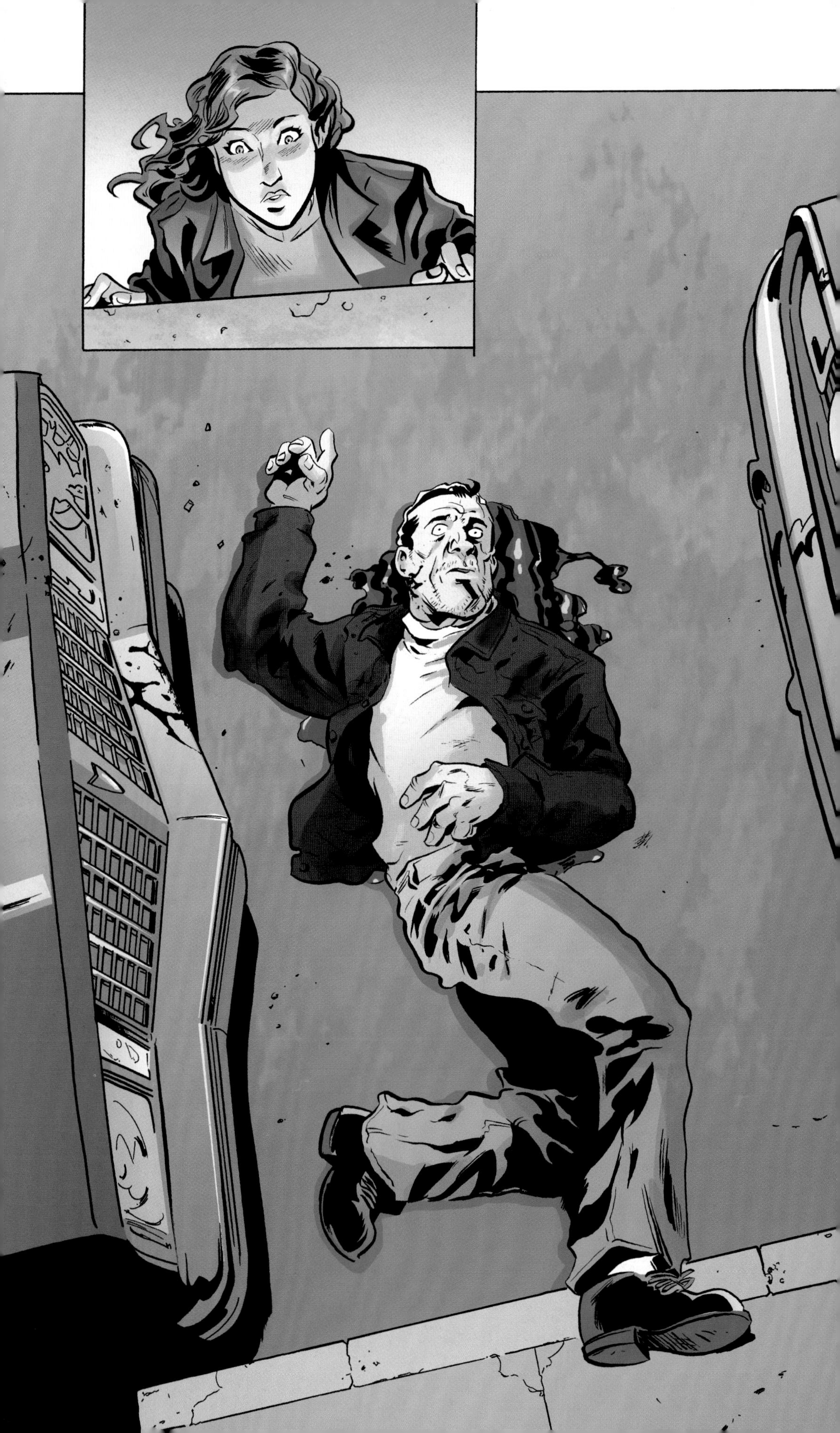

CHAPTER 4

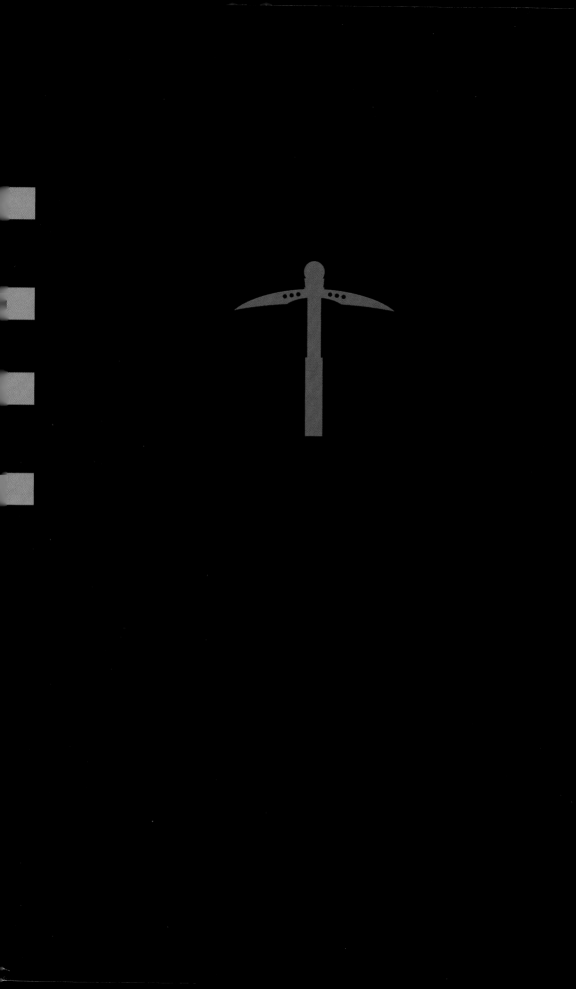

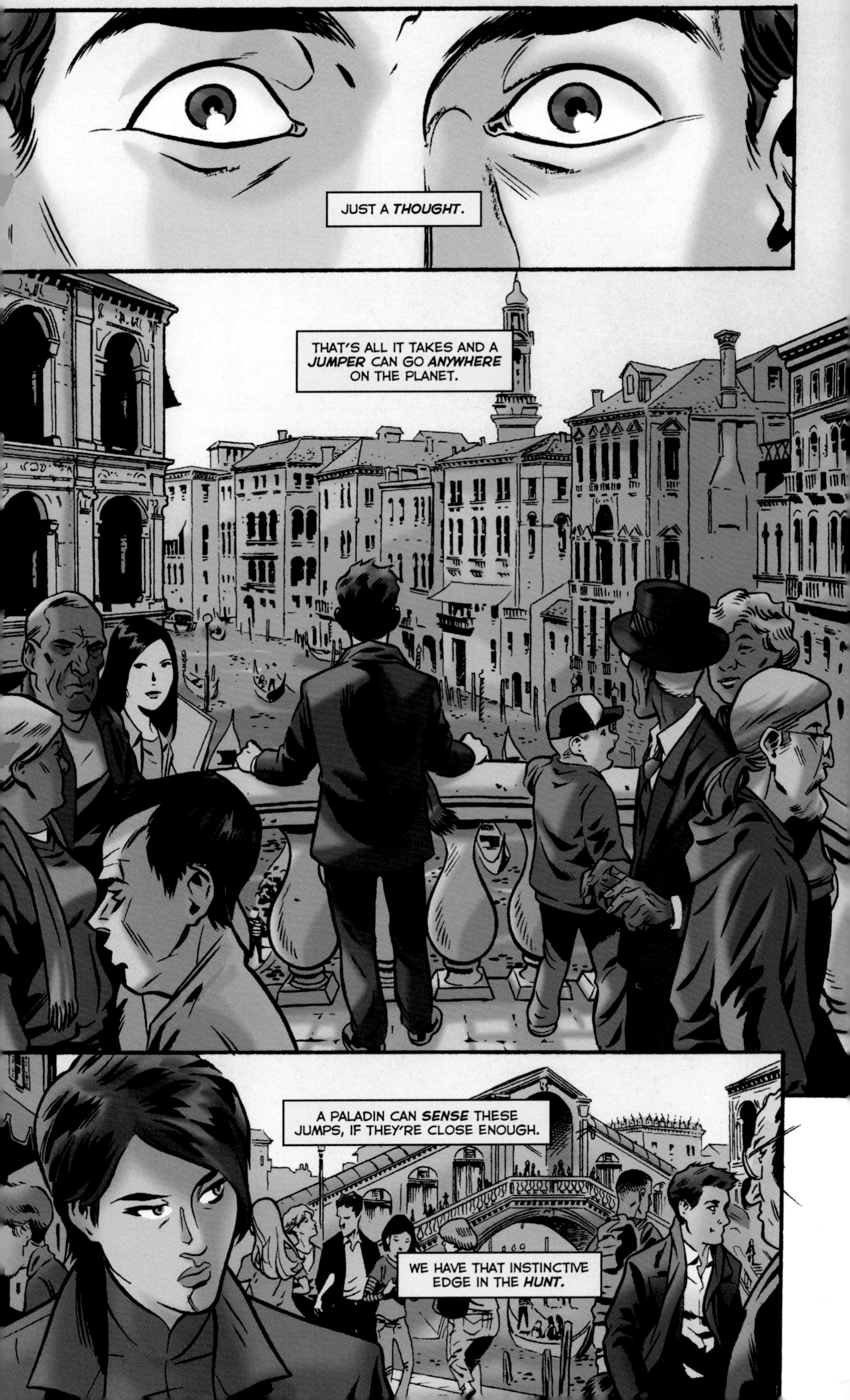
JUST A *THOUGHT*.
THAT'S ALL IT TAKES AND A *JUMPER* CAN GO *ANYWHERE* ON THE PLANET.
A PALADIN CAN *SENSE* THESE JUMPS, IF THEY'RE CLOSE ENOUGH.
WE HAVE THAT INSTINCTIVE EDGE IN THE *HUNT*.

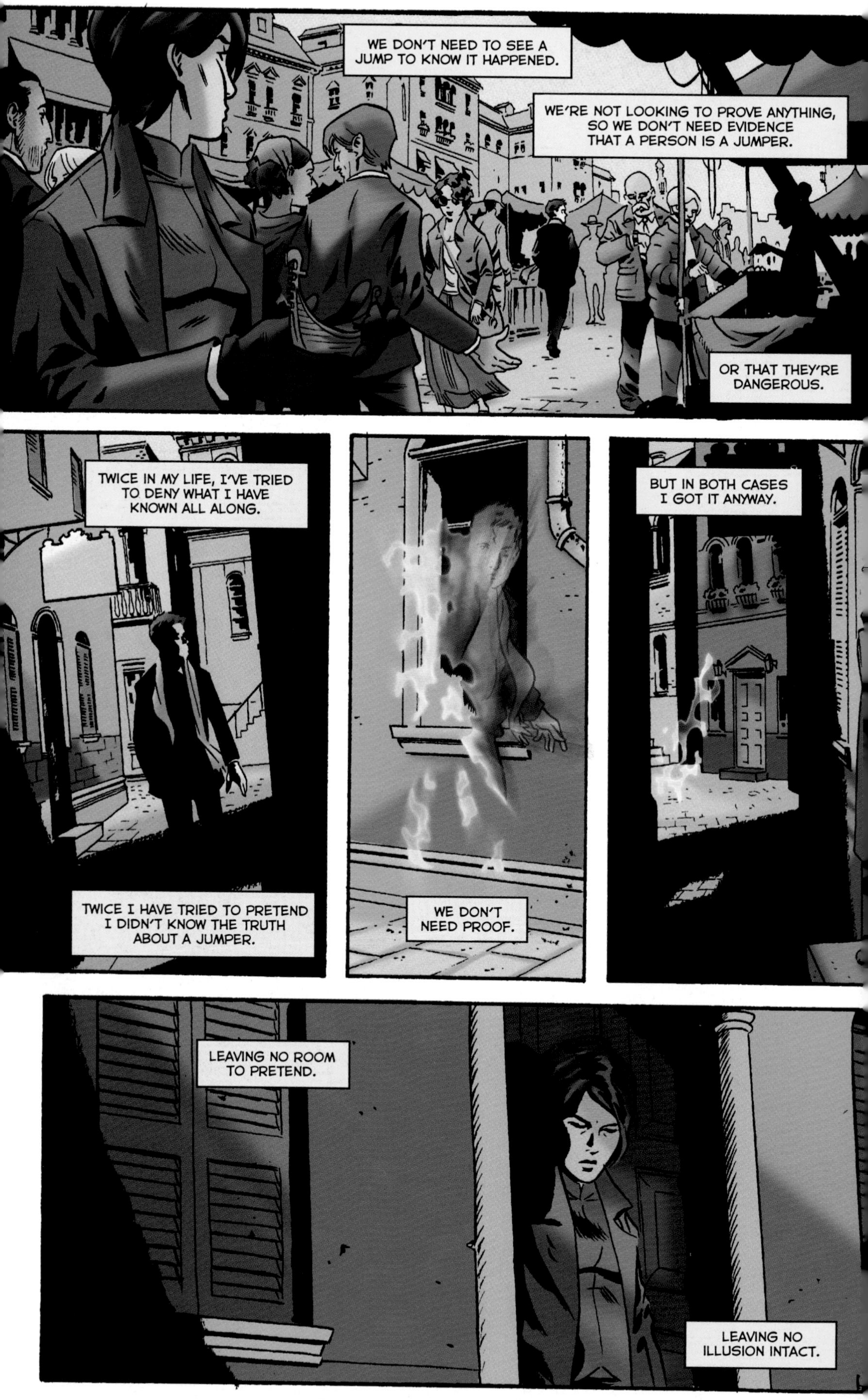
WE DON'T NEED TO SEE A JUMP TO KNOW IT HAPPENED.
WE'RE NOT LOOKING TO PROVE ANYTHING, SO WE DON'T NEED EVIDENCE THAT A PERSON IS A JUMPER.
OR THAT THEY'RE DANGEROUS.
TWICE IN MY LIFE, I'VE TRIED TO DENY WHAT I HAVE KNOWN ALL ALONG.
TWICE I HAVE TRIED TO PRETEND I DIDN'T KNOW THE TRUTH ABOUT A JUMPER.
WE DON'T NEED PROOF.
BUT IN BOTH CASES I GOT IT ANYWAY.
LEAVING NO ROOM TO PRETEND.
LEAVING NO ILLUSION INTACT.

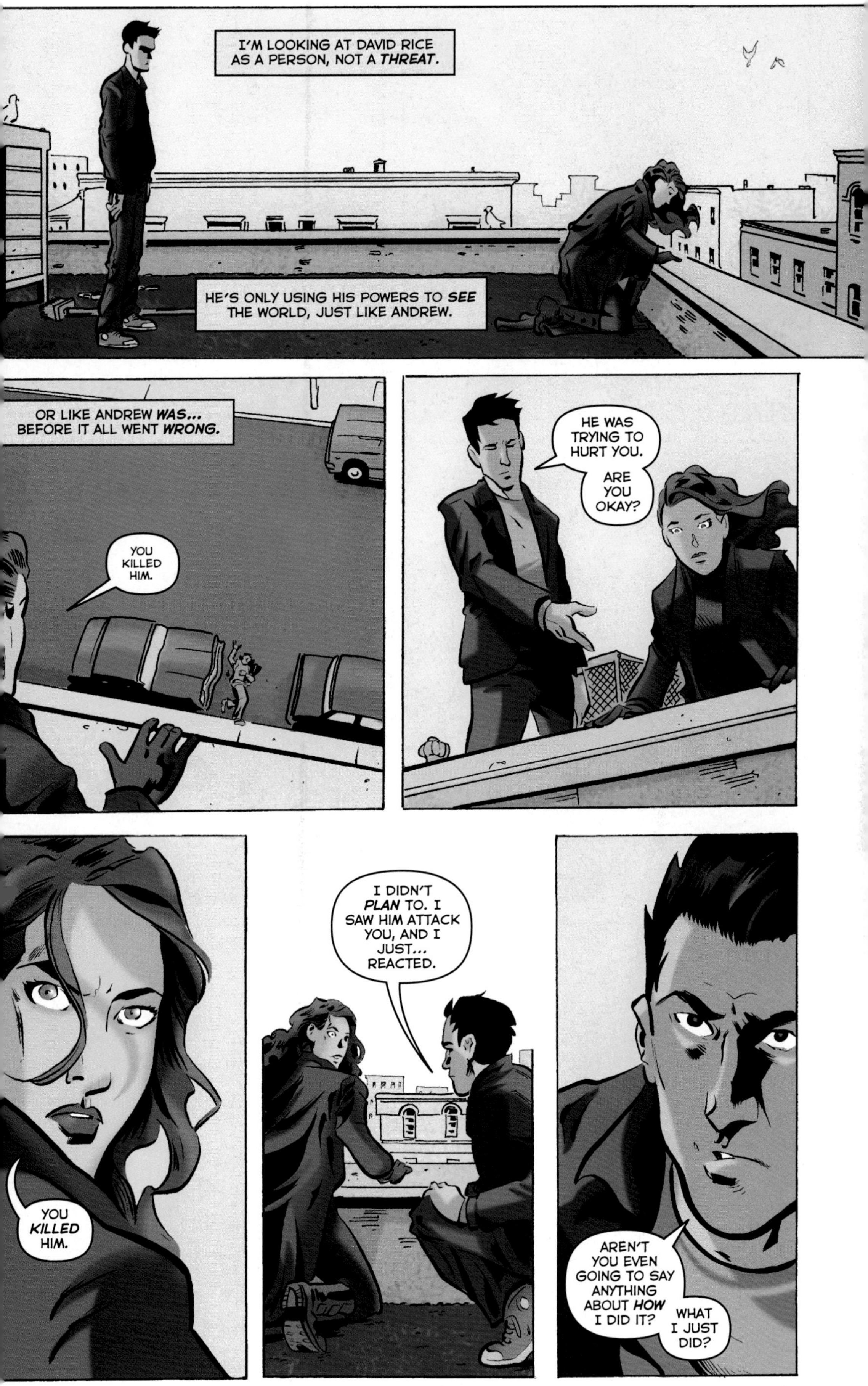

I'M LOOKING AT DAVID RICE AS A PERSON, NOT A *THREAT*.
HE'S ONLY USING HIS POWERS TO *SEE* THE WORLD, JUST LIKE ANDREW.
OR LIKE ANDREW *WAS*... BEFORE IT ALL WENT *WRONG*.
YOU KILLED HIM.
HE WAS TRYING TO HURT YOU.
ARE YOU OKAY?
YOU *KILLED* HIM.
I DIDN'T *PLAN* TO. I SAW HIM ATTACK YOU, AND I JUST... REACTED.
AREN'T YOU EVEN GOING TO SAY ANYTHING ABOUT *HOW* I DID IT?
WHAT I JUST DID?

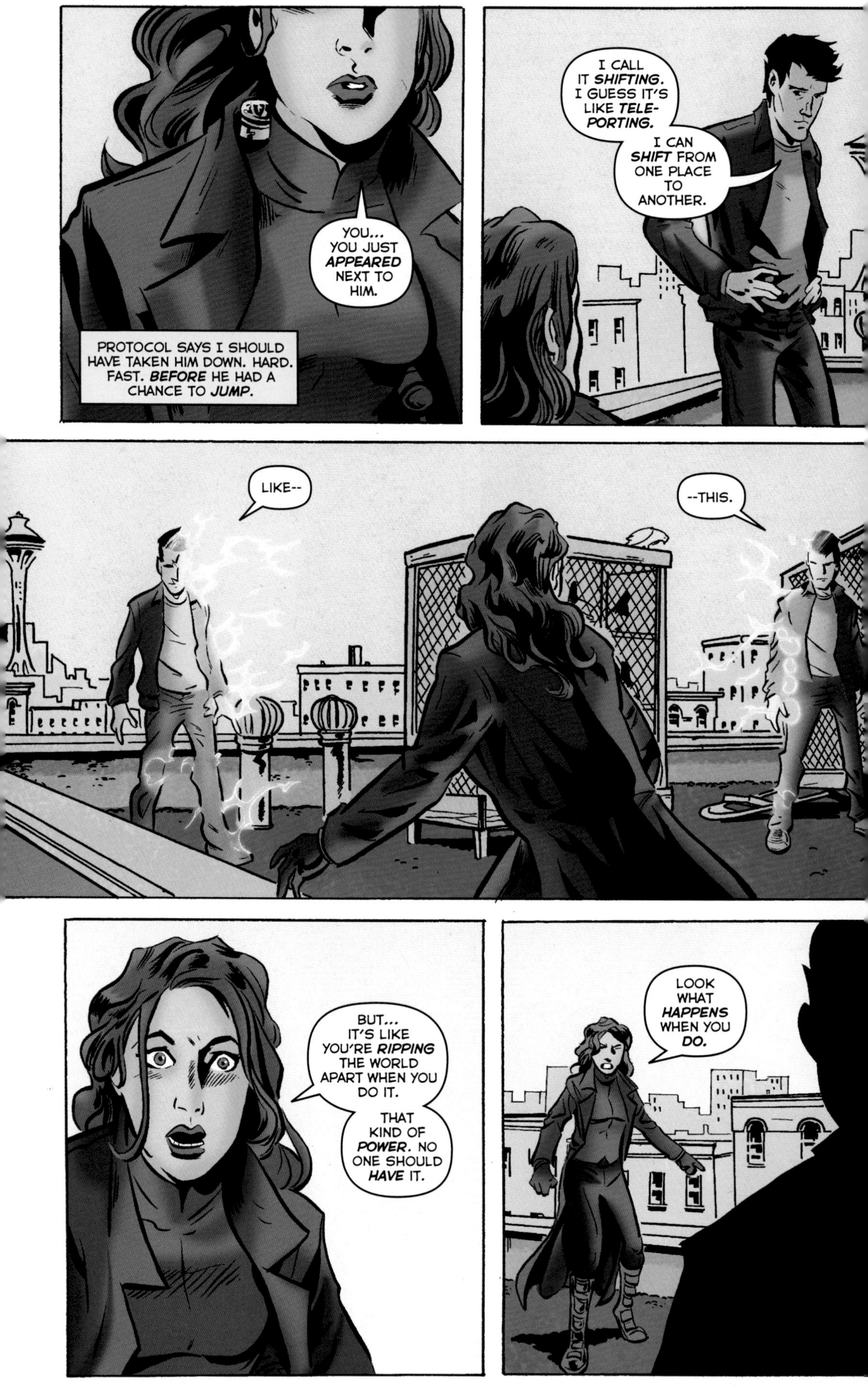
YOU... YOU JUST APPEARED NEXT TO HIM.
PROTOCOL SAYS I SHOULD HAVE TAKEN HIM DOWN. HARD. FAST. BEFORE HE HAD A CHANCE TO JUMP.
I CALL IT SHIFTING. I GUESS IT'S LIKE TELE-PORTING.
I CAN SHIFT FROM ONE PLACE TO ANOTHER.
LIKE--
--THIS.
BUT... IT'S LIKE YOU'RE RIPPING THE WORLD APART WHEN YOU DO IT.
THAT KIND OF POWER. NO ONE SHOULD HAVE IT.
LOOK WHAT HAPPENS WHEN YOU DO.

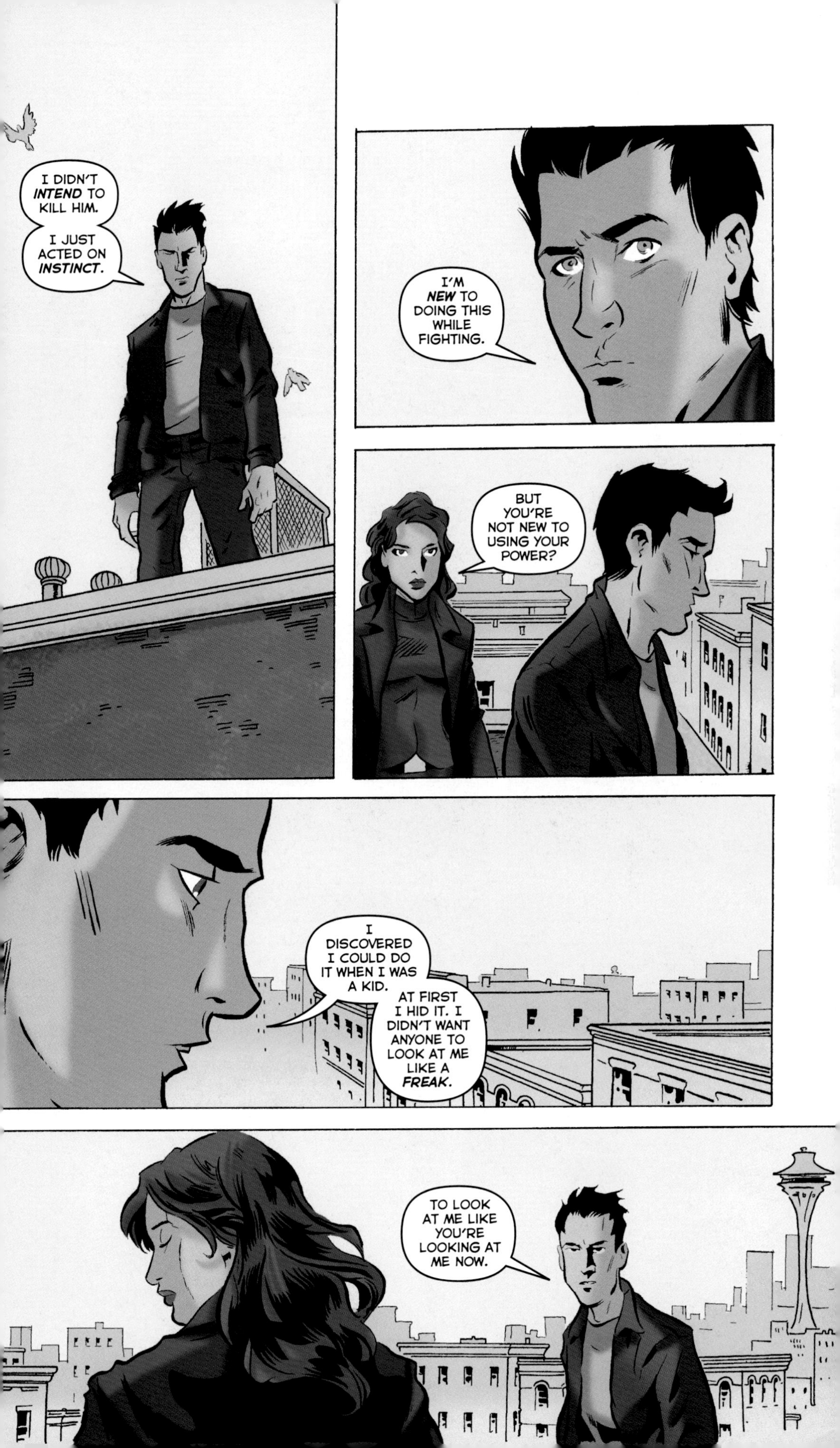
I DIDN'T INTEND TO KILL HIM.
I JUST ACTED ON INSTINCT.
I'M NEW TO DOING THIS WHILE FIGHTING.
BUT YOU'RE NOT NEW TO USING YOUR POWER?
I DISCOVERED I COULD DO IT WHEN I WAS A KID.
AT FIRST I HID IT. I DIDN'T WANT ANYONE TO LOOK AT ME LIKE A FREAK.
TO LOOK AT ME LIKE YOU'RE LOOKING AT ME NOW.

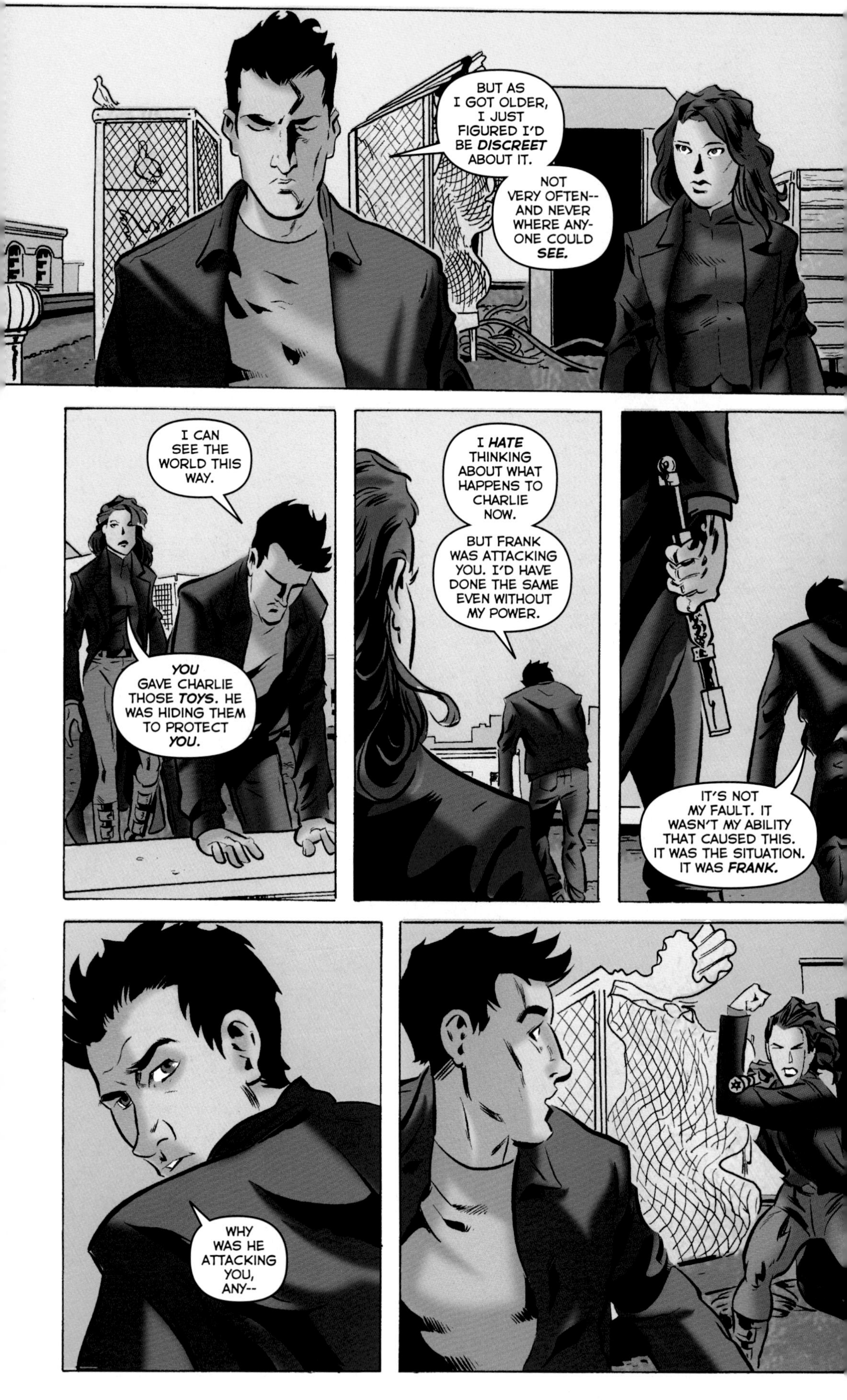

BUT AS I GOT OLDER, I JUST FIGURED I'D BE *DISCREET* ABOUT IT.
NOT VERY OFTEN-- AND NEVER WHERE ANY-ONE COULD *SEE.*
I CAN SEE THE WORLD THIS WAY.
YOU GAVE CHARLIE THOSE *TOYS*. HE WAS HIDING THEM TO PROTECT *YOU*.
I *HATE* THINKING ABOUT WHAT HAPPENS TO CHARLIE NOW.
BUT FRANK WAS ATTACKING YOU. I'D HAVE DONE THE SAME EVEN WITHOUT MY POWER.
IT'S NOT MY FAULT. IT WASN'T MY ABILITY THAT CAUSED THIS. IT WAS THE SITUATION. IT WAS *FRANK.*
WHY WAS HE ATTACKING YOU, ANY--

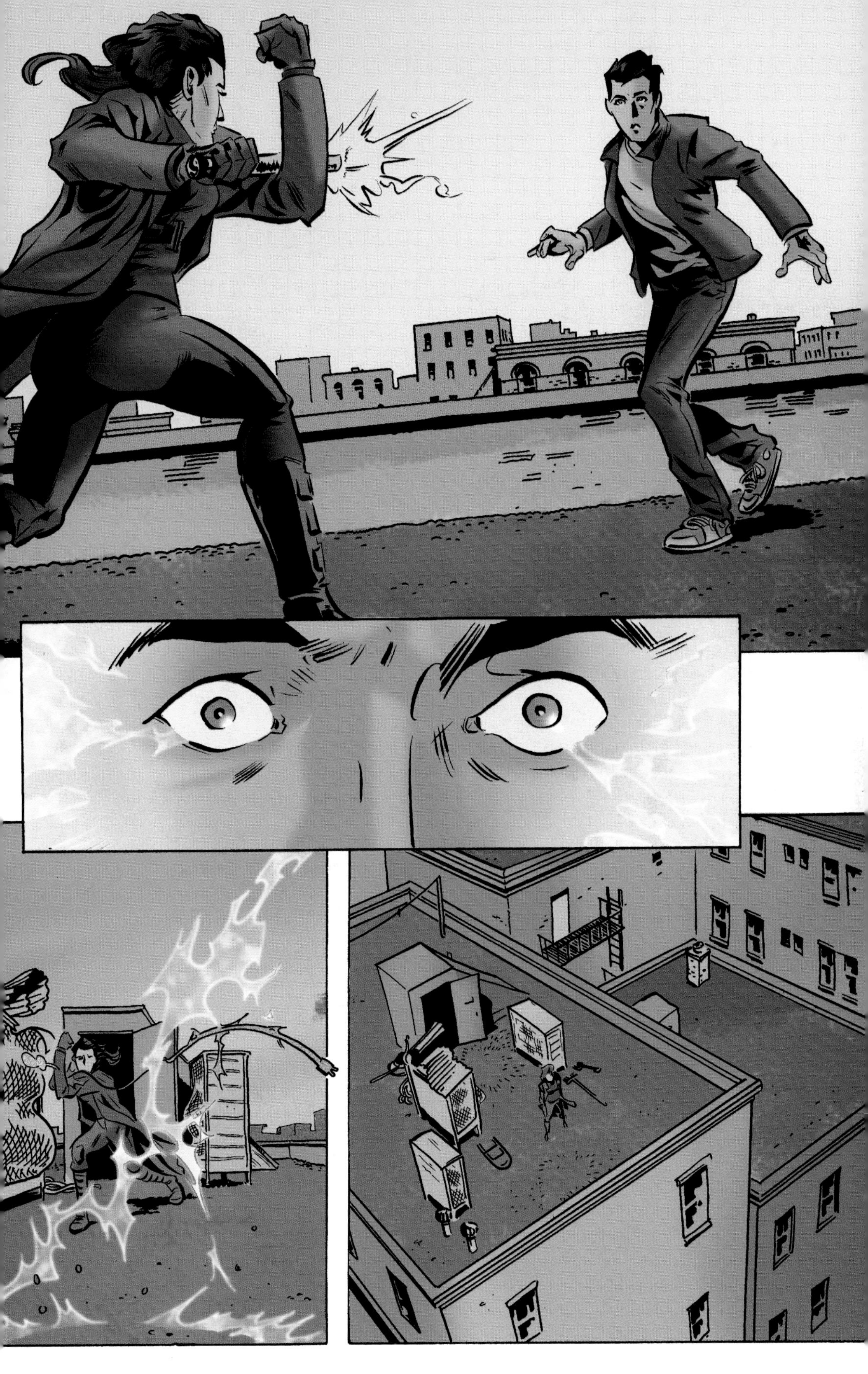

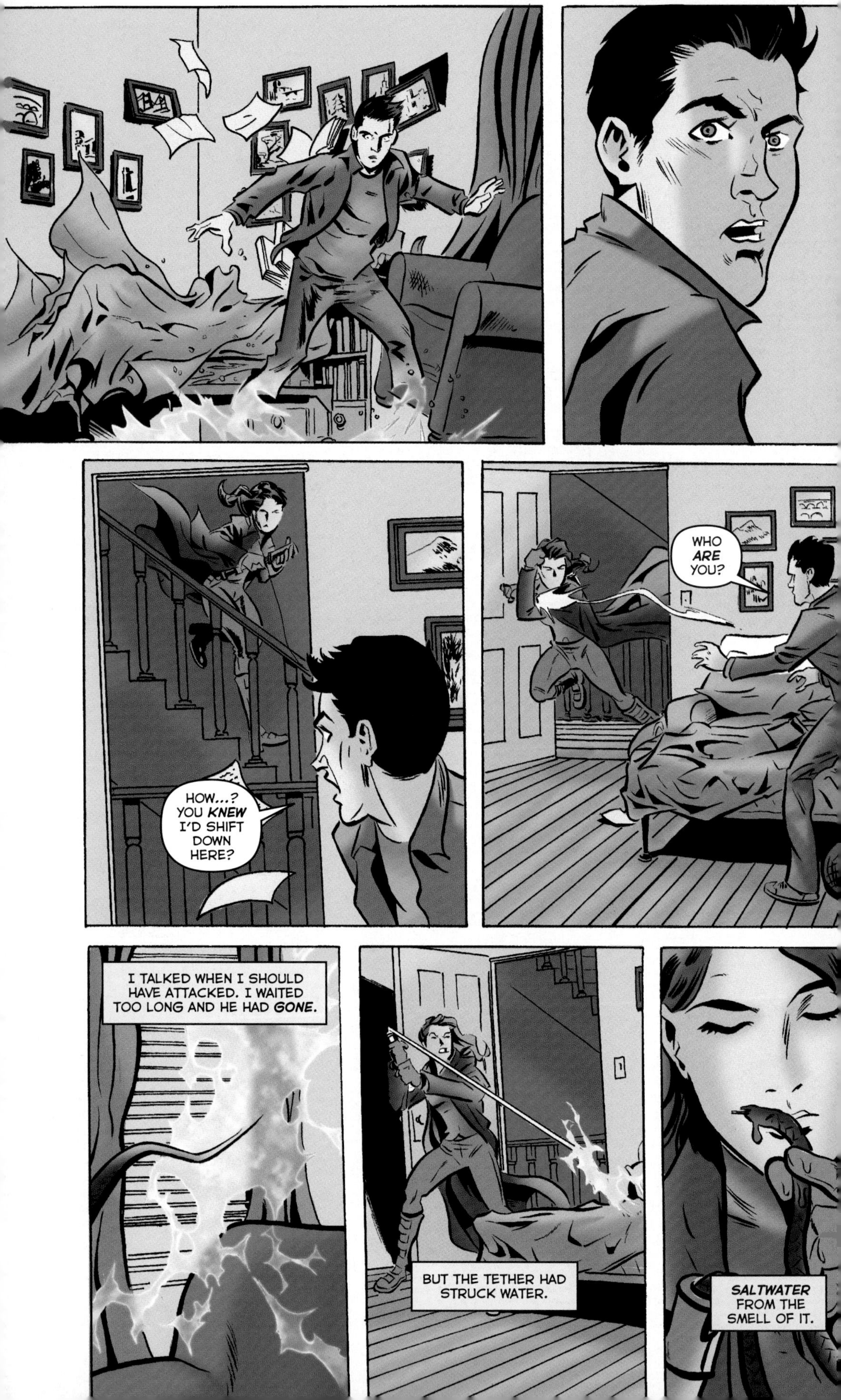
HOW...? YOU KNEW I'D SHIFT DOWN HERE?
WHO ARE YOU?
I TALKED WHEN I SHOULD HAVE ATTACKED. I WAITED TOO LONG AND HE HAD GONE.
BUT THE TETHER HAD STRUCK WATER.
SALTWATER FROM THE SMELL OF IT.

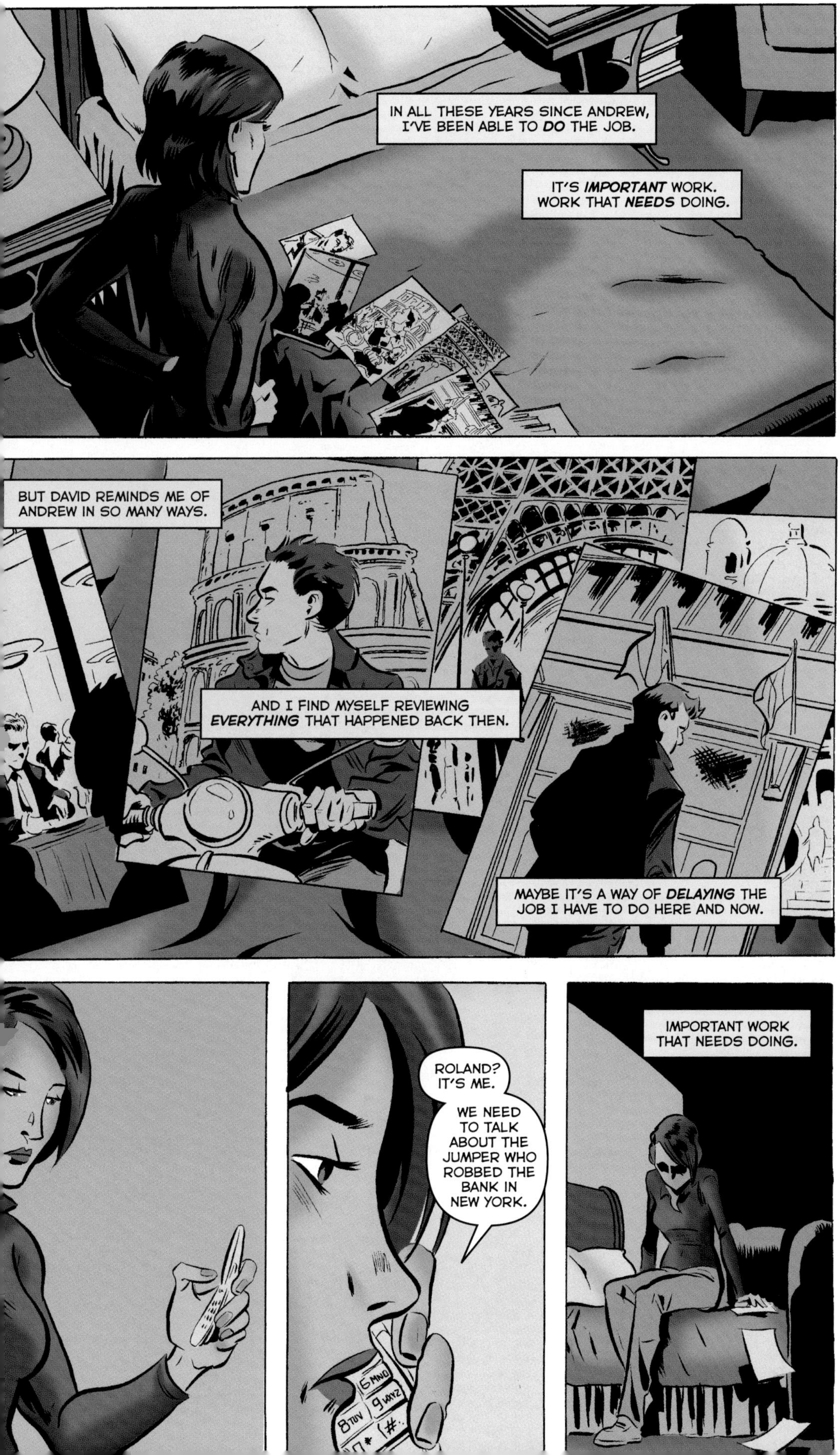
IN ALL THESE YEARS SINCE ANDREW, I'VE BEEN ABLE TO DO THE JOB.
IT'S IMPORTANT WORK. WORK THAT NEEDS DOING.
BUT DAVID REMINDS ME OF ANDREW IN SO MANY WAYS.
AND I FIND MYSELF REVIEWING EVERYTHING THAT HAPPENED BACK THEN.
MAYBE IT'S A WAY OF DELAYING THE JOB I HAVE TO DO HERE AND NOW.
ROLAND? IT'S ME.
WE NEED TO TALK ABOUT THE JUMPER WHO ROBBED THE BANK IN NEW YORK.
IMPORTANT WORK THAT NEEDS DOING.

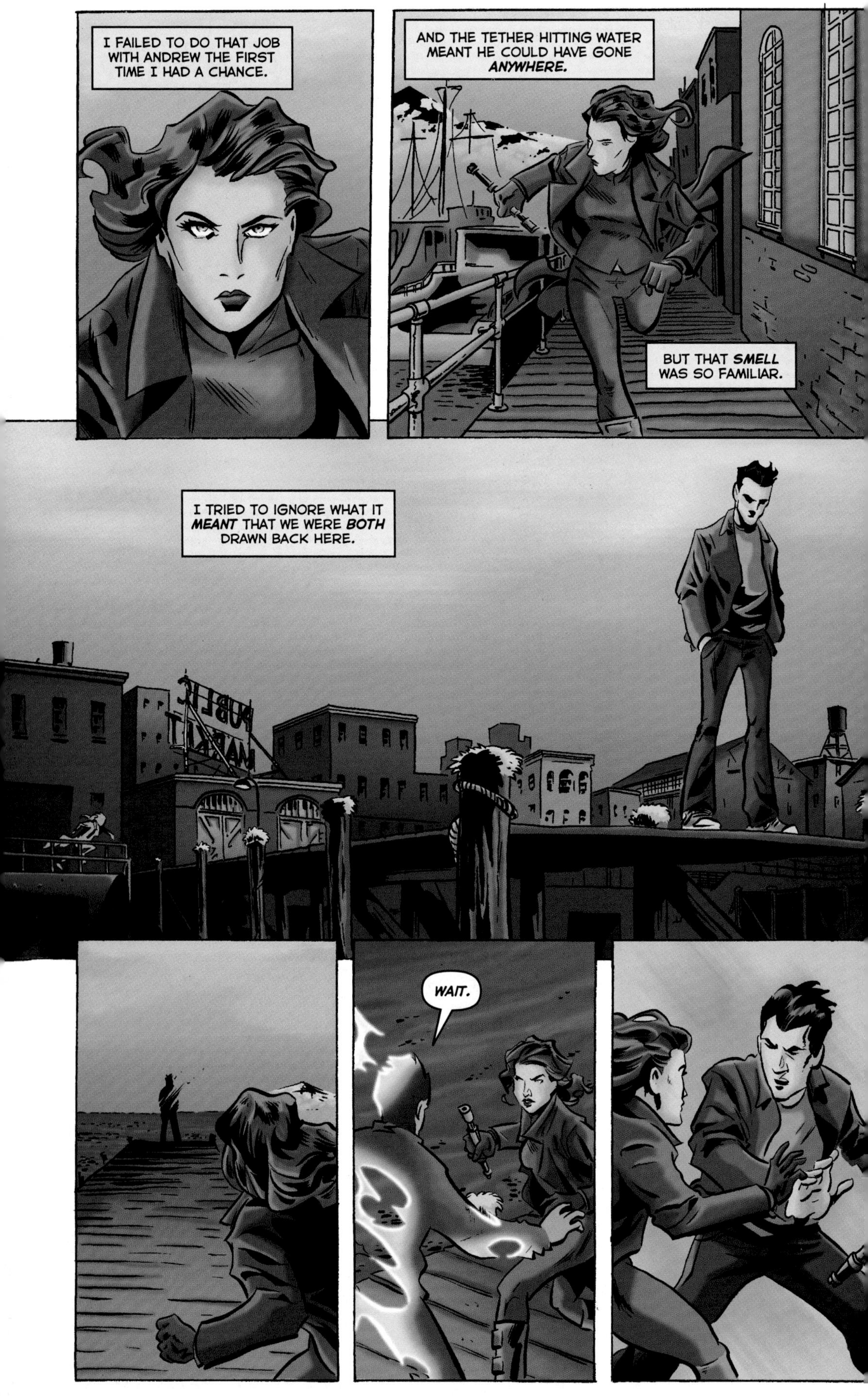
I FAILED TO DO THAT JOB WITH ANDREW THE FIRST TIME I HAD A CHANCE.
AND THE TETHER HITTING WATER MEANT HE COULD HAVE GONE *ANYWHERE.*
BUT THAT *SMELL* WAS SO FAMILIAR.
I TRIED TO IGNORE WHAT IT *MEANT* THAT WE WERE *BOTH* DRAWN BACK HERE.
PUBLIC MARKET
WAIT.

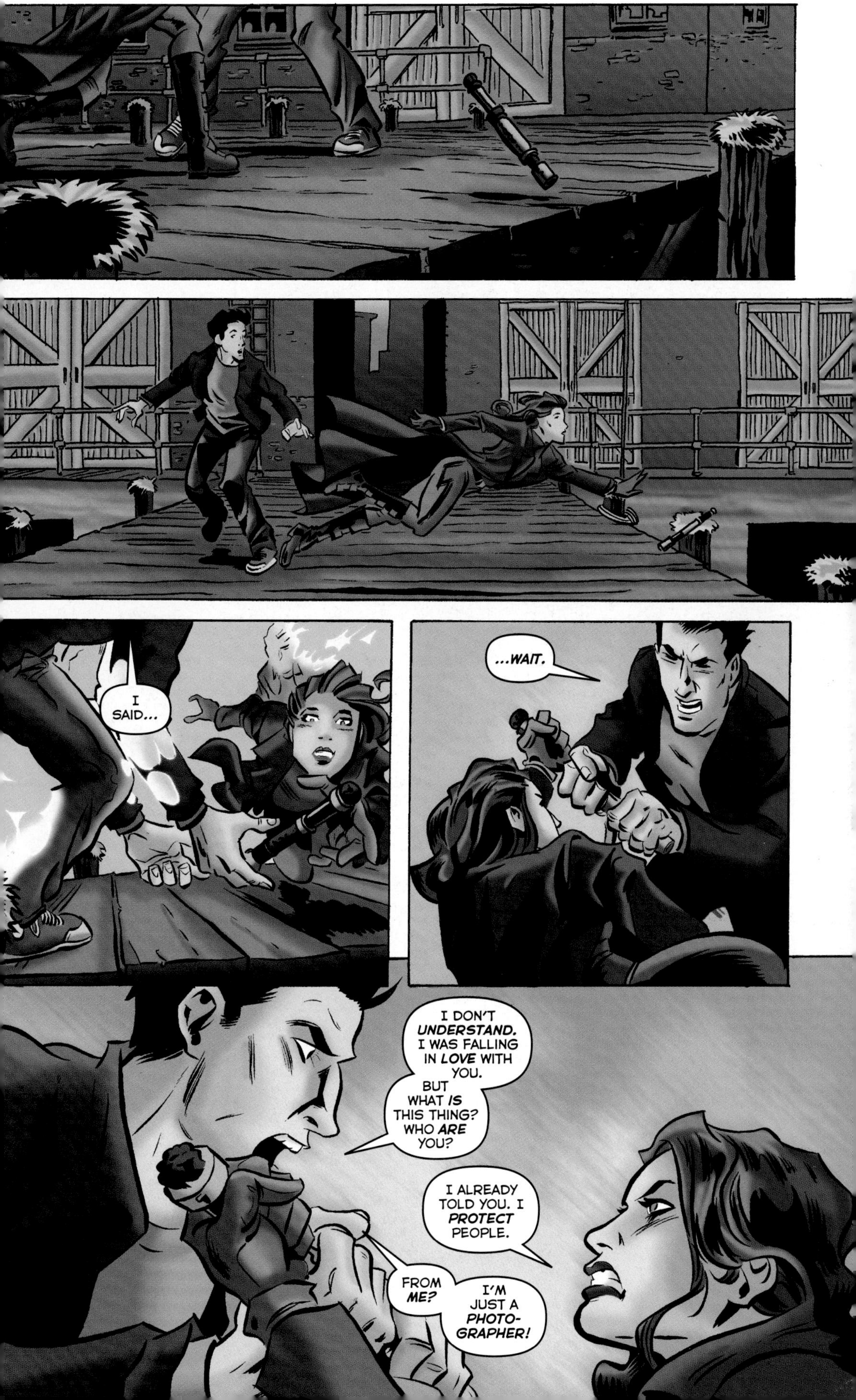
I SAID...
...WAIT.
I DON'T UNDERSTAND. I WAS FALLING IN LOVE WITH YOU.
BUT WHAT IS THIS THING? WHO ARE YOU?
I ALREADY TOLD YOU. I PROTECT PEOPLE.
FROM ME?
I'M JUST A PHOTO-GRAPHER!

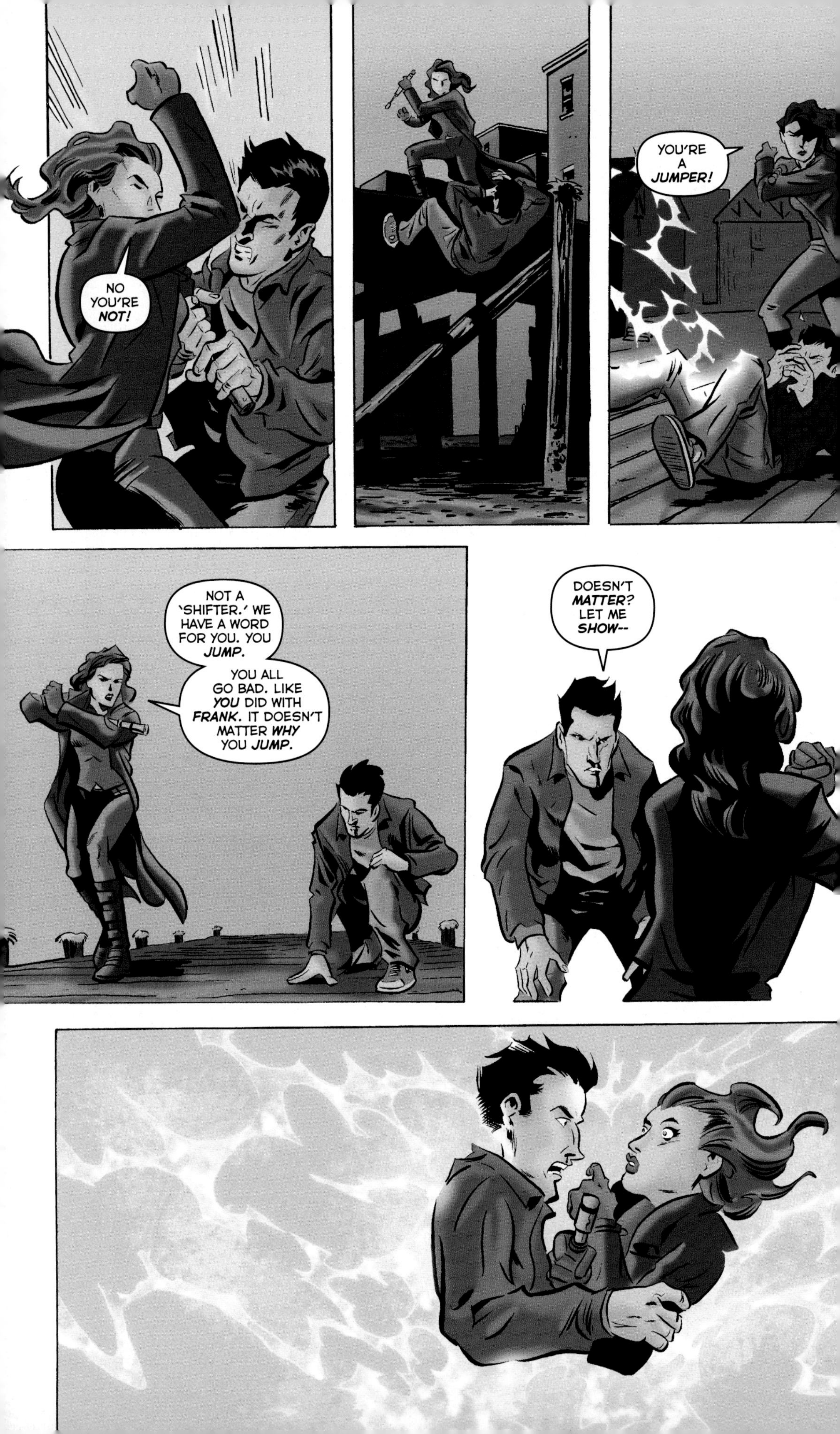
NO YOU'RE NOT!
YOU'RE A JUMPER!
NOT A 'SHIFTER.' WE HAVE A WORD FOR YOU. YOU JUMP.
YOU ALL GO BAD. LIKE YOU DID WITH FRANK. IT DOESN'T MATTER WHY YOU JUMP.
DOESN'T MATTER? LET ME SHOW--

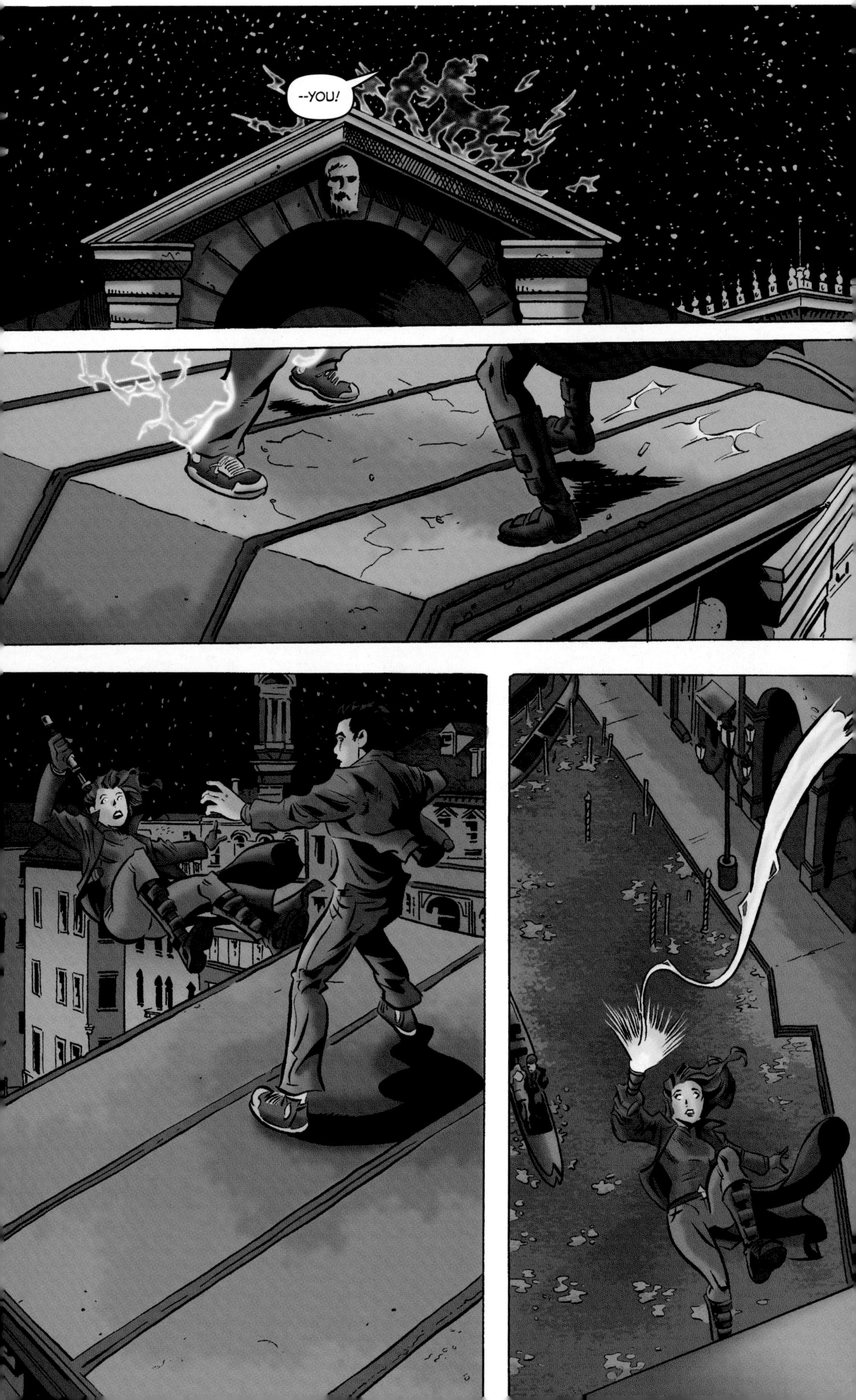
--YOU!

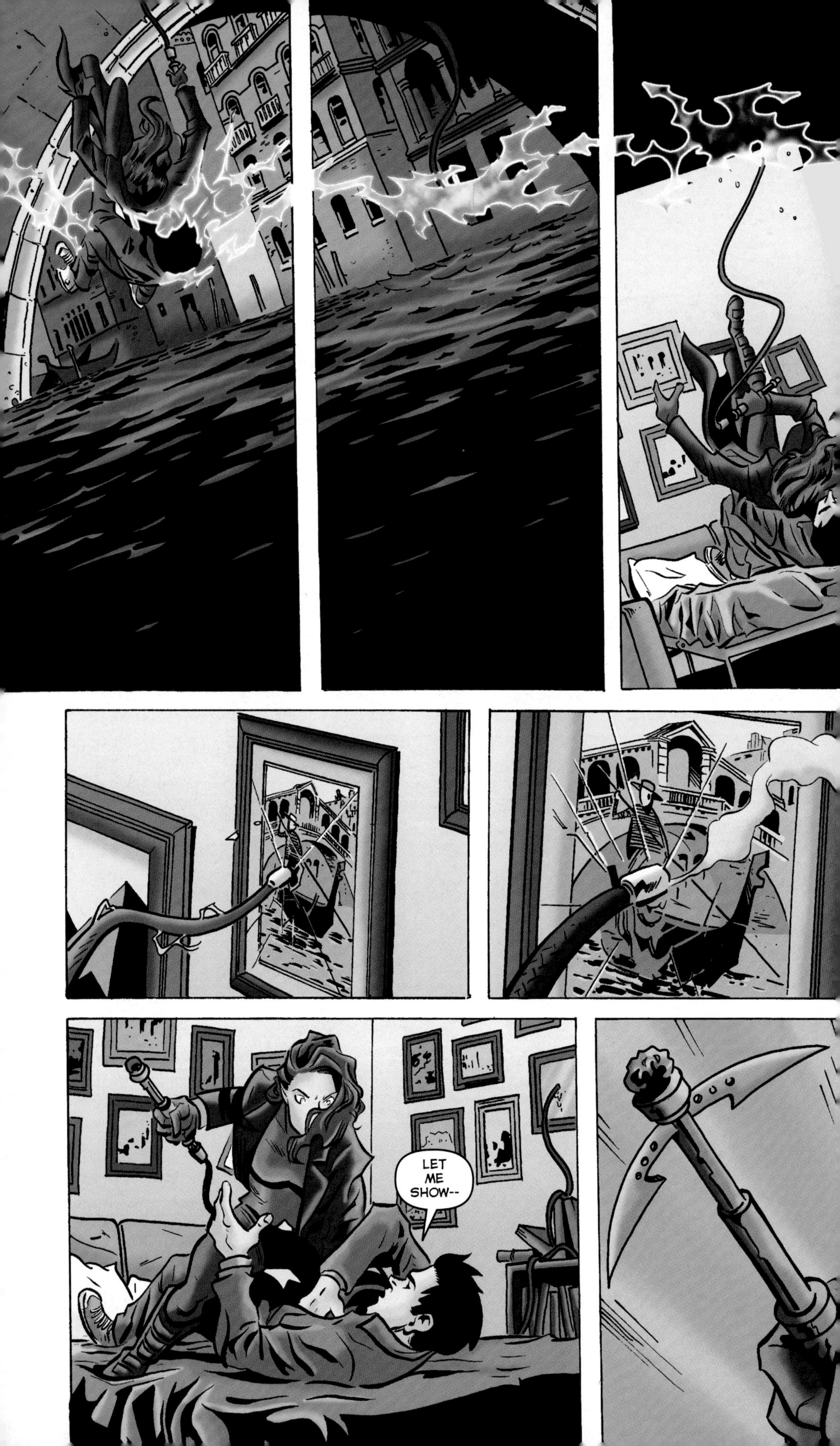
LET ME SHOW--

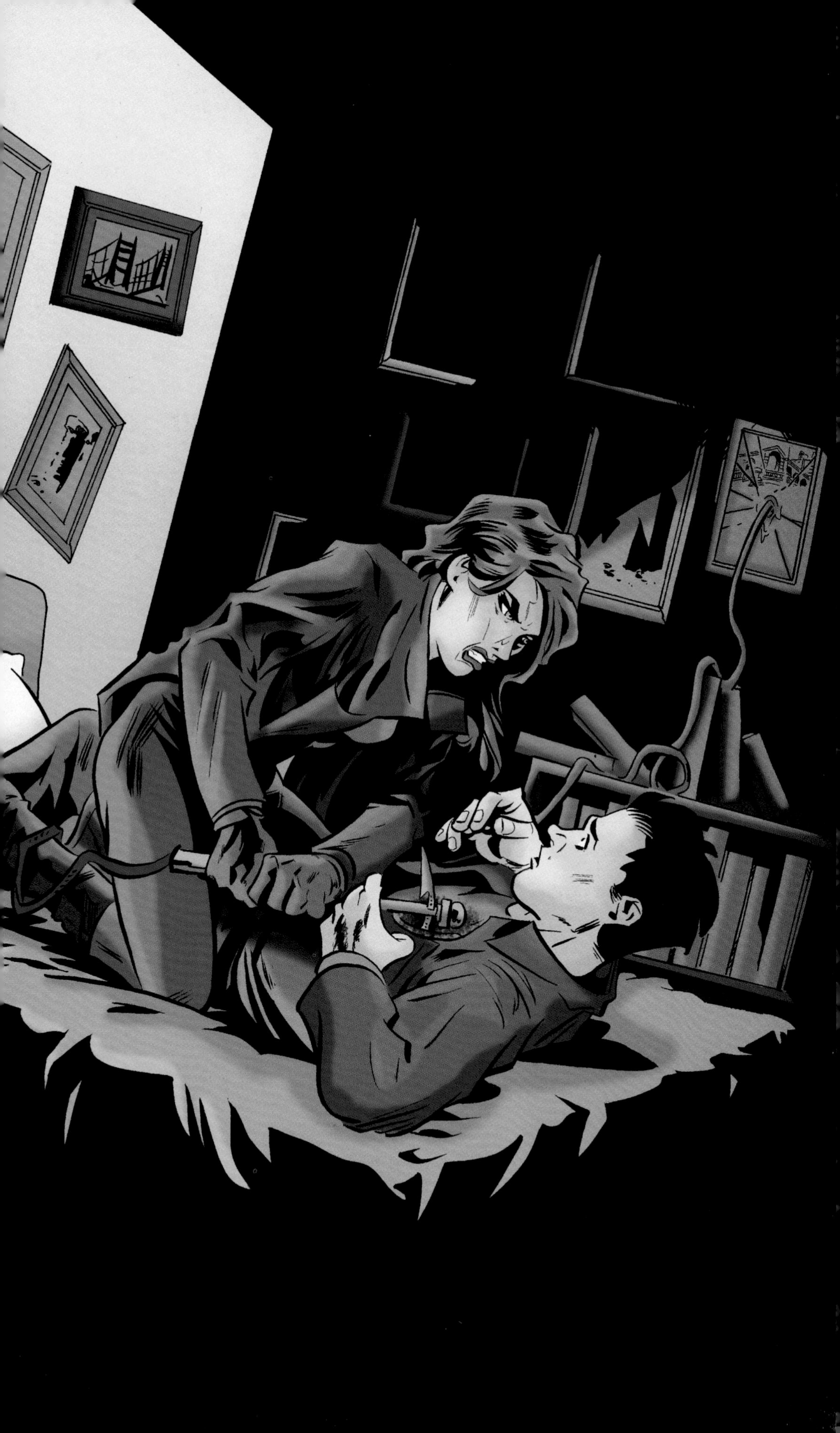

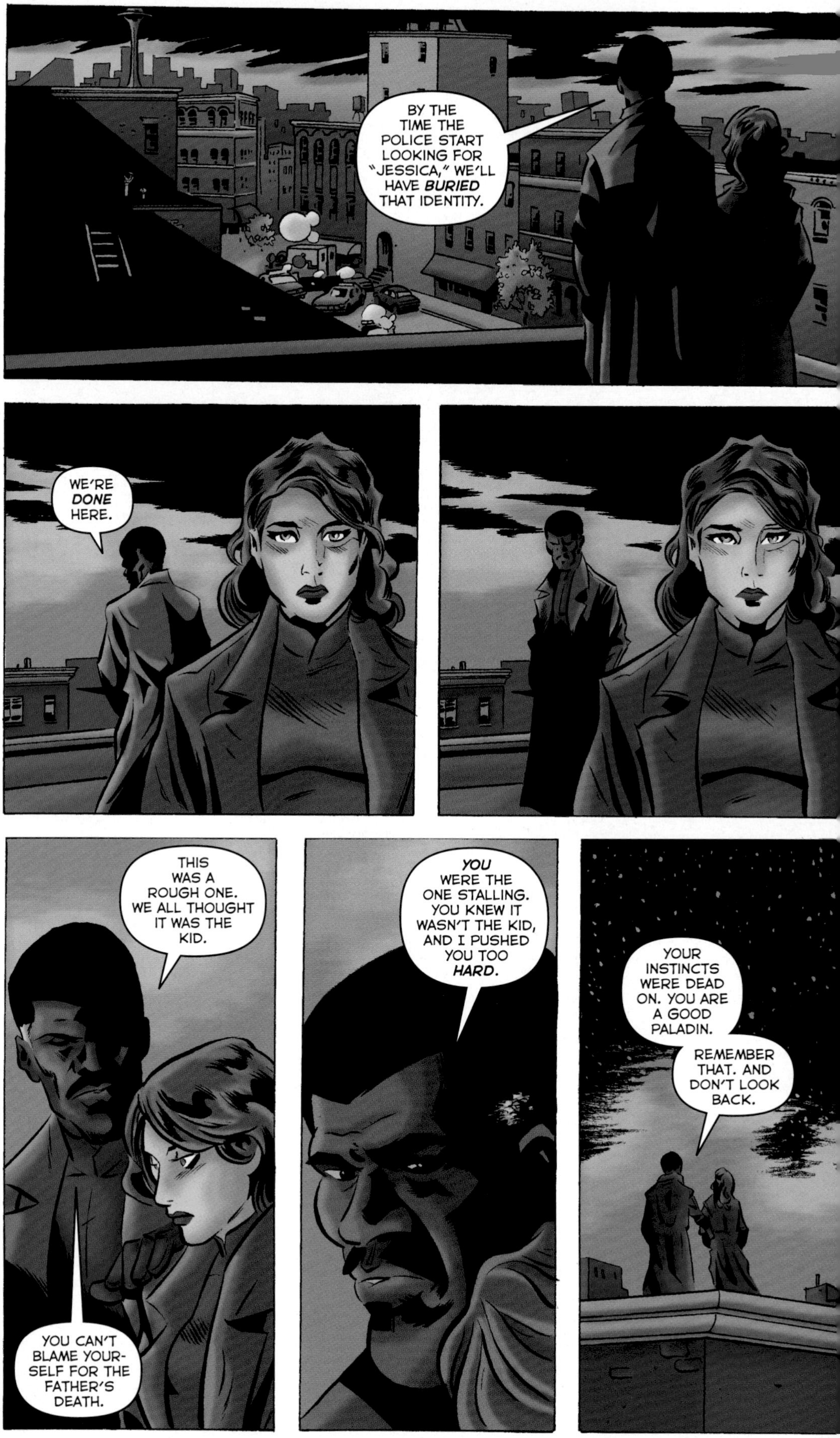
BY THE TIME THE POLICE START LOOKING FOR "JESSICA," WE'LL HAVE *BURIED* THAT IDENTITY.
WE'RE *DONE* HERE.
THIS WAS A ROUGH ONE. WE ALL THOUGHT IT WAS THE KID.
YOU CAN'T BLAME YOUR-SELF FOR THE FATHER'S DEATH.
YOU WERE THE ONE STALLING. YOU KNEW IT WASN'T THE KID, AND I PUSHED YOU TOO *HARD*.
YOUR INSTINCTS WERE DEAD ON. YOU ARE A GOOD PALADIN.
REMEMBER THAT. AND DON'T LOOK BACK.

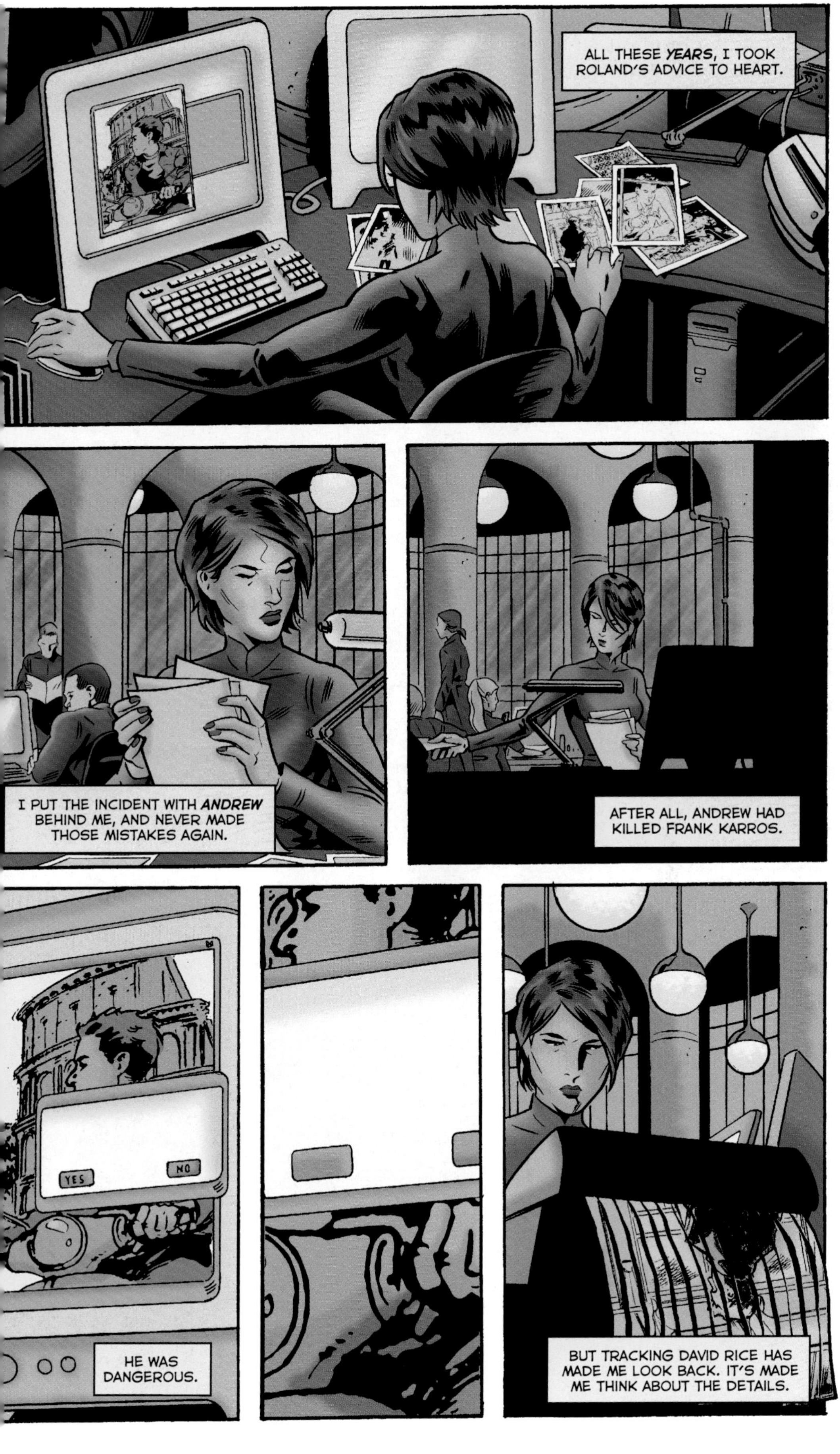

ALL THESE YEARS, I TOOK ROLAND'S ADVICE TO HEART.
I PUT THE INCIDENT WITH ANDREW BEHIND ME, AND NEVER MADE THOSE MISTAKES AGAIN.
AFTER ALL, ANDREW HAD KILLED FRANK KARROS.
YES
NO
HE WAS DANGEROUS.
BUT TRACKING DAVID RICE HAS MADE ME LOOK BACK. IT'S MADE ME THINK ABOUT THE DETAILS.

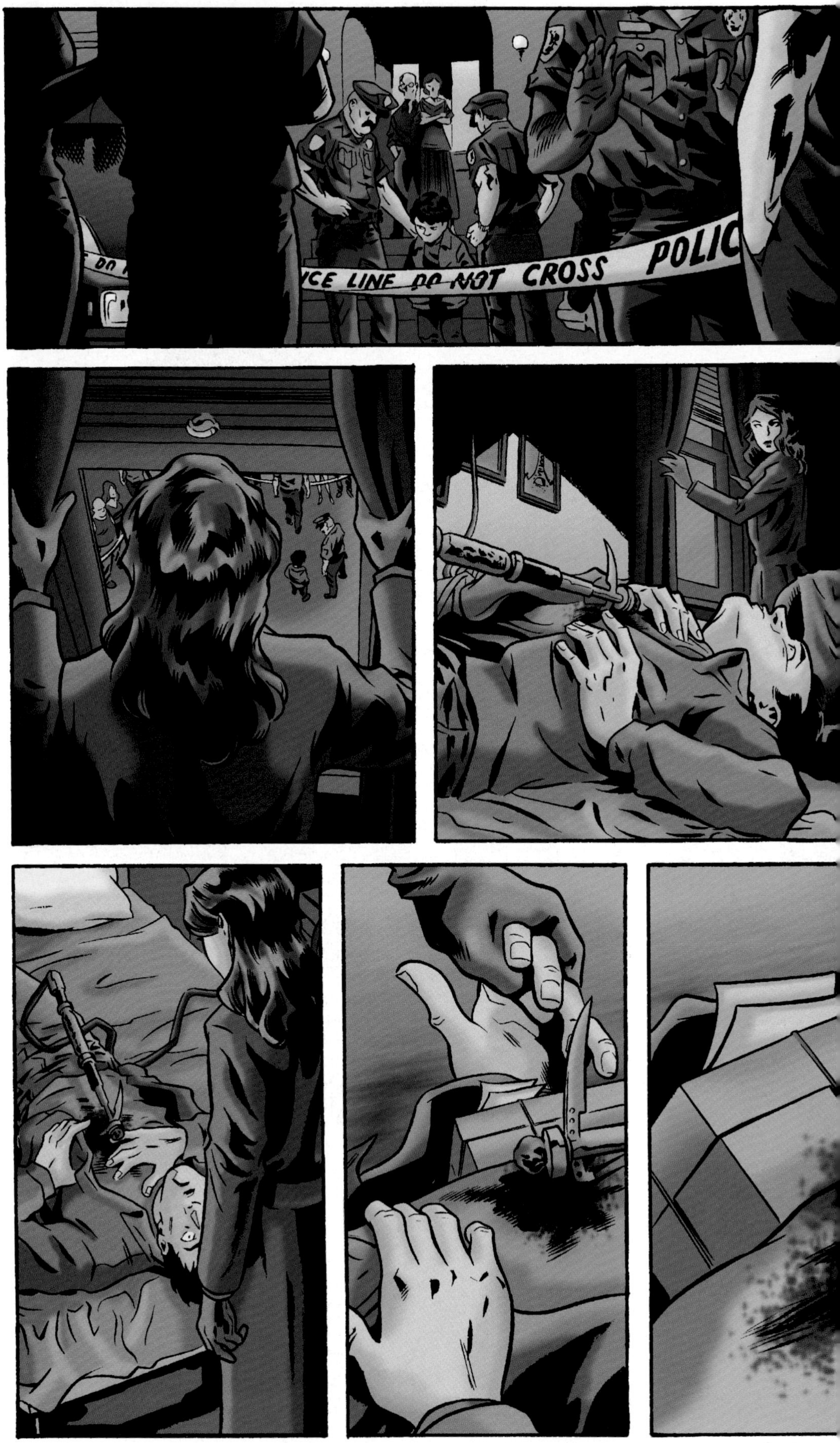
ICE LINE DO NOT CROSS
POLIC

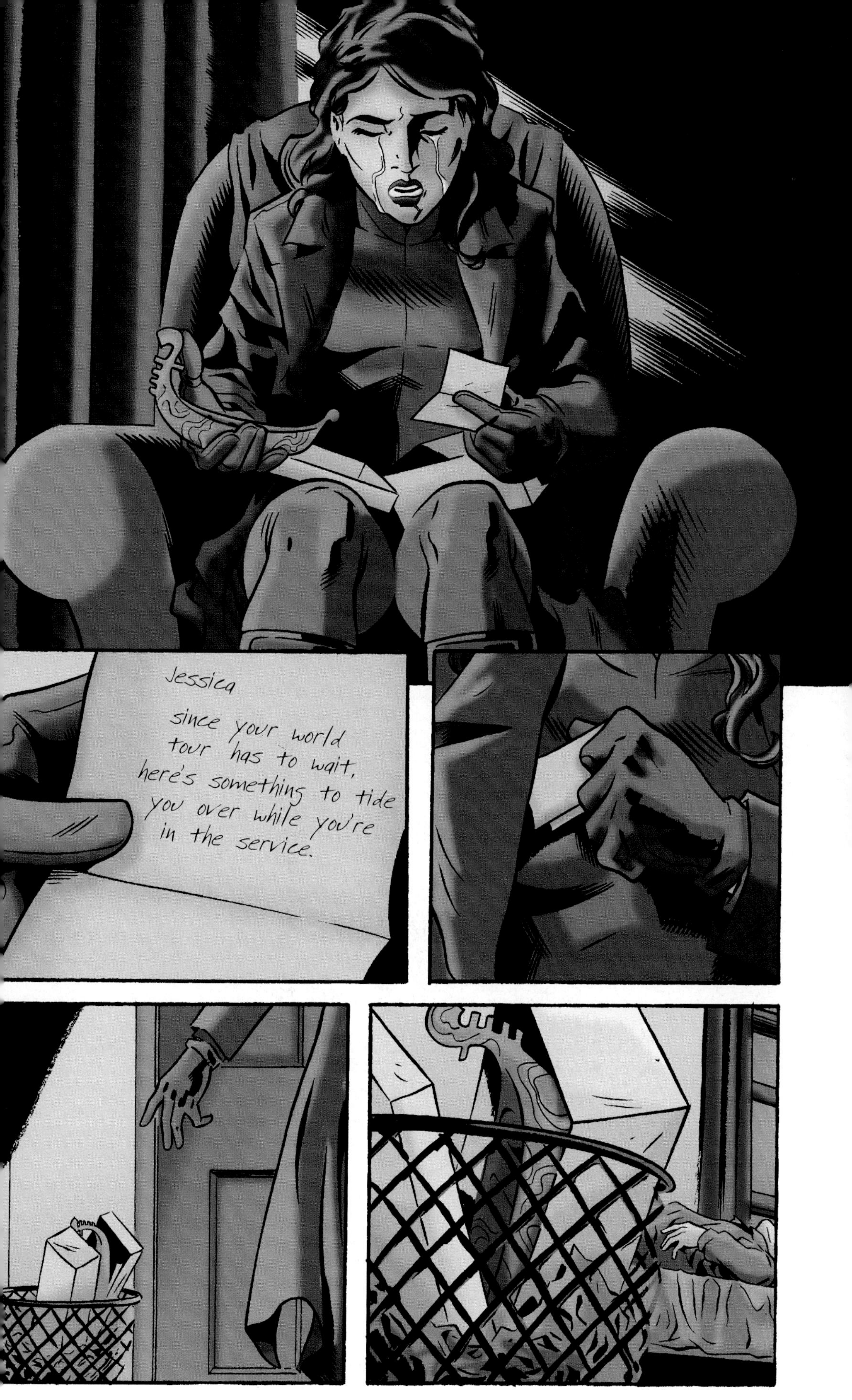
Jessica
since your world tour has to wait, here's something to tide you over while you're in the service.

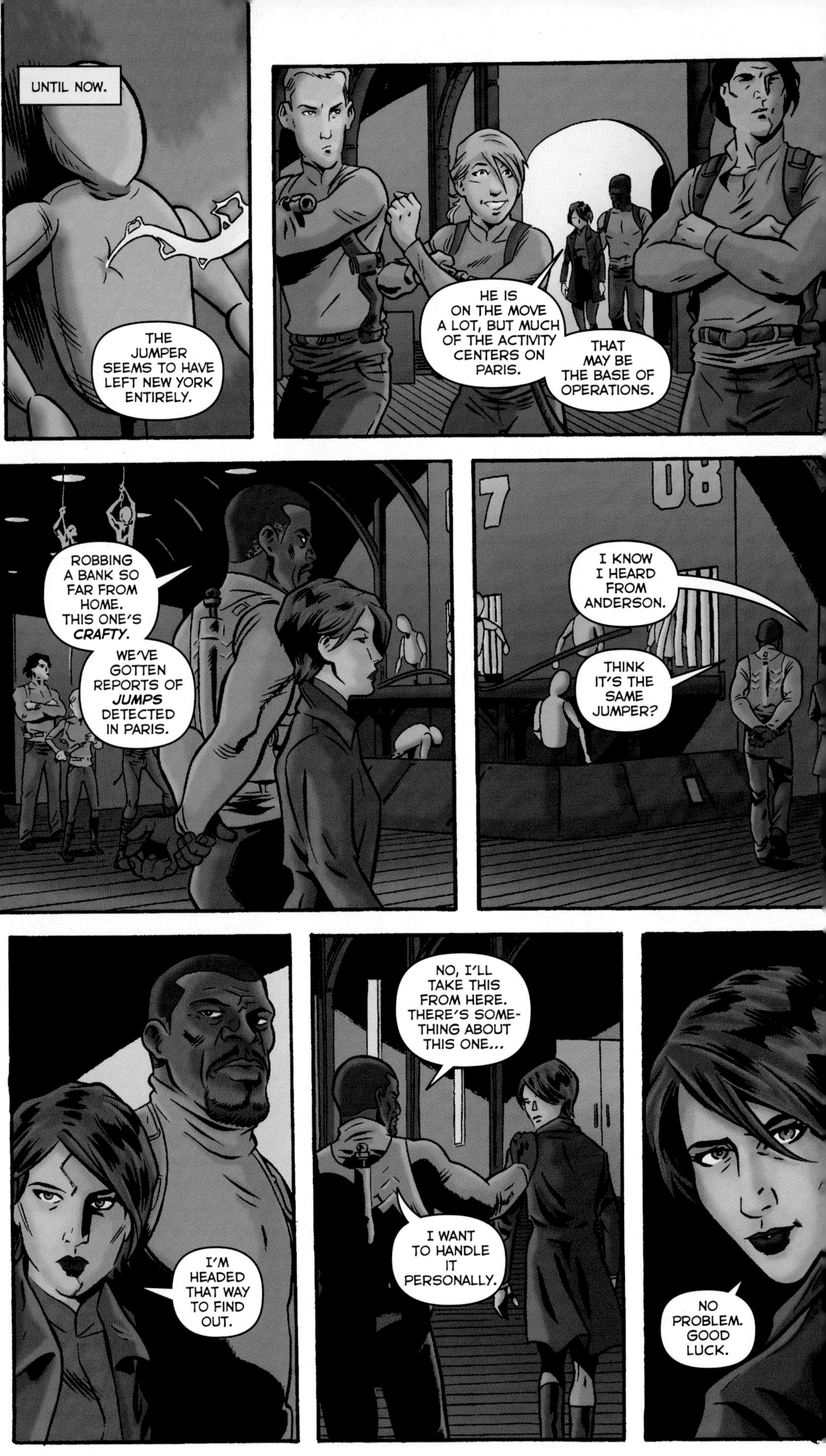
UNTIL NOW.
THE JUMPER SEEMS TO HAVE LEFT NEW YORK ENTIRELY.
HE IS ON THE MOVE A LOT, BUT MUCH OF THE ACTIVITY CENTERS ON PARIS.
THAT MAY BE THE BASE OF OPERATIONS.
ROBBING A BANK SO FAR FROM HOME. THIS ONE'S *CRAFTY.*
WE'VE GOTTEN REPORTS OF *JUMPS* DETECTED IN PARIS.
08
7
I KNOW I HEARD FROM ANDERSON.
THINK IT'S THE SAME JUMPER?
I'M HEADED THAT WAY TO FIND OUT.
NO, I'LL TAKE THIS FROM HERE. THERE'S SOME-THING ABOUT THIS ONE...
I WANT TO HANDLE IT PERSONALLY.
NO PROBLEM. GOOD LUCK.

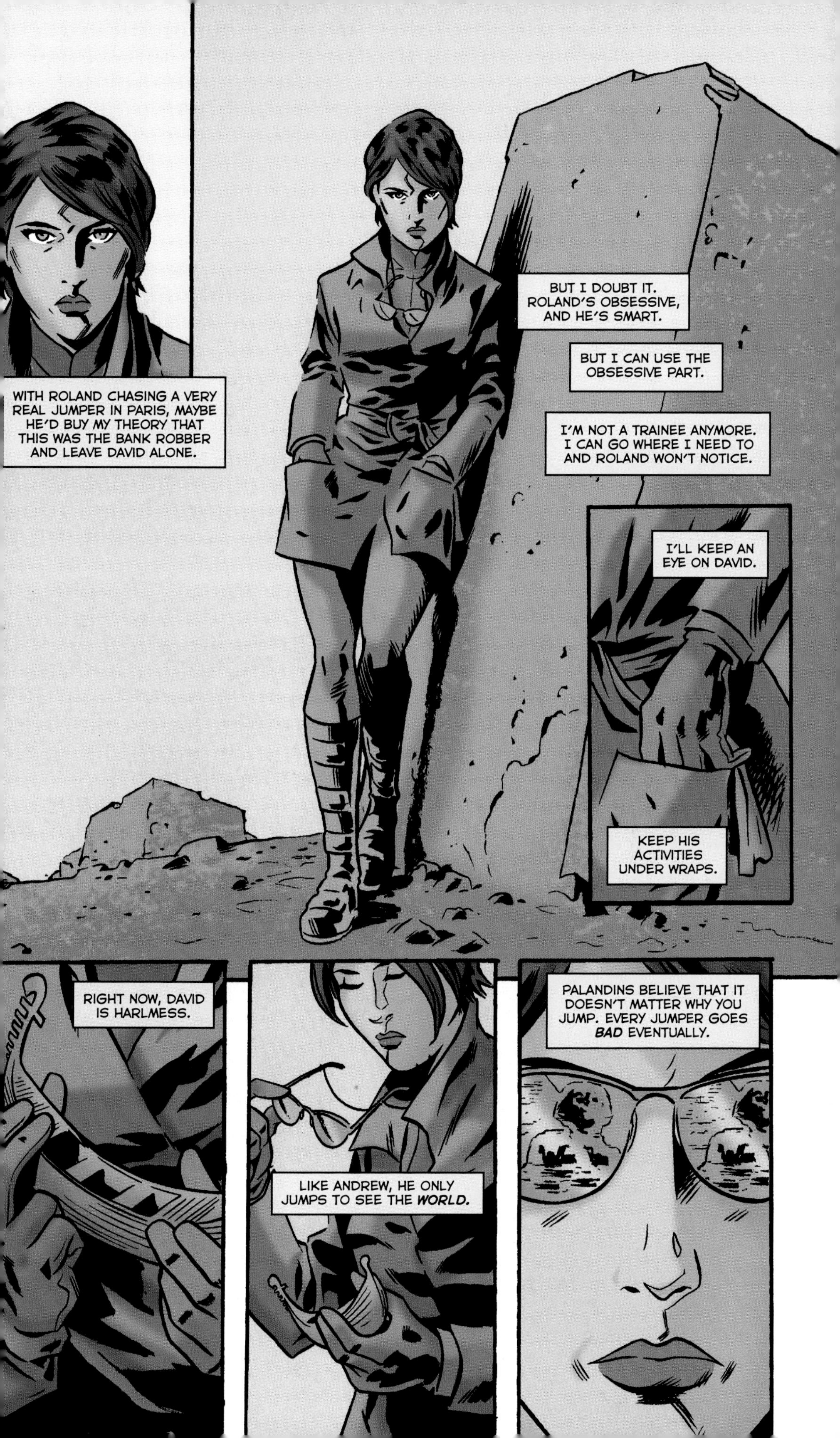
WITH ROLAND CHASING A VERY REAL JUMPER IN PARIS, MAYBE HE'D BUY MY THEORY THAT THIS WAS THE BANK ROBBER AND LEAVE DAVID ALONE.
BUT I DOUBT IT. ROLAND'S OBSESSIVE, AND HE'S SMART.
BUT I CAN USE THE OBSESSIVE PART.
I'M NOT A TRAINEE ANYMORE. I CAN GO WHERE I NEED TO AND ROLAND WON'T NOTICE.
I'LL KEEP AN EYE ON DAVID.
KEEP HIS ACTIVITIES UNDER WRAPS.
RIGHT NOW, DAVID IS HARLMESS.
LIKE ANDREW, HE ONLY JUMPS TO SEE THE *WORLD.*
PALANDINS BELIEVE THAT IT DOESN'T MATTER WHY YOU JUMP. EVERY JUMPER GOES *BAD* EVENTUALLY.

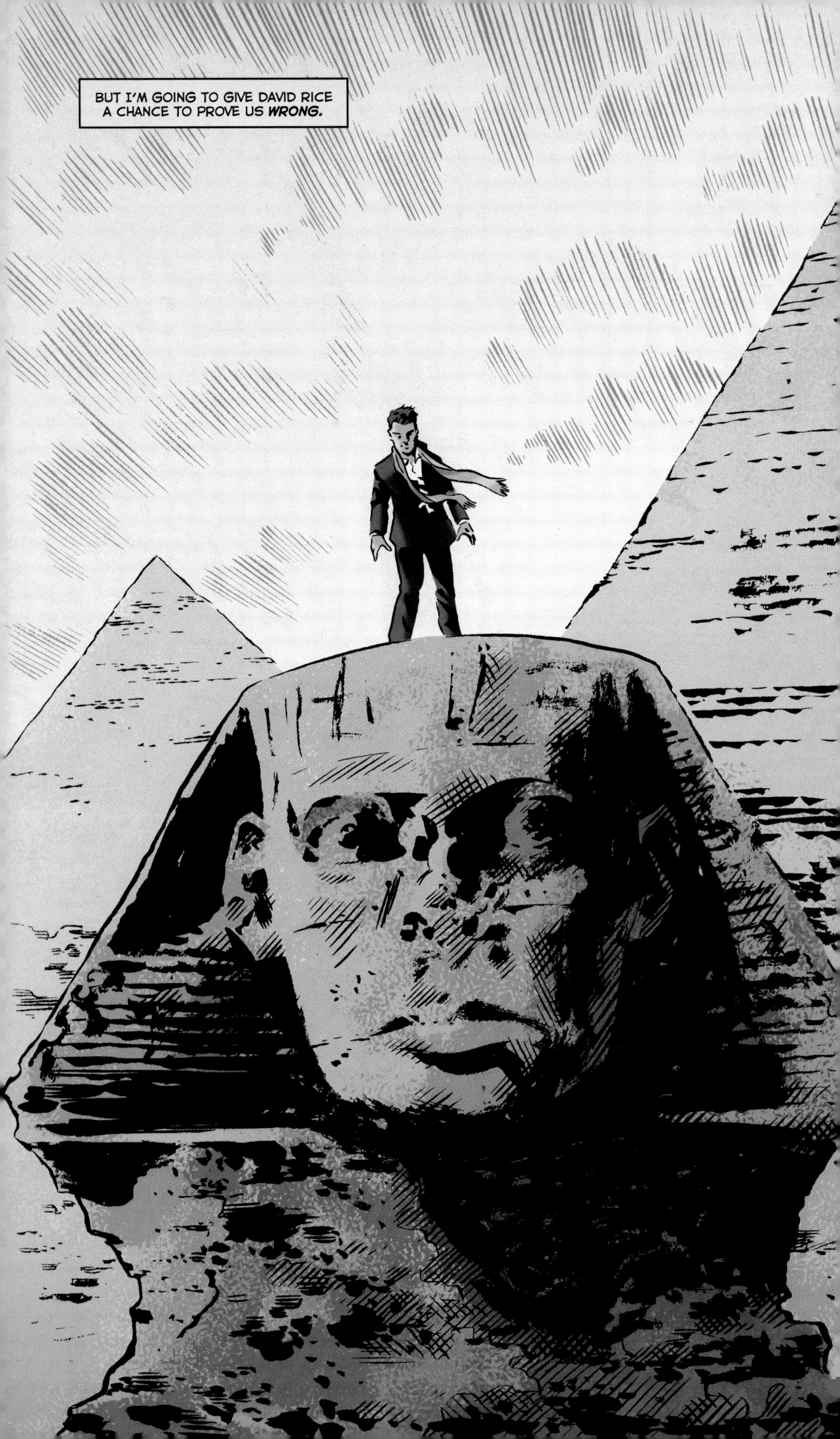
BUT I'M GOING TO GIVE DAVID RICE A CHANCE TO PROVE US *WRONG.*

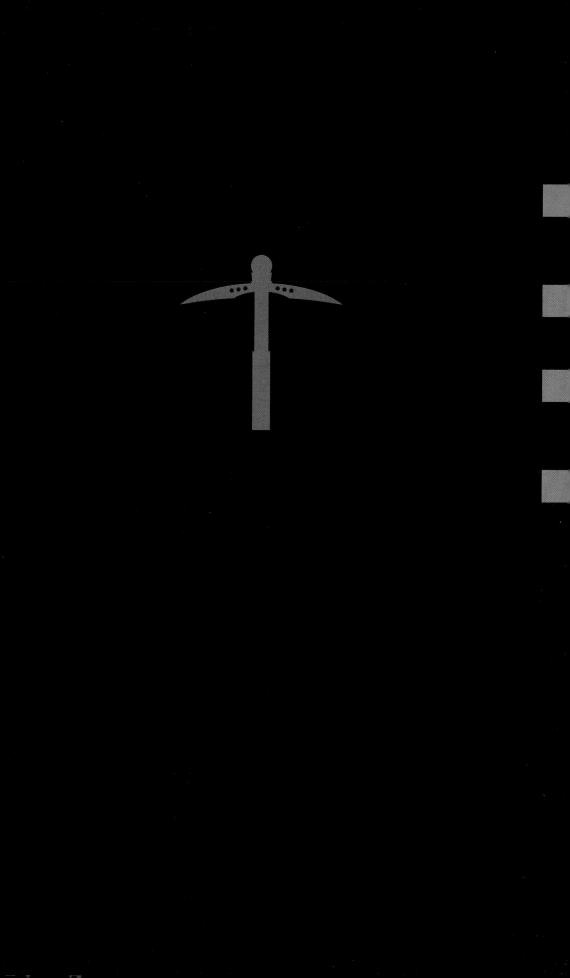

THE ALL-NEW

ONI
PRESS
DOTCOM

IS FINALLY
HERE.

(WELL, NOT "HERE," OBVIOUSLY.
THIS IS A COMIC BOOK. IT'S MADE OF PAPER.
WE MEAN ON YOUR COMPUTER.
THE ONE WITH AN INTERNET CONNECTION.)

IT HAS PREVIEWS, REVIEWS, AND
SPECIAL DOWNLOADS
FOR ALL YOUR FAVORITE ONI PRESS
TITLES! AND YOU'LL ONLY FIND 'EM AT
ONIPRESS.COM!

OTHER BOOKS FROM ONI PRESS

Courtney Crumrin and the Night Things
By Ted Naifeh

COURTNEY CRUMRIN, VOL. 1:
THE NIGHT THINGS
By Ted Naifeh
128 pages, digest, BW interiors
$11.95
ISBN 978-1-929998-60-9

DAMNED
Volume One
"Three Days Dead"

THE DAMNED, VOL. 1:
THREE DAYS DEAD
By Cullen Bunn & Brian Hurtt
160 pages, 6x9, BW interiors
$14.95
ISBN 978-1-93266-46-3

The Leading Man

LEADING MAN
By B. Clay Moore & Jeremy H
136 pages, standard, color inte
$14.95
ISBN 978-1-932664-57-7

The Annotated
Northwest Passage
Scott Chantler

NORTHWEST PASSAGE
By Scott Chantler
272 pages, hardcover
$19.95
ISBN 978-1-932664-61-4

PAST LIES

PAST LIES
By Nunzio DeFilippis, Christina Weir
& Christopher Mitten
168 pages, digest, BW interiors
$14.95
ISBN 978-1-932664-34-8

GREG RUCKA
QUEEN & COUNTRY
DEFINITIVE EDITION
VOLUME 01

QUEEN & COUNTRY,
DEFINITIVE EDITION, VOL.
By Greg Rucka, Steve Rolst
Brian Hurtt, & Leandro Fernan
376 pages, 6x9, BW interior
$19.95
ISBN 978-1-932664-87-4

SCOTT PILGRIM'S
PRECIOUS LITTLE LIFE
VOL. 1
BRYAN LEE O'MALLEY

SCOTT PILGRIM, VOL. 1: SCOTT PILGRIM'S
PRECIOUS LITTLE LIFE
By Bryan Lee O'Malley
168 pages, digest, BW interiors
$11.95
ISBN 978-1-932664-08-9

THREE STRIKES

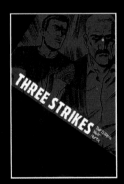

THREE STRIKES
By Nunzio DeFilippis, Christina Weir
& Brian Hurtt
144 pages, digest, BW interiors
$14.95
ISBN 978-1-929998-82-1

WASTELAND
ANTONY JOHNSTON
CHRISTOPHER MITTEN
BOOK 01
CITIES IN DUST

WASTELAND, VOL. 1:
CITIES IN DUST
By Antony Johnston & Christophe
160 pages, standard size, BW in
$11.95
ISBN 978-1-932664-59-1

Available at finer comics shops everywhere. For a comics store near you, call 1-888-COMIC-BOOK or visit www.the-master-list.com